ACQUISITIONS AND GROUP STRUCTURES

ACQUISITIONS AND GROUP STRUCTURES

Marie-Anne Denicolo LLB (Hons), Solicitor

JORDANS

2003

Published by
Jordan Publishing Limited
21 St Thomas Street
Bristol BS1 6JS

British Library Cataloguing-in-Publication Data

A catalogue record for this book is available from the British Library.

ISSN 1353–355X
ISBN 0 85308 826 8

Printed in Great Britain by Hobbs The Printers Ltd of Southampton

PREFACE

The purpose of this book is to provide an introduction to the legal and taxation implications of selling and acquiring unincorporated businesses and private companies (Parts I–III) and of operating through groups of companies (Part IV). Although many of the principles described in this book apply to the acquisition of all companies, it does not deal with the different procedures and additional obligations involved where either the seller or the buyer is a public company listed on The Stock Exchange.

Although it is hoped that the book will provide a useful guide to trainee solicitors and others who are involved in this type of work in commercial practice, it is written primarily as a complement to The College of Law's Legal Practice Course elective 'Acquisitions and Group Structures'. Those studying this elective will have completed the compulsory business course; some references are, therefore, made to the LPC Resource Book *Business Law and Practice* (Jordans) which accompanies the compulsory course.

The success and popularity of the 'Acquisitions and Group Structures' elective must surely be attributable to the comprehensive content of this Resource Book, which was originally written by Denis Heshon. The original work was a clear, accurate and helpful guide and I have endeavoured to achieve the same standards with my editorship. If I have succeeded in achieving this aim, my success is due in no small part to the kind assistance of a number of long-suffering colleagues, not least being the members of the Acquisitions team at The College of Law.

In the interests of brevity, I have used the masculine pronoun throughout to include the feminine.

The law is stated as at 31 July 2002.

MARIE-ANNE DENICOLO

CONTENTS

PREFACE   v

TABLE OF CASES   xi

TABLE OF STATUTES   xiii

TABLE OF STATUTORY INSTRUMENTS   xv

TABLE OF EC LEGISLATION AND TREATIES   xvii

TABLE OF ABBREVIATIONS   xix

PART I   **GENERAL CONSIDERATIONS**   1

Chapter 1   TYPES OF ACQUISITION   3
     1.1   Introduction   3
     1.2   An unincorporated business – distinguishing between acquisition
of a business and mere acquisition of assets   4
     1.3   Company – share acquisition, business acquisition or mere
acquisition of assets?   6

Chapter 2   ROLES OF THE PARTIES' ADVISERS   15
     2.1   Solicitor's role   15
     2.2   Procedural overview   15
     2.3   Accountant's role   24

Chapter 3   INVESTIGATING THE TARGET   27
     3.1   What are the buyer's objectives?   27
     3.2   Scope of the investigation   27
     3.3   Accountants' investigation and report   29
     3.4   Enquiries before contract   31
     3.5   Searching the file at the Companies Registry 34
     3.6   Internal registers   36
     3.7   Credit reports   36
     3.8   Checking the solvency of the seller   36
     3.9   Property matters   37
     3.10   Environmental matters   40

Chapter 4   SELLER'S LIABILITY AND BUYER'S REMEDIES   47
     4.1   Introduction   47
     4.2   Are any protections for the buyer implied into the contract? 47
     4.3   Express contractual protection   47
     4.4   How may the seller limit his liability?   57
     4.5   Criminal liability for false or misleading statements 64
     4.6   Negligent statements   65
     4.7   Seller's liability under guarantees   67
     4.8   Restrictions on the seller   67

PART II   **ACQUIRING A BUSINESS**   73

Chapter 5   THE ACQUISITION AGREEMENT   75
               5.1   Introduction   75
               5.2   Structure of the agreement   75
               5.3   Assets and liabilities   76
               5.4   Consideration   83
               5.5   Conditional contracts   84
               5.6   Completion   85
               5.7   Insurance   86
               5.8   Employees and pensions   86
               5.9   Warranties   87
               5.10   Some procedural requirements for corporate sellers and buyers   89

Chapter 6   EMPLOYEES AND PENSIONS ON A BUSINESS ACQUISITION   93
               6.1   Introduction   93
               6.2   What are an employee's rights on the termination of his
                      employment?   93
               6.3   The Transfer of Undertakings (Protection of Employment)
                      Regulations 1981 (implementing the Acquired Rights Directive)   98
               6.4   Effect of a relevant transfer – Regulation 5   100
               6.5   What the transferee acquires   102
               6.6   Dismissal of an employee resulting from a relevant transfer –
                      Regulation 8   104
               6.7   Transfer-connected dismissals and post-transfer variations to
                      terms and conditions   105
               6.8   Due diligence and protection in the acquisition agreement   108
               6.9   Pensions   110
               6.10   Flowchart   112

Chapter 7   TAXATION ON A BUSINESS ACQUISITION   113
               7.1   Introduction   113
               7.2   Implications for the seller of an unincorporated business   113
               7.3   Implications on the sale of a business by a company   117
               7.4   Implications for the buyer of a business   119
               7.5   Warranties   123

PART III   **ACQUIRING A COMPANY BY SHARE PURCHASE**   125

Chapter 8   THE ACQUISITION AGREEMENT   127
               8.1   Introduction   127
               8.2   Structure of the agreement   127
               8.3   Sale of shares   128
               8.4   Purchase price   128
               8.5   Conditional contracts   131
               8.6   Warranties   132
               8.7   Completion   137
               8.8   Restrictive covenants   137

Chapter 9   PROCEDURAL ASPECTS AND STATUTORY REQUIREMENTS   139
               9.1   Introduction   139
               9.2   Compliance with the Financial Services and Markets Act 2000   139
               9.3   Compliance with the Companies Act 1985   140
               9.4   Completion   146

Chapter 10	EMPLOYEES AND PENSIONS ON A SHARE ACQUISITION	151
	10.1 Effect of a share acquisition on employees	151
	10.2 Pre-contract enquiries	151
	10.3 Changes contemplated by the buyer	152
	10.4 Provision in the acquisition agreement	157
	10.5 Pensions	157
Chapter 11	TAXATION ON A SHARE ACQUISITION	159
	11.1 Introduction	159
	11.2 Liability of the seller on the sale of shares	159
	11.3 Reducing the charge	160
	11.4 How is the seller taxed when the consideration is deferred?	164
	11.5 Tax implications for the buyer	166
	11.6 Warranties and indemnities	167
PART IV	**GROUPS**	169
Chapter 12	AN INTRODUCTION TO GROUPS	171
	12.1 How do groups come about?	171
	12.2 Why are groups so popular?	171
	12.3 Disadvantages	172
	12.4 Company law status of groups	172
	12.5 Group accounts	173
	12.6 Obligations of the parent company and its directors to subsidiaries	174
	12.7 Group indebtedness	175
Chapter 13	TAXATION OF GROUPS	177
	13.1 Introduction	177
	13.2 Defining a group	177
	13.3 Group relief	179
	13.4 Capital gains	182
	13.5 Small companies rate of corporation tax	185
	13.6 VAT group registration	185
INDEX		187

TABLE OF CASES

References in the right-hand column refer to paragraph numbers.

Allen and Others v Amalgamated Construction Co Ltd (Case C-234/98) [2000] IRLR 19, ECJ — 6.3.1

Berriman v Delabole Slate Ltd [1985] IRLR 305, CA — 6.6.2, 6.7.3, 6.7.4, 6.10
Botzen v Rotterdamsche Droogdok Maatschappij BV [1986] 2 CMLR 50, ECJ — 6.4.2
Brady v Brady [1988] 2 All ER 617, HL — 9.3.1
Briggs v Oates [1991] 1 All ER 411, ChD — 10.3.2
British Fuels Ltd v Baxendale and Another; Wilson and Others v St Helens Borough Council
  [1999] 2 AC 52, HL — 6.7, 6.7.2, 6.7.4
Brookes and Others v Borough Care Services and CLS Care Services Ltd [1998] IRLR 636, EAT — 6.3.1

Caparo Industries plc v Dickman [1990] 2 WLR 358, HL — 4.6.2
Carisway Cleaning Contracts Ltd v Richards and Another (EAT/629/97) (1998) unreported,
  19 June, EAT — 6.4.2
Credit Suisse First Boston (Europe) Ltd v Lister [1998] IRLR 700, CA — 6.7.2
Credit Suisse First Boston (Europe) Ltd v Padiachy and Others [1998] IRLR 504, QBD — 6.7.2

Duncan Webb Offset (Maidstone) Ltd v Cooper and Others [1995] IRLR 633 — 6.4.2

Eurocopy plc v Teesdale and Others [1992] BCLC 1067, CA — 4.4.2

Faccenda Chicken Ltd v Fowler [1986] IRLR 69, CA — 10.3.2

General Billposting Co Ltd v Atkinson [1909] AC 118, HL — 10.3.2
Government of Zanzibar v British Aerospace (Lancaster House) Ltd and Others [2000] 1 WLR
  2333, QBD — 4.3.1
Green v Elan Care Ltd [2002] All ER (D) 17, Mar, EAT — 6.6.2

Hadley v Baxendale (1854) 9 Exch 341 — 4.3.1, 4.4.1
Harrison Bowden Ltd v Bowden [1994] ICR 186, EAT — 6.6.1
Hedley Byrne and Co Ltd v Heller and Partners Ltd [1964] AC 465, HL — 4.6.1

Ibex Trading Co Ltd (in administration) v Walton and Others [1994] IRLR 564, EAT — 6.6.1

Levison and Others v Farin and Others [1978] 2 All ER 1149, QBD — 4.4.2
Litster v Forth Dry Dock and Engineering Co Ltd [1989] IRLR 161, HL — 6.4.2, 6.7.3, 6.8, 6.10

Marren (Inspector of Taxes) v Ingles [1980] 3 All ER 95, HL — 11.4.3
Morgan Crucible Co plc v Hill Samuel and Co Ltd [1991] 2 WLR 665, CA — 4.6.2
Morris v John Grose Group Ltd [1998] IRLR 499, EAT — 6.6.1

Redmond Stichting (Dr Sophie) v Bartol and Others [1992] IRLR 366, ECJ — 6.3.2
Ronbar Enterprises Ltd v Green [1954] 2 All ER 266, CA — 4.8.3
Rylands v Fletcher (1866) LR 3 HL 330, HL — 3.10.3

Secretary of State for Employment v Spence [1987] QB 179, CA — 6.4.2, 6.7.3, 6.10
Secretary of State for Trade and Industry v Cook and Others [1997] ICR 288, EAT — 6.4.2
Senior Heat Treatment Limited v Bell [1997] IRLR 614, EAT — 6.4.2
Shepherd (Inspector of Taxes) v Law Land plc [1990] STC 795, ChD — 13.3.4
Spijkers v Gebroeders Benedik Abattoir CV [1986] ECR 1119, ECJ — 6.3.2

Stirling District Council v Allan and Others [1995] IRLR 301, Ct of Sess (Inner House) 6.7.3

Thomas Witter Ltd v TBP Industries Ltd [1996] 2 All ER 575, ChD 4.3.1
Transport and General Workers' Union v James McKinnon Jr (Haulage) Ltd and Others
     [2001] IRLR 597, EAT 6.5.2
Trego v Hunt [1896] AC 7, HL 4.8.1

Walford v Miles [1992] 2 WLR 174, HL 2.2.1
Warner v Adnet Ltd [1998] IRLR 394, CA 6.6.3
Wheeler v Patel and Another [1997] IRLR 211, EAT 6.6.1, 6.6.2
Whent and Others v T. Cartledge Limited [1997] IRLR 153, EAT 6.5.1

Zim Properties Ltd v Procter (Inspector of Taxes); Procter (Inspector of Taxes) v Zim Properties
     Ltd [1985] STC 90, ChD 4.3.2, 11.6.2

TABLE OF STATUTES

References are to paragraph numbers.

Civil Liability (Contribution) Act 1978	4.3.3
s 1	4.3.3
s 2	4.3.3
Companies Act 1985	3.5.2, 5.10.2, 8.6.1,
	9.1, 9.3.1, 12.4, 12.5
s 22	9.4.3
s 23	12.4.1
s 35A	3.5.2
s 80	3.6, 9.3.2
s 89	3.6, 9.3.2
s 121	9.3.2
s 151	1.3.7, 9.3.1, 12.4.2
(1), (2)	9.3.1
s 152(1)(a)	9.3.1
(i)–(iv)	9.3.1
s 153	9.3.1
(1)	9.3.1
(a), (b)	9.3.1
(2)	9.3.1
(3)	9.3.1
(a)	9.3.1
ss 155–158	9.3.1
s 258(1)	12.5.1
s 303	10.3.2
s 309	5.10.2, 9.3.6
s 313	5.10.2
s 314	9.3.4
s 316(2)	9.3.4
(3)	5.10.2
s 317	5.10.2, 9.3.3, 9.4.3
s 319	5.10.2, 9.3.5, 9.4.3, 10.3.2
s 320	5.10.2, 9.3.3, 9.4.3, 12.4.3
s 322	5.10.2
s 324	9.4.3
s 330	12.4.4
s 346	5.10.2
(3)(a)	9.3.3
s 381A	5.10.2
s 392	9.4.4
s 459	12.6
s 736	12.4.5
s 741	12.7.2
Sch 15A	5.10.2
Companies Act 1989	2.2.6
Competition Act 1980	4.8.5
Competition Act 1998	2.2.6, 4.8.5, 4.8.6, 9.4.4
s 2	4.8.5
(2)	4.8.5
s 18	4.8.5
s 60	4.8.5
Consumer Credit Act 1974	5.9.2
Consumer Protection Act 1987	4.4.1

Contracts (Rights of Third Parties) Act	
1999	4.3.4
Employment Rights Act 1996	6.2.2, 6.10
s 1	6.2, 6.2.2, 6.8.1, 6.10, 10.2
s 86	6.2.1, 10.3.1
s 98	6.2.2
(1)	6.6.2
(4)	6.6.2, 6.10, 10.3.1
s 138	6.2.2
s 139	6.2.2
s 182	6.3.2
Environment Act 1995	3.10.2, 3.10.4
Environmental Protection Act 1990	3.10.2,
	3.10.3, 3.10.4
Pt II	3.10.2
Pt IIA	3.10.2
s 7	3.10.2
(4)	3.10.2
s 81	3.10.2
s 157	3.10.3
Fair Trading Act 1973	2.2.6, 5.9.2
s 63(2)	2.2.6
s 64	2.2.6
s 68(4)	2.2.6
s 84	2.2.6
Finance Act 1930	
s 42	13.4.1
Finance Act 1993	13.3.6
Finance Act 1994	11.5.3
s 137	11.5.3
Sch 5	11.5.3
Finance Act 1996	7.4.8, 11.5.3, 13.6
Finance Act 1998	11.3.2
Finance Act 2002	11.3.4
Financial Services Act 1986	9.2
Financial Services and Markets Act	
2000	1.3.6, 2.1, 4.5, 9.2, 9.2.1, 9.2.2
s 21	1.3.6, 9.2.1
s 397(1)–(3)	4.5
Income and Corporation Taxes Act	
1988	
s 13	13.5
s 148	6.2.1, 10.3.2
s 188	6.2.1, 10.3.2
s 360	11.5.3
s 362	7.4.8
s 380	7.2.1

Income and Corporation Taxes Act
    1988 *cont*
    s 385   7.2.1
    s 386   1.2.1, 7.2.2
    s 388   7.2.1
    s 393   1.3.7, 7.3.1, 13.3.3
        (1)   11.5.1
    s 393A   13.3.3
    s 402   11.3.5, 13.3, 13.3.5
    ss 403A–403C   13.3.4
    s 410   13.3.4
    s 413(3)   13.3.2
    s 416   13.5
    s 768   11.5.1
        (4)   11.5.1
    s 832(1)   13.2.1
    s 838   13.2
    Sch 18   13.2.4
Insolvency Act 1986
    s 213   12.7.2
    s 214   12.7.2

Landlord and Tenant Act 1927
    s 19   5.3.1
Landlord and Tenant Act 1988   5.3.1
Law of Property Act 1925
    s 136   5.3.6, 5.3.7
Law of Property (Miscellaneous
    Provisions) Act 1994   8.3.1
Local Land Charges Act 1975   3.9.2

Misrepresentation Act 1967
    s 1   4.3.1
    s 2(1)   4.3.1, 4.6.1
        (2)   4.3.1
    s 3   4.3.1

Pollution Prevention and Control Act
    1999   3.10.2
    Sch 3   3.10.2

Resale Prices Act 1976   4.8.5
Restrictive Trade Practices Act 1976   4.8.5, 9.4.4

Stamp Act 1891
    s 59   7.4.7
    Sch 1   7.4.7

Taxation of Chargeable Gains Act 1992   11.3
    s 10A   11.3.2
    s 48   11.4.1
    s 49   4.3.2
    s 52(4)   7.4.5
    s 116   11.3.3
    s 135   11.3.3
    s 137   11.3.3
        (2)   11.3.3
    s 138   11.3.3
    ss 152–158   7.2.1
    s 152   1.3.6
    s 162   1.2.1, 7.2.2
    s 170   13.4.1
    s 171   11.3.5, 13.4.1
    s 175   13.4.2
    s 177A   13.3.6
    s 179   13.4.1
    s 179A   13.4.1
    s 179B   13.4.1
Trade Descriptions Act 1968   5.9.2
Trade Descriptions Act 1972   5.9.2

Unfair Contract Terms Act 1977   4.4.1
    s 3   4.3.1, 4.4.1
    s 8   4.3.1
    s 12   4.4.1
    Sch 1, para 1(e)   4.4.1

Value Added Tax Act 1994
    s 4(1)   7.4.6
    s 19(2)   7.4.6
    s 43   13.6

Water Industry Act 1991   3.10.2
Water Resources Act 1991   3.10.2, 3.10.3
    s 161   3.10.2
    s 217   3.10.3

TABLE OF STATUTORY INSTRUMENTS

References in the right-hand column are to paragraph numbers.

Collective Redundancies and Transfer of Undertakings (Protection of Employment) (Amendment)
   Regulations 1999, SI 1999/1925 — 6.2.2
Companies (Tables A to F) Regulations 1985, SI 1985/805
   Table A, arts 64–69 — 9.4.1
        art 70 — 5.10.1
        art 94 — 5.10.2
        art 95 — 5.10.2

Environmental Protection (Prescribed Processes and Substances) Regulations 1991, SI 1991/472 — 3.10.2

Fair Trade Act (Amendment) (Mergers Pre-Notification) Regulations 1994, SI 1994/1934 — 2.2.6

Transfer of Undertakings (Protection of Employment) Regulations 1981, SI 1981/1794 — 1.2.3, 1.3.6, 6.3, 6.3.1, 6.3.2, 6.5.1, 6.7.2, 6.7.4, 6.8, 6.8.2
   reg 2(1) — 6.3.1
   reg 3 — 6.3.2, 6.10
     (1) — 6.3.2
   reg 4A — 6.4.2
   reg 5 — 6.3.1, 6.4, 6.4.2
     (1)–(2) — 6.4.1
     (3) — 6.4.2
   reg 6 — 6.5.1, 6.7.5
   reg 8 — 6.6, 6.6.1, 6.7.3, 6.10
     (1) — 6.4.2, 6.6, 6.6.1, 6.6.3, 6.8
     (2) — 6.5.1, 6.6, 6.6.2, 6.6.3
   reg 9 — 6.5.1, 6.7.5
   reg 10 — 6.7.5
   reg 11 — 6.7.5
   reg 12 — 6.3.2

Value Added Tax (Special Provisions) Order 1995, SI 1995/957
   art 5 — 1.2.2, 7.4.6

TABLE OF EC LEGISLATION AND TREATIES

References in the right-hand column are to paragraph numbers.

Legislation, etc

Directive 77/187 (Acquired Rights Directive)	6.3, 6.3.2, 6.5.2, 6.6.1
Art 1(1)	6.3.2
Regulation 4064/89 (Merger Regulation)	2.2.6
Regulation 1310/97	2.2.6

Treaties

European Coal and Steel Community Treaty – Paris 1951	2.2.6
European Community Treaty (as amended by the Treaty of Amsterdam)	5.9.2
Art 81	4.8.5, 4.8.6
(2)	4.8.5
(3)	4.8.5
Art 82	4.8.5, 4.8.6

TABLE OF ABBREVIATIONS

ACAS	Advisory, Conciliation and Arbitration Service
ACT	advance corporation tax
BATNEEC	'best available techniques not entailing excessive cost'
CA 1985	Companies Act 1985
CA 1989	Companies Act 1989
CGT	capital gains tax
DGFT	Director General of Fair Trading
DIB	discrete investment business
EIS	Enterprise Investment Scheme
EPA 1990	Environmental Protection Act 1990
ERA 1996	Employment Rights Act 1996
ETO reason	economic, technical or organisational reason
FII	franked investment income
FSA 1986	Financial Services Act 1986
FSMA 2000	Financial Services and Markets Act 2000
ICTA 1988	Income and Corporation Taxes Act 1988
IPC	integrated pollution control
IPPC	integrated pollution prevention control
MCT	mainstream corporation tax
MTF	Merger Task Force
OFT	Office of Fair Trading
PAYE	pay as you earn
PPCA 1999	Pollution Prevention and Control Act 1999
RPB	recognised professional body
RTPA 1976	Restrictive Trade Practices Act 1976
SDRT	stamp duty reserve tax
SRO	self-regulating organisation
TCGA 1992	Taxation of Chargeable Gains Act 1992
Transfer Regulations	Transfer of Undertakings (Protection of Employment) Regulations 1981
UCTA 1977	Unfair Contract Terms Act 1977
VAT	value added tax
VATA 1994	Value Added Tax Act 1994
VCT	Venture Capital Trust

PART I

GENERAL CONSIDERATIONS

Reading

Ch 1 & 12
Ch 2 & 3
Ch 4
Ch 5
Ch 6 & 10
Ch 8 & 9
Ch 7 & 11   11.3.4   11.4
Ch 13 & 12
Ch 5 & 8   2, 3, 4, 6, 10

Chapter 1

TYPES OF ACQUISITION

1.1 INTRODUCTION

The term 'acquisition' is used to describe a wide variety of transactions including the sale and purchase of public companies whose shares are listed on The Stock Exchange. Listed companies are dealt with in the LPC Resource Book *Corporate Finance: Public Companies and the City* (Jordans). This book is concerned with two types of acquisition – the sale and purchase of a business as a going concern (a business acquisition) and the sale and purchase of a private company by share transfer (a share acquisition) in both cases from an unlisted company or private individuals.

A business acquisition involves the buyer acquiring the assets that make up the business. The contract is made between the buyer and the owner of the business, who may be an individual, a partnership or a company. The business is purchased as a going concern together with all its assets, including goodwill.

A share acquisition is where the buyer acquires the shares in the company that owns the business. The contract is made between the buyer and the owners of the shares. In such a transaction the shares in the company are transferred; there is no change in the ownership of the business – the business remains in the ownership of the company.

1.1.1 A business acquisition

There are effectively two possibilities here – the business may be owned by an individual or partnership (ie it is unincorporated) or the business may be owned by a company.

In either case, the buyer may be an individual, a partnership or a company.

Unincorporated business

> *Example 1*
> Mike Baldwin is a sole trader. He owns a motor repair business and trades under the name 'MB Motors'. He sells 'MB Motors' to Ken Barlow.

> *Example 2*
> Reginald and Maureen Holdsworth are partners in a grocery business. They sell the business to Bettabuys Limited.

Business owned by a company

> *Example 3*
> Computers R Us Limited is a medium-sized company which manufactures computers and also produces a wide range of software packages. In view of the

Chapter 1 contents
Introduction
An unincorporated business – distinguishing between acquisition of a business and mere acquisition of assets
Company – share acquisition, business acquisition or mere acquisition of assets?

prevailing economic climate, the board of directors decides to concentrate on the software business. The board arranges for Computers R Us Limited to sell the computer manufacturing business to Avaricious Limited.

1.1.2 A share acquisition

Example 4
Steve and Andy are equal shareholders in Street Printers Limited, a small print and design company. They are approached by Big Limited, a much larger printing company, with a generous offer for the company. Steve and Andy sell all of their shares in Street Printers Limited to Big Limited.

1.1.3 Choice

The remainder of this chapter considers the choices which the parties involved in the proposed acquisition of an unincorporated business or a company may be faced with and the factors which may influence them in deciding how to proceed.

1.2 AN UNINCORPORATED BUSINESS – DISTINGUISHING BETWEEN ACQUISITION OF A BUSINESS AND MERE ACQUISITION OF ASSETS

Let us assume that the commercial enterprise to be acquired is an unincorporated business that is being run by a sole trader or by a partnership. The parties may decide that the business is to be sold as a going concern, together with all its assets, including goodwill. Such a transaction is referred to, in this book, as a business acquisition. Alternatively, the buyer may not wish to acquire the entire business. He may wish to limit the transaction to the purchase of certain assets of the business. For example, the business assets may include three premises and some machinery. The buyer may want only two of the premises and may not wish to acquire some items of machinery that may be antiquated. This transaction is unlikely to be classed as a sale of a business as a going concern but as a mere sale/acquisition of assets, particularly if the buyer does not acquire the goodwill.

It is important for a number of reasons to distinguish between the sale of a business as a going concern and a mere sale of assets. This distinction is not always easy to make in practice.

1.2.1 Transfer of business in return for shares

Two reliefs, one from capital gains tax (CGT) and the other from income tax, are potentially available where a business is transferred to a company in return for shares. They are not available on a mere sale of assets.

Rolling the gain into shares
Section 162 of the Taxation of Chargeable Gains Act 1992 (TCGA 1992) enables chargeable gains on the disposal of the business to be 'rolled into' the price at which the shares are taken to have been acquired, thus postponing any liability to CGT until the shares are themselves disposed of (see **7.2.2**). For the relief to operate, however,

it is essential that all of the assets of the business are transferred to the company (cash may, however, be ignored for this purpose).

Carrying forward unutilised trading losses

Where a business is transferred to a company wholly or mainly in return for shares, s 386 of the Income and Corporation Taxes Act 1988 (ICTA 1988) allows the former proprietor(s) to carry forward any unutilised trading losses against income received from the company, such as salary as a director or dividends as a shareholder (see **7.2.2**). If, on the other hand, the transfer is not wholly or mainly in return for shares (at least 80% of the consideration must be in shares) or is of assets only, the discontinuance of the business will terminate the ability to carry forward losses.

1.2.2 VAT

Another important factor for both seller and buyer to take into account is VAT (see Chapter 7). If the sale involves a 'transfer of a business as a going concern' (as defined in art 5 of the Value Added Tax (Special Provisions) Order 1995), the transfer is treated as a supply neither of goods nor of services (see **7.4.6**). VAT is therefore not chargeable. It is important to distinguish between the transfer of a business as a going concern and a mere transfer of assets. In the latter case, VAT will be chargeable on the assets passing such as plant and machinery, goodwill and stock.

1.2.3 Employees

The distinction between the sale of a business as a going concern and a mere asset sale has a significant bearing on how the employees of the business are affected and on the potential liability of the buyer and seller to those employees.

Asset sales

Where there is a sale of assets only, the transaction is less likely to be caught by the Transfer of Undertakings (Protection of Employment) Regulations 1981 (the Transfer Regulations) than if the business is sold as a going concern (see below).

The common law position, which will apply where the Transfer Regulations do not, is that, unless the seller redeploys his employees, the employee's contracts will be terminated and the seller will be open to all potential claims arising from the termination of their employment, notably wrongful dismissal, unfair dismissal and redundancy.

Business sales

Where, on the other hand, the business is sold as a going concern, the position is entirely different. The effect of the Transfer Regulations (discussed in Chapter 6) is to transfer automatically to the buyer the contracts of those employees employed immediately before the transfer. In other words, full responsibility for the employees may pass to the buyer of the business, whether he likes it or not.

1.3 COMPANY – SHARE ACQUISITION, BUSINESS ACQUISITION OR MERE ACQUISITION OF ASSETS?

It is possible to acquire a business as a going concern from a company in much the same way as from a sole trader or partnership. Equally, the parties may want to structure the transaction as a mere asset sale. The VAT and employment factors discussed above will again be relevant to this decision.

An alternative to the company itself selling the business (or assets) is for the shareholders of the company (the 'target company') to sell their shares to the buyer. The shares may be held by individuals (in which case they are the sellers) or by another company. If all the shares in the target company are owned by another company (the 'parent') the company is called a wholly owned subsidiary (the seller in this case is the parent company).

The buyer of the assets/business or the shares may be an individual (or individuals) or, perhaps more commonly, a company. If all the shares of the company (the 'target company') are acquired by another company, it becomes a wholly owned subsidiary of the buyer.

The remainder of this chapter concentrates on a business acquisition and a share acquisition and does not consider further a mere sale/acquisition of assets.

The buyer can enter into a contract with the target company for the sale of its business as a going concern. Alternatively, the buyer can contract with the owners of the shares of the target company for the purchase of those shares. In either case, the buyer will achieve its commercial objective of acquiring the business that is being run by the target company, although the legal effect of the two types of acquisition is vastly different.

1.3.1 Legal effect of a business acquisition

When buying a business from a company, the buyer is acquiring a collection of assets, such as premises, plant and machinery, vehicles, stock, goodwill etc. The selling company, stripped of its business, remains in the same hands.

1.3.2 Legal effect of a share acquisition

In contrast, where all the shares of the target company are acquired, the only legal effect of this is that the ownership of the company has changed hands. The target company itself is otherwise in exactly the same shape as it was prior to the acquisition and, in particular, it still owns the business. Whatever assets, liabilities, rights or obligations which the target company had before the acquisition, it will continue to have after it.

1.3.3 Receipt of consideration

It should also be noted that different persons receive the consideration depending on the type of sale. On the sale of the business, it is the target company itself that receives the sale proceeds, whereas, on the sale of the target company's shares, it is the shareholders of the target company.

1.3.4 Does the choice always exist?

Before analysing the advantages and disadvantages of these methods of acquiring a company, it is worth pointing out that there will be situations where the choice may not realistically be available to the parties. This will be the case if, for example, a company has a number of different businesses (perhaps run as separate 'divisions') only one of which the buyer wishes to buy.

1.3.5 The balance between the parties

The parties may have opposing views on the form that the acquisition should take. This stems from the fact that, in relation to many of the factors which influence the decision as to how to proceed, what is an advantage to one party is a disadvantage to the other and vice versa. Although this is very much a generalisation, the owners of a company will often prefer to sell their shares, whereas a buyer will often prefer to acquire the business from the company. In these circumstances, the relative bargaining power of the parties is likely to dictate the outcome.

1.3.6 Comparison between share sales and business sales: seller

Clean break from business

SHARES

Following the disposal of shares, the seller loses his connection with the company. The company itself continues to exist and, in particular, liabilities (hidden or otherwise) continue to be enforceable against it. It is the buyer who will now have a close eye on the state of the company and, thus, the value of his investment.

BUSINESS

This contrasts with the disposal of a business by a company; the shareholders continue to own the company which itself has a continuing liability for the debts of the business. It is a feature of any business sale that legal liability to third parties for debts and obligations of the business remains with the seller. Even where the buyer has contracted to assume responsibility for certain liabilities in the acquisition agreement, this will not affect third parties who can still take action against the seller unless they have expressly released him from liability. Although the seller would have a right of indemnity from the buyer in these circumstances, this may be difficult to enforce, particularly if the buyer is insolvent. In addition, the buyer may have expressly excluded responsibility for certain specific matters for which the seller will, accordingly, remain 'on the hook', as indeed he will for any unforeseen liabilities which may materialise.

WIDER PROTECTIONS ON A SHARE ACQUISITION

Too much can be made, however, of the share sale advantage of a clean break. The very nature of a share sale means that the buyer will seek wide protections from the seller in the acquisition agreement, so that if the target company does turn out to be riddled with undisclosed problems, the buyer has a right of comeback from the seller. Additionally, a clean break will not be possible where the seller has guaranteed obligations of the target company if he is unable to negotiate releases from such obligations on completion.

Scope of warranties

Although the acquisition agreement will invariably contain warranties and indemnities by the seller in favour of the buyer, whether it is a business sale or a share sale, it follows from what has been said above that the scope of these protections needs to be wider in the context of a share sale. For example, on a business sale, there is no need for complex taxation warranties and indemnities for the simple reason that most contingent tax liabilities will remain with the seller. For the same reasons, the investigation into the affairs of the target company needs to be more extensive on a share sale.

Transfer of title

SHARES

Although the pre-contract investigation and the contract documentation will invariably be more extensive on a share sale, the actual mechanics of transferring title are much simpler; a stock transfer form is all that is necessary to transfer title to shares.

BUSINESS

On a business transfer, on the other hand, each separate asset of the business must be transferred and this can involve complications, particularly where consents are required from third parties. Where, for example, leasehold property is involved, the landlord's consent to assignment may be required and this can often significantly delay the transaction. Some assets, such as stock and loose plant and machinery, are transferable by delivery but formal transfers of assets such as land and certain intellectual property rights will be necessary to transfer title.

Restrictions in the Financial Services and Markets Act 2000

SHARES

The requirements of the Financial Services and Markets Act 2000 (FSMA 2000) are more onerous on a share sale than on a business sale. For example, s 21 of the FSMA 2000 places restrictions on the issue of 'investment advertisements' (see **9.2.1**). The definition of an 'investment' in this context includes shares but not businesses. This is something which a potential seller of shares will need to bear in mind if searching for a buyer for his company.

Solicitors (or other professional advisers) who give advice in relation to a proposed sale of shares will also need to ensure that they comply with the FSMA 2000 requirements for authorisation to carry out 'investment business'. The definition of investment business is wide enough to catch a solicitor who is acting in an acquisition of shares (see **9.2.3**).

BUSINESS

Although the provisions of the FSMA 2000 do not extend to the sale of a business, it should be appreciated that, in relation to a target company, the decision to dispose of the business rather than the shares may be taken at a fairly late stage in the negotiations. In other words, compliance with the provisions of the FSMA 2000 may be necessary even if the transaction ultimately proceeds as a business sale.

Employees

SHARES

On a share sale, there is no change of employer; the target company is the employer before and after the change of control, which has no direct effect on the contracts of employment of the work-force. The share sale itself will not, therefore, give rise to any potential claims by the employees and it is the buyer, as the new owner of the company, who will be affected (at least indirectly) by any liabilities and obligations of the target company which arise in the future in relation to those employees. The seller no longer has a direct interest except in relation to warranties given to the buyer in the acquisition agreement.

BUSINESS

The position on the sale of a business has already been noted (see **1.2.3**). The effect of the Transfer Regulations is that the transfer itself does not operate to terminate the contracts of employment and responsibility for the employees passes to the buyer.

EMPLOYEES' CLAIMS

In both types of acquisition, actions by the seller or the buyer, before or after the acquisition, may result in claims by the employees. For example, it may be part of the deal that certain employees are dismissed prior to the transfer or there may be a substantial change in the terms and conditions of employment imposed on the work-force after the transfer. These issues are fully explored in Chapter 6 (business sales) and Chapter 10 (share sales).

Taxation factors

SHARES: DIRECT RECEIPT OF CONSIDERATION

Where the company is owned by individual shareholders, a sale of the shares ensures that the consideration is received by them directly. The taxation consequences of a sale of shares by individuals are relatively straightforward. Shares are chargeable assets for CGT purposes and any disposal which realises a gain will involve (subject to exemptions) a charge to tax at the disposing shareholder's marginal income tax rate. The seller may be able to exempt some or all of the gain if he qualifies for reliefs.

Where the company is owned by another company, a sale of shares results in the selling company receiving the consideration directly. Any capital gain realised by the selling company is likely to be exempt from corporation tax, however, provided the seller is disposing of a substantial shareholding in a trading company. The availability of this exemption (which is discussed fully in Chapter 11) will clearly be an important consideration where ownership of the shares of the target company is in corporate hands.

BUSINESS: TWO-TIER TAXATION

On a business sale, if the company owns the business, then it, as the seller, receives the purchase price. For the benefit to accrue to the shareholders of the selling company, further steps have to be taken, such as the company declaring a dividend or the shareholders liquidating the company. Apart from the administrative inconvenience involved, this also complicates the tax position since there are effectively two separate charging points.

First, the selling company suffers corporation tax on the sale of the business. The disposal of capital assets of the business may give rise to a chargeable gain; proceeds from the disposal of stock are chargeable as income receipts; and the sale of assets in respect of which capital allowances have been claimed, such as plant and machinery, may trigger balancing charges (treated as income receipts) if the assets are sold for more than their tax written down value.

Secondly, there will be a further charge when the proceeds of the sale of the business, as reduced by the above tax charges, are distributed to the shareholders. If the net proceeds are distributed in a winding up there is a disposal by the shareholders of their shares for CGT purposes. The alternative possibility of distribution by dividend involves a Schedule F income tax charge on the shareholders (although they have a tax credit).

REINVESTING THE PROCEEDS

Business

Roll-over relief from CGT/corporation tax under s 152 of the TCGA 1992 is available on the disposal of qualifying assets (including land, fixed plant and machinery and goodwill) used in the trade where the disposal proceeds are applied in the acquisition of replacement qualifying assets (see **7.2.1**). The relief operates to roll the gain into the replacement asset, thus postponing any charge to CGT until the replacement asset is disposed of (without itself being replaced).

Shares: individual sellers

Shares are not qualifying assets for the purpose of the above roll-over relief. However, an individual shareholder who reinvests a chargeable gain from the disposal of shares (or indeed any gain) in subscribing for shares which qualify for the Enterprise Investment Scheme (EIS) would be able to claim a deferral relief. A similar deferral relief is available if the individual invests in Venture Capital Trust shares (VCT). (See **7.2.1** under 'Deferral relief on reinvestment in EIS and VCT shares' and **11.3.1**.)

Shares: corporate sellers

Deferral relief on reinvestment in EIS and VCT shares is not available to a corporate seller which reinvests a chargeable gain in shares. However, as mentioned above, capital gains arising on the disposal by companies of substantial shareholdings in trading companies are exempt from tax.

Taxation considerations are considered in more detail in Chapter 7 (business) and Chapter 11 (shares).

1.3.7 Comparison between share sales and business sales: buyer

Many of the points mentioned above are equally relevant when considering the matter from the buyer's standpoint.

Trade continuity

The main advantage of acquiring the entire share capital of the target company is the lack of disruption to the trade which this causes. From an outsider's point of view, very little will appear to have changed and customers and suppliers will usually be content to carry on dealing with the company as before. A business sale, on the other hand, is more likely to prompt them to review their dealings with the new owners, who may have to work harder to build up confidence again.

BUSINESS

The benefit of existing contracts entered into by the seller will not be transferred to the buyer automatically on a sale of the business. Also, the terms of many contracts require the consent of the third party for an assignment of the benefit to be effective. There may be certain contracts which the buyer sees as crucial to the continued well-being of the business and he may be reluctant to rely on the third party continuing to honour the contract despite the change in ownership of the business. There is always the danger that if a formal approach is made, the third party may feel inclined to seek to renegotiate the terms of the contract as a price for consenting to the assignment.

Where the assets of the business include leasehold property, it will often be necessary to obtain the consent of the landlord to the assignment of the lease. The landlord will wish to ensure that he is not taking any greater risk by having the new owner as tenant and will often agree to the assignment only if the buyer is able to arrange suitable guarantees. Obtaining a landlord's consent may cause delay to the transaction.

The buyer must also remember that, on a business sale, he must arrange for all appropriate insurances to be transferred or alternatively take out fresh cover.

SHARES

None of the above matters need be of concern to the buyer of shares because the assets of the company and outstanding contracts remain unaffected legally by the change in ownership of the company. The buyer of shares does need to be careful on two counts, however. First, he has no guarantee that those third parties who are accustomed to dealing with the company but who are not contractually obliged to do so will continue to deal with it after the change in ownership. Secondly, some contracts contain clauses which permit a party to terminate the contract where control of the company changes hands. Change of control clauses are quite common, for example, in distribution and franchise agreements.

Choice of assets and liabilities

ASSETS

On a share sale, all the underlying assets of the company are indirectly acquired by the buyer, whether he wants them or not. A business sale provides greater flexibility in the sense that the buyer is able to pick and choose the assets he wishes to buy. For example, the buyer may already have some perfectly adequate plant and machinery and may, therefore, wish to exclude certain items of plant and machinery belonging to the seller from the sale.

LIABILITIES

Perhaps the major advantage to a buyer of acquiring the business relates to liabilities. On a share purchase, all the liabilities of the company (hidden or otherwise) remain with it and indirectly become the responsibility of the buyer. Extensive investigations and wide-ranging warranties and indemnities are insufficient to protect the buyer fully. The seller may, for example, not be able to meet a warranty claim or it may prove difficult (and costly) to establish that a particular matter is covered by a warranty.

On a business acquisition, on the other hand, the buyer will only be liable for those matters for which he agrees to take responsibility in the acquisition agreement (liability will then be to the seller and not direct to third parties).

Financial assistance

Section 151 of the Companies Act 1985 (CA 1985) prohibits a company from giving direct or indirect financial assistance to a person who is acquiring or proposing to acquire shares in the company. This important provision is considered fully in **9.3.1**, but it is worth noting here that the buyer's arrangements for financing the acquisition may have a bearing on whether the matter proceeds as a share sale or a business sale.

If the buyer is proposing to finance the acquisition at least partly by borrowing, a business sale will enable him to offer the assets acquired as security for the loan. If, on the other hand, he acquires shares, charging the assets of the target company will come within the prohibition in s 151 – the target company, by granting a charge in favour of the lender, would be giving indirect assistance to the buyer to enable the buyer to acquire its shares.

There are some exceptions to this general prohibition on the giving of financial assistance and there is also a special mechanism enabling a private limited company to give such assistance (see **9.3.1**).

Taxation factors

From a buyer's perspective, most of the taxation advantages lie with a business transfer.

BASE COSTS FOR CGT

On a business acquisition, chargeable assets, such as land, will have a higher base cost for CGT purposes on their subsequent disposal. In an arm's length transaction, the buyer will acquire these assets at market value. When the buyer comes to dispose of them at market value in the future he will be charged to CGT, based on any increase in value since the date he acquired the business.

Contrast this with the position on a share acquisition. Although the buyer acquires the shares at market value, the base cost of the assets which the company owns is the cost at which they were originally acquired by the company. It follows that on a subsequent arm's length disposal of any of these assets by the company, corporation tax will be charged, based on the increase in value since originally acquired by the company. There is, in effect, a deferred tax liability in respect of which a prudent buyer should seek a discount on the price of the shares. The importance of this consideration to the buyer will depend on his future plans for the company and, in particular, whether he is contemplating imminent disposals of any assets by the company (perhaps in an attempt to rationalise the business).

CAPITAL ALLOWANCES

On a business acquisition, the purchase of certain assets, such as plant and machinery and industrial buildings, will enable the buyer to obtain tax relief (as an income deduction) in the form of writing down allowances on the price paid for them. This is a mirror of the corresponding disadvantage to the seller, ie that a balancing charge will arise on the amount by which the actual price paid exceeds the tax written down value (see **7.4.1**).

APPORTIONMENT OF THE PURCHASE CONSIDERATION

On the acquisition of a business, it will be necessary to apportion the total consideration between the various assets acquired (see **7.4.5**). This must be done on a fair and reasonable basis but there is some flexibility here which can be used to gain tax advantages. For example, it will usually be in the buyer's interest to weight the consideration in favour of:

(1) plant and machinery qualifying for capital allowances;
(2) trading stock which will form a deduction against income profits for the buyer;
(3) capital items qualifying for capital gains tax roll-over relief on replacement of business assets.

The apportionment is a matter of negotiation with the seller, and inevitably the parties may be pulling in different directions. For example, a high allocation to plant and machinery qualifying for capital allowances may result in a balancing charge on the seller, thus increasing his tax liability on income profits. A similar result flows from an allocation in favour of stock. The seller may be keen to avoid this, particularly if taper relief on his capital gains is of benefit.

PRESERVING TAX LOSSES

Section 393 of the ICTA 1988 permits trading losses of a company to be carried forward and set against trading profits from the same trade in the future. A feature of a share acquisition is that the tax identity of the company continues and this will enable accumulated tax losses of the target company to be carried forward and set against profits generated after the buyer has acquired the shares (although see **11.5.1** for certain restrictions on this carry forward). This may be a significant factor for a buyer who is confident that he will be able to change the company's fortunes and make it profitable; he will view the accumulated losses as an asset.

The carry forward of losses is not generally possible on a business transfer.

VAT

A charge to VAT may arise on the disposal of business assets alone but not on the disposal of a business as a going concern (see **1.2.2**). VAT is not normally chargeable on a share sale.

STAMP DUTY

On the acquisition of shares, the buyer pays stamp duty at 0.5% of the purchase price to the nearest £5 (ie £5 per £1,000 or part thereof) (see **11.5.2**).

On the acquisition of a business, the buyer pays stamp duty on assets (except assets where title passes by delivery, and exempt assets) and liabilities transferred unless the total value of dutiable items does not exceed £60,000. The buyer pays stamp duty at 1% where the total value of dutiable items is more than £60,000 but does not exceed £250,000; 3% where it is more than £250,000 but does not exceed £500,000; and 4% where it exceeds £500,000 (see **7.4.7**).

1.3.8 Hive-down – a compromise

A hive-down combines characteristics of both business sales and share sales. 'Hiving down' describes the process whereby the target company sells some or all of its assets and undertaking to a brand new company, usually set up as a wholly owned subsidiary of the target company. The buyer then acquires the shares of this new company.

The feature of a hive-down which makes it similar to a business transfer is that only those assets (and liabilities) which the seller wishes to sell and which the buyer wishes to buy will be hived down. Unlike a normal share sale, the buyer will not need to worry about liabilities or other 'skeletons in the cupboard' cropping up unexpectedly; the company he is buying will be 'clean' as it will have no history. It is principally for this reason that hive-downs are popular with receivers, liquidators and administrators of insolvent companies; they are able to attract buyers by hiving down only the profitable parts of the business which can be passed on to the buyer, who need not be unduly worried about the past troubles of the insolvent company. Hive-downs are by no means restricted to this situation, however. It was noted above that, where a buyer wishes to buy one of several businesses owned by a company, a share sale is not a viable alternative; in this situation a hive-down may suit both parties.

Chapter 2

ROLES OF THE PARTIES' ADVISERS

2.1 SOLICITOR'S ROLE

Chapter 2 contents
Solicitor's role
Procedural overview
Accountant's role

The extent of a solicitor's involvement in an acquisition is dependent upon the instructions of the client and varies from case to case. The objective which the parties' solicitors will be expected to achieve is the legal transfer of ownership from seller to buyer of either the shares or the assets of the business as appropriate. The client will also expect his solicitor to identify risks of a legal nature and to seek to protect him from those risks as far as possible.

It is the solicitor's input into the commercial (as opposed to purely legal) aspects of the transaction which varies enormously in practice. The stage at which the client instructs the solicitor tends to be equally as variable. These two factors are often linked, in that if the client sees the solicitor's role as excluding the commercial side of the transaction, he may only instruct the solicitor at a relatively late stage in proceedings, perhaps after the substance of the deal has been negotiated.

The reality is, however, that it is difficult to isolate the legal aspects from the commercial aspects and it is for this reason that most solicitors prefer to be involved as early as possible in the parties' negotiations. This is particularly so where the solicitor is asked to give taxation advice in relation to the acquisition. The way the acquisition is structured can have a significant bearing on the parties' tax position; if the client delays in instructing the solicitor, it may be too late to choose the most tax-effective method. The solicitor will also wish to ensure that his client does not enter into any binding commitments and that all negotiations are subject to contract. Finally, there is a danger that, if the solicitor is not instructed at an early stage, the client may inadvertently commit a breach of the FSMA 2000 (see **9.2**).

Another function which the client will often ask the solicitor to carry out is to coordinate the various professional advisers involved in the proposed acquisition. The acquisition 'team' may include accountants (see **2.3**), surveyors and environmental auditors (where real property is involved), patent agents (intellectual property aspects) and actuaries (pension aspects). Where a listed public company is involved, the team will be much larger including, for example, stockbrokers and merchant bankers. The solicitor will need to liaise carefully with the other members of the acquisition team and is ideally placed to act as coordinator. Once again, the earlier he becomes involved the easier this will be. Specific aspects of the solicitor's role in an acquisition are discussed below.

2.2 PROCEDURAL OVERVIEW

No two acquisitions are the same. However, a typical acquisition – whether it be of a business or of shares – bears a superficial resemblance to a conveyancing transaction. It can be broken down into the same five distinct stages: pre-contract; contract; pre-completion; completion; and post-completion. In practice, contract and completion often take place simultaneously so that the pre-completion stage disappears.

2.2.1 Pre-contract

Heads of agreement

Once negotiations have reached a certain point, the parties may wish to record the main points on which they have agreed and the basis on which they are prepared to proceed with the transaction. The parties often feel more confident that the whole exercise will not prove to be a waste of time, money and effort if they are able to point to a document setting out at least some of the fundamental issues (eg price). Drawing up the document may serve to focus the minds of the parties and establish whether there is a sufficient measure of agreement between them to make it worthwhile continuing with the proposed acquisition. It may also be helpful to show the heads of agreement to professional advisers acting for the parties and, indeed, to those who may have been approached by the buyer to finance the proposed acquisition.

Heads of agreement are by no means universally employed in acquisitions, however. The parties' solicitors often take the view that the time involved in producing them can be more usefully employed in drafting and negotiating the main agreement, which – unlike the heads of agreement – will incorporate appropriate protections for their clients. Regrettably, it is relatively common for the parties to enter into heads of agreement before taking any professional advice.

Two considerations will often arise in connection with heads of agreement: first, whether the terms (or some of them) are to be legally binding, and secondly, whether the buyer is to be granted an exclusive right to bargain with the seller.

'SUBJECT TO CONTRACT'

It is extremely unlikely that the buyer, in particular, will want all the heads to be binding. The signing of heads of agreement will invariably precede the buyer requisitioning a detailed investigation of the target, the outcome of which may prompt him to seek to withdraw from the transaction or to renegotiate the price. He will not wish to be fully committed until he has completed the investigation and is satisfied that he is adequately protected by appropriate warranties and indemnities included in the main agreement. Indeed, if the heads were fully binding, there would be little incentive for the seller to sign a further agreement.

Normal practice is for the document containing the heads of agreement to be marked 'subject to contract' and (because of the uncertainty as to the precise effect of this phrase) for it to include a statement that the provisions are not intended to be legally binding.

The parties may, however, want some of the provisions which are included in the heads of agreement to be legally binding, in which case this needs to be expressly stated. For example, provisions relating to confidentiality, exclusivity of bargaining (see below), and liability for costs in the event of an abortive transaction, will need to be legally binding from the outset.

EXCLUSIVE BARGAINING

A buyer who is considering acquiring the target may be reluctant to spend the time and money necessary to undertake a full investigation into the target's affairs unless he is granted an exclusive bargaining right for a certain period, ie the seller agrees that, during this period, the seller will not enter into or continue negotiations for the sale of the target with anyone else.

It is clear from the House of Lords' case of *Walford v Miles* [1992] 2 WLR 174 that such a clause (commonly known as a 'lock-out clause') is enforceable provided it is sufficiently certain. Some doubt had been thrown on this by the Court of Appeal which found a lock-out agreement to be void on the grounds that it was no more than an agreement to negotiate (it being a long-established contractual principle that an agreement to agree is unenforceable).

In the House of Lords, Lord Ackner concurred with the view that an agreement to negotiate is void for uncertainty, pointing out that the essence of negotiations is that the parties are entitled to withdraw from those negotiations at any time and for any reason. He described these sort of agreements as 'lock-in' agreements. Lord Ackner, on the other hand, saw no such difficulty with 'lock-out' agreements, ie agreements not to negotiate with anyone else for a fixed period, provided they are sufficiently certain. The House of Lords decided unanimously that the lock-out clause in question was not sufficiently certain because it did not specify how long it was to last.

In addition, consideration must be given in order to make the clause enforceable.

Due diligence

Before the buyer enters into a contractual commitment to buy the target business or company ('the target') he will want to acquire as much information about it as is possible in the circumstances (time constraints and expense being the main limiting factors). The buyer's solicitor will be involved in gathering much of this information. It will usually be in the seller's interest to co-operate fully in this exercise and to reply, via his solicitor, to the buyer's specific enquiries; this process is called due diligence and is considered in detail in Chapter 3.

Confidentiality agreement

It is important, where there is a large team involved in an acquisition, that there is some control over the flow of information. The solicitor is ideally placed to act as 'information controller', ie the person through whom all requests for information are made and who collates all the information passing to and from the other side.

A problem which often arises during this information-gathering process, however, is that the seller may be understandably reluctant to pass on sensitive information concerning the business in advance of an unconditional exchange of contracts. The proposed buyer may even be a competitor of the target, in which case the seller may be concerned about revealing information, such as customer lists and important contracts, which the competitor would be able to use to his own advantage if the acquisition fell through. The extent to which the seller is wise to disclose sensitive information depends very much on the nature of the business, the type of information requested and the identity of the buyer.

A related point is that the seller (and indeed the buyer) may wish to keep the proposed deal itself a closely guarded secret. The seller will often not want customers or suppliers to know that the business is on the market; he may also be particularly concerned that his work-force does not get to know about the negotiations for fear that this may cause a spate of rumour and uncertainty. In these circumstances, the buyer may be hampered in carrying out full enquiries as there will be obvious practical difficulties in the seller extracting relevant data and allowing the buyer's advisers access to papers and premises, etc without alerting others (employees in particular) that an acquisition is contemplated.

Where the seller is prepared to allow sensitive information to pass prior to unconditional exchange he is well advised to require the buyer to enter into a confidentiality agreement. The initial draft of the agreement is prepared by the seller and may contain some or all of the following:

(1) a definition of confidential information (this is likely to exclude information in the public domain and information already known to the proposed buyer);

(2) an obligation on the buyer not, without the seller's consent, to disclose or use such information except for authorised purposes (as defined) in connection with the acquisition. A list of authorised persons entitled to receive the information, such as certain employees and professional advisers of the buyer, may be included (with an assurance by the buyer that he will notify them of the terms of the confidentiality agreement). In addition, the seller may prevent the buyer from soliciting customers, suppliers or employees of the target for a specified period (although care needs to be taken that these provisions are not void as being in restraint of trade);

(3) an undertaking by the buyer to return or destroy such information (including copies) if the acquisition does not proceed;

(4) an agreement that the parties will not, without the written consent of the other party, make any announcement or disclosure of the fact that negotiations are taking place.

The various undertakings of the buyer may be contained in a formal agreement between the parties or, quite commonly, in a letter to the seller. Whichever form is chosen, consideration must be given for this part of the heads of agreement to be enforceable.

A confidentiality agreement provides comfort to a seller who is in a sensitive position commercially; nevertheless, it may prove extremely difficult for the seller to monitor breaches and, indeed, to assess the loss where he can prove that breaches have occurred.

2.2.2 Contract

When both parties are prepared to commit themselves contractually to effect the acquisition, they will enter into an acquisition agreement. At the same time, the seller will hand over a disclosure letter to the buyer.

Acquisition agreement

In the acquisition agreement (or 'sale and purchase' agreement) the parties agree to transfer title to the shares (share acquisition) or the assets of the business (business acquisition). This aspect of the agreement tends to be short; nevertheless, the agreement will invariably be very lengthy (particularly on a share transfer) as a result of the protections sought by the buyer in the form of warranties and indemnities from the seller.

The normal practice is for the buyer's solicitor to prepare the first draft of the agreement, which he then submits to the seller's solicitor for approval (the opposite to the normal conveyancing practice). The principle reason for this is that much of the agreement is taken up with protections for the buyer.

Disclosure letter

The disclosure letter, which is closely linked to the acquisition agreement, is prepared by the seller's solicitor. The purpose of this document is to disclose matters relating to the target and its affairs which, were they to remain undisclosed, would result in the seller being in breach of warranty (see **4.4.2**). The seller attaches copies of documents referred to in the letter (the 'disclosure bundle') and this can make it a lengthy document.

The disclosure letter may be written by the seller or by the seller's solicitor. In the latter case it should incorporate an appropriate disclaimer that all information has been provided by the client and that the solicitor accepts no responsibility for its contents. The letter is handed to the buyer at the same time as the acquisition agreement is entered into. It has such an important bearing on the seller's potential liability under the agreement that the seller's solicitor should send it to his opposite number in draft form well in advance of this; a final version will be discussed and agreed by the parties' solicitors in much the same way as the acquisition agreement itself. Indeed, the disclosures may prompt the buyer to renegotiate the deal (perhaps asking for a reduction in the price) or to seek to include further protections in the main agreement, usually by way of specific indemnities.

Negotiation and drafting

It will be clear from what has been said above that an acquisition is very document-based. An important aspect of a solicitor's role, whether he acts for the seller or the buyer, is negotiating, agreeing and then drafting the different versions of the documents as the transaction progresses, particularly the main acquisition agreement (and, to a lesser extent, the disclosure letter) until a final form of each agreement can be agreed. Understandably, the initial draft is likely to favour heavily the party producing it. For example, the main acquisition agreement, when prepared by the buyer's solicitor, is unlikely to contain limitations on the seller's liability for breaches of warranty; it will be up to the seller's solicitor to draft this section of the agreement and negotiate for its inclusion.

In practice, one of the main difficulties with this process is that the parties' solicitors cannot conduct these negotiations in isolation. Clearly, the solicitor must involve his client at all stages, but he will also need to liaise closely with the other members of the acquisition team. For example, the solicitor will be unwise to agree detailed amendments to warranties relating to taxation without first consulting the tax specialists in his own firm and, commonly, the accountant member of the team as well.

Briefly, the order of events in which the respective solicitors negotiate the contract documentation is often as follows.

(1) The buyer's solicitor prepares the draft acquisition agreement. He submits this to his client and, with his client's agreement, forwards it to the seller's solicitor.

(2) The seller's solicitor considers the draft with his client and amends it, returning the draft (as marked-up) to the buyer's solicitor.

(3) The seller's solicitor prepares a draft disclosure letter based on information provided by his client which, after obtaining approval of his client, he forwards to the buyer's solicitor.

(4) Both parties' solicitors agree final versions (there may have been many drafts before getting to this stage).

Each stage in the process will involve discussions with the other members of the acquisition team.

2.2.3 Pre-completion

Completion normally and, indeed, ideally, takes place immediately after the acquisition agreement has been signed (simultaneous exchange and completion). However, there may be a gap between contract and completion where, for example, the parties enter into the acquisition agreement conditionally upon the happening of certain events (see **5.5** and **8.5**). The parties will be concerned mainly during this period with the satisfaction of any such conditions. The buyer's solicitor will also repeat some of the searches carried out during the due diligence process (see **9.4.2**).

2.2.4 Completion

On completion, title to the assets which are the subject of the acquisition is formally transferred by the seller to the buyer in return for the buyer providing the purchase price or consideration.

On a share sale, the seller's solicitor will hand over duly signed stock transfer forms and there will be a completion board meeting of the target company to deal with such matters as the resignation and appointment of directors and the approval of the share transfers (see **9.4.3**). The method by which completion takes place will normally be included as a clause of the acquisition agreement itself. Provisions dealing with what is to happen on completion are, therefore, negotiated by the parties at the pre-contract stage in the usual way. In addition, completion board minutes (and, if necessary, general meeting minutes) will also have been negotiated and agreed by the parties. They will usually be referred to in the acquisition agreement as being in the 'agreed form' and will often be annexed to or contained in schedules to the acquisition agreement.

On a business sale, any land which is included in the sale must be transferred by deed (assignment, transfer or conveyance as appropriate). Assignment of certain intellectual property rights (eg copyrights, patents and trademarks) is necessary. Goodwill and the benefit of contracts may also be formally assigned. On the other hand, no formal documentation is required to transfer title to assets such as loose plant and machinery and stock – title to these passes on delivery (see **5.6.1**).

2.2.5 Post-completion

On a share sale, the buyer's solicitor will ensure that stock transfer forms are duly stamped; that the internal registers of the target company are updated, to reflect, for example, the change in members and directors; and that the appropriate forms (eg Form 288a or b on a change of director) are filed at the Companies Registry (see **9.4.4**). On a business sale involving the transfer of land, the buyer's solicitor must make appropriate registrations at HM Land Registry or the Land Charges Department.

2.2.6 Ensuring compliance with EC and domestic 'merger' provisions

Both parties' solicitors must consider whether the proposed acquisition is likely to be affected by the provisions of EC or UK law which seek to control 'mergers'. The term 'merger' in this context covers share sales and business sales, but it will generally only be large-scale transactions which will be affected. This is not to say, however, that merger control is limited to listed companies; it may well apply to acquisitions of sufficient importance involving private companies.

The parties to a merger can either notify the relevant authorities in advance of completion or post-completion. In practice they often notify in advance if referral is a real possibility.

UK control

Mergers are regulated by the Fair Trading Act 1973, as amended by the Companies Act 1989 (CA 1989). However, where EC Regulation 4064/89 (as amended by EC Regulation 1301/97) applies (ie where the merger has a 'Community dimension', see below at 'Council Regulation 4064/89') this overrides the UK legislation, or that of any other Member State.

WHEN WILL AN ACQUISITION BE CONTROLLED BY THE FAIR TRADING ACT 1973?

The Fair Trading Act 1973 defines a merger as occurring when two or more enterprises (one of which must be carried on in the UK or by or under the control of a body corporate incorporated in the UK) cease to be distinct enterprises (s 64). The term 'enterprise' is widely defined as 'the activities, or part of the activities of a business' (s 63(2)). Most typical share sale and business sale arrangements are clearly within the general definition. However, for a merger to be caught by the legislation, either of the following must apply:

(1) the merger will result in at least 25% of all goods or services of a particular description which are supplied in the UK, or a substantial part of it, being supplied by or to the same person (the 'market share' test); or

(2) the value of assets transferred exceeds £70 million (the 'assets' test).

The 'market share' test involves an assessment of when goods or services are of a separate description and, accordingly, form a distinct market. This makes it very difficult for the parties' advisers to be certain when the criterion is met. Where the market for particular goods or services is small, acquisitions which are relatively minor in terms of overall value may, nevertheless, be the subject of regulation.

The 'assets' test is based on the value of gross assets, without deduction for liabilities; the price of the target is not a relevant factor.

WHAT IS THE SCHEME OF CONTROL?

The Director General of Fair Trading (DGFT) (and the Secretary of State in cases relating to national security) can refer a proposed or a completed merger to the Competition Commission which, if it feels (after carrying out a full investigation) that the merger is not in the public interest, may recommend to the Secretary of State that the merger be prohibited or, if it is completed, unscrambled.

The sequence of events is as follows.

(1) The DGFT, after investigation, makes recommendations to the Secretary of State about any merger (whether prospective or completed) which comes to his

attention. The parties are not obliged to notify the merger to the Office of Fair Trading (OFT); the onus is on the DGFT to ensure that he is aware of mergers which meet the criteria.

(2) The Secretary of State has a discretion to refer the merger to the Competition Commission. In October 2000, the Secretary of State announced that it would be his policy to accept the DGFT's advice save in exceptional circumstances. The general rule is that the Secretary of State must make the reference no later than 4 months after the merger has taken place. Normally, however, he makes the reference in advance of the merger and this prompts the parties to delay completion. In significant merger cases, decisions of the Secretary of State can be found on the OFT's website (www.oft.gov.uk).

(3) If the merger is referred to it, the Competition Commission investigates whether the merger is against the public interest (see below).

(4) The Competition Commission reports on the matter to the Secretary of State and the report is laid before Parliament.

(5) The Secretary of State, who is obliged to consider any advice from the DGFT (but is not bound by the advice), decides whether to approve or prohibit the merger (where the merger has been completed he can order it to be undone). He is not obliged to follow the Competition Commission's recommendations.

What factors does the Competition Commission take into account in deciding whether the merger is in the public interest?

Section 84 of the Fair Trading Act 1973 obliges the Competition Commission to take into account all relevant circumstances including the desirability of the following:

(1) maintaining and promoting effective competition between persons supplying goods and services in the UK;

(2) promoting the interests of consumers, purchasers and other users of goods and services in the UK in respect of the prices charged for them and in respect of their quality and the variety of goods and services supplied;

(3) promoting, through competition, the reduction of costs and the development and use of new techniques and new products, and of facilitating the entry of new competitors into existing markets;

(4) maintaining and promoting the balanced distribution of industry and employment in the UK;

(5) maintaining and promoting competitive activity in markets outside the UK on the part of producers of goods, and suppliers of goods and services, in the UK.

Pre-notification procedure and undertakings

The CA 1989 (as amended by the Fair Trading Act (Amendment) (Mergers Pre-Notification) Regulations 1994 (SI 1994/1934) introduced some important amendments to the procedure which may be of benefit to the parties to a proposed merger.

First, the parties may serve a 'merger' notice (containing prescribed information) on the DGFT giving him advance notice of a merger. The effect of serving the notice is that, unless the Secretary of State refers the merger to the Competition Commission within a specified time period, he loses the right to make such a reference. The time-limit is 20 days from receipt of the notice (although this may be extended by a maximum of 15 days). This is a useful device which enables parties who are concerned about the possibility of a reference, with all the attendant uncertainties and delays that it would bring, to force the hand of the Secretary of State. It is, however, a requirement that the proposed merger must be made public before the notice is served.

Secondly, the Secretary of State has the power to accept undertakings from the parties (eg providing for parts of the business or undertaking to be sold off after completion) rather than making a merger reference.

EC control

COUNCIL REGULATION 4064/89 (AS AMENDED BY REGULATION 1310/97)

The Regulation gives the European Commission exclusive jurisdiction (eg overriding UK merger control in the Fair Trading Act 1973) with regard to 'concentrations with a Community dimension'. 'Concentration' is widely defined but it will arise where control (itself widely defined) of an undertaking is acquired, directly or indirectly. Whether a concentration has a 'Community dimension' is measured in terms of aggregate turnover (eg the aggregate world-wide turnover of all the undertakings concerned must exceed €5,000 million).

The Regulation imposes an obligation on the parties to notify the European Commission's Merger Task Force (MTF) before the concentration is put into effect. The MTF will then decide whether the concentration is compatible with the common market. It is expressly provided that a concentration will be declared incompatible with the common market if it creates or strengthens a dominant position so that effective competition would be significantly impeded in the common market or in a substantial part of it.

The European Commission has the power to order the unscrambling of concentrations which have been put into effect in breach of the Regulation and to impose fines (of up to 10% of turnover) for contraventions of the Regulation.

THE EUROPEAN COAL AND STEEL COMMUNITY TREATY

The European Coal and Steel Community Treaty governs certain acquisitions and mergers involving coal and steel undertakings (to the exclusion of national merger legislation), requiring authorisation from the European Commission.

See LPC Resource Book *Corporate Finance: Public Companies and the City* (Jordans) for more detail on the area of merger regulation.

2.2.7 Summary of procedure for conditional contracts

BUYER'S SOLICITOR   **SELLER'S SOLICITOR**

Take instructions	Take instructions

Agree heads of agreement

Due diligence	Draft confidentiality agreement

Agree confidentiality agreement

Reply to enquiries

Draft acquisition agreement	Draft disclosure letter

Agree acquisition agreement and disclosure letter

STAGE 1

STAGE 2

EXCHANGE ACQUISITION AGREEMENT
SELLER DELIVERS DISCLOSURE LETTER

STAGE 3

Ensure compliance with conditions

Repeat searches

STAGE 4

COMPLETION

STAGE 5

POST-COMPLETION MATTERS

If the parties are able to exchange and complete simultaneously, stage 3 above would not be necessary, although repeat searches would be carried out prior to stage 2.

2.3 ACCOUNTANT'S ROLE

The precise roles of accountants acting for the parties in an acquisition vary considerably. Indeed, the client may instruct more than one firm of accountants and assign a different role to each firm. There follows a summary of some of the main functions the accountant may be expected to perform.

2.3.1 Valuing the target

The seller's accountant may be asked to put a value on the target business or company, which can be used as a starting point for negotiations with potential buyers. The buyer's accountant will go through a similar exercise on behalf of his client and his valuation will determine the parameters within which the buyer is prepared to negotiate.

The value of the business is, of course, what a buyer is prepared to pay for it, which itself depends on the buyer's motives for acquiring it. For example, the buyer's principal motive may be to prevent the target from being acquired by a competitor; or the buyer may wish to acquire a competitor in order to reduce competition, or to acquire a supplier in order to protect the source of supply. In these instances, a valuation based on established principles is unlikely to coincide with the worth of the business to the buyer. Similarly, the seller may have his own special reasons for selling which may impact more on the negotiations than a formal valuation.

A detailed analysis of the principles of valuation is outside the scope of this book. However, it is important that the parties' solicitors understand the basis on which any valuations have been undertaken as this can have an important effect on the provisions which are included in the main acquisition agreement.

The two main categories of valuation are assets-based valuations and earnings-based valuations.

Assets-based valuation

A valuation based on the net assets of the target is rare as it will not usually reflect the true value of the target as a going concern. It is appropriate on a business sale only in so far as the assets include goodwill; and the valuation of this intangible asset is itself likely to be earnings based (see below).

An assets-based valuation of a company may be appropriate where a company is in financial difficulty or has been making consistently low profits. In these circumstances, the 'break up' value of the business may be more than its value as a going concern. Also, certain types of company lend themselves more easily to this method of valuation, for example property and investment companies.

Earnings-based valuation

The potential of the target to generate profits in the future is the crucial factor in an earnings-based valuation. The main pointer towards this potential is the level of profit achieved by the target in the years leading up to the proposed earnings. Appropriate adjustments to the profit figures appearing in the accounts will be necessary, however, when using these historical figures to forecast future profits. For example, the profits may be significantly understated for this purpose if the award of large salaries to directors, who are also shareholders, has been used as the main method of extracting profits from the company. On the other hand, profits may be overstated where, for example, goods or services have been supplied to the target on favourable terms by connected persons, which arrangements will discontinue after completion.

The next stage is to apply a multiplier to the figure reached above in an attempt to capitalise the future profit-generating capacity of the target. Sometimes, the valuer will have recourse to information published about comparable quoted companies in the same industry, in determining the appropriate multiplier.

There are several other methods of valuing the target and there are additional factors involved when valuing holdings of shares of less than 100%.

2.3.2 Completion accounts

Where the price of the target has been arrived at on the basis of either net assets or profits, the parties may not wish to rely on out-of-date audited accounts or unaudited management accounts containing this information. In these circumstances, they will sometimes provide for the drawing up of completion accounts following completion and if the 'net assets' or 'earnings' are not as anticipated, for appropriate adjustments to be made to the price (see **8.4.2**).

The seller's accountant, who will probably be the target company's auditor, will usually prepare the completion accounts on the basis set out in the acquisition agreement. The seller's accountant will then try to agree the accounts with the buyer's accountant; if they cannot reach agreement, it is usually provided that the dispute is to be referred to an independent accountant.

Where the valuation of the target is based on its future profit-generating capacity, the parties may agree that some of the consideration is deferred until after completion, the amount then payable being calculated by reference to profits actually achieved for specified periods after completion (this is called an 'earn out' and is discussed in detail in **8.4.2**). These arrangements will again involve input from both parties' accountants in advising on the details of the scheme to be included in the acquisition agreement and, once again, preparing and agreeing accounts for the periods concerned.

2.3.3 Investigation and report

The prospective buyer will often commission a full accountant's investigation and report into the affairs of the target business or company before committing himself to the acquisition. This aspect is dealt with in Chapter 3.

Chapter 3

INVESTIGATING THE TARGET

3.1 WHAT ARE THE BUYER'S OBJECTIVES?

During the initial negotiations on the terms of the proposed acquisition, the buyer may not have any detailed knowledge of the target. He will often be relying in these early stages on what he has been told by the seller, what is publicly known about the target, any sales information released by the seller, any knowledge of the target's business which he has acquired from previous dealings, perhaps as a supplier or even a competitor, and a search of the company's file at the Companies Registry.

The parties or their advisers may draw up heads of agreement to record the results of their preliminary discussions and to provide a helpful basis on which to proceed to the signing of the main agreement (see Chapter 2). The buyer will not, however, want to enter into a binding commitment to acquire the target until he has acquired as much information as possible about it and this information-gathering stage is often known as 'due diligence'. The aim of due diligence is to enable the buyer to decide whether or not to go ahead with the proposed acquisition and, if so, on what terms. In particular, the results of the investigation may prompt the buyer to renegotiate the price for the target.

Whilst the due diligence process can provide the buyer with an enormous insight into the business he is planning to buy, it is important to remember the basic common law principle of 'caveat emptor' (buyer beware). Due to the harshness of this principle, the buyer will seek to protect himself in two ways, namely, like any prudent buyer, by obtaining as much information as possible on the target and, secondly, backing that up with extensive warranties and indemnities in the acquisition agreement. The purpose of the warranties and indemnities is to provide the buyer with contractual protection should the target not turn out to be as expected (see Chapter 4). It is important to remember that the two are not mutually exclusive and, indeed, that a thorough investigation of the target should reveal areas where the buyer is at risk and needs to protect himself by including warranties and indemnities.

3.2 SCOPE OF THE INVESTIGATION

3.2.1 Business or shares?

Share sale

The extent of the investigation needs to be more extensive on the acquisition of the entire share capital of a company than on the acquisition of a business. This is because the buyer of shares acquires a 'live' company with all its assets and, perhaps more significantly, its liabilities, whether actual or contingent, fixed or unquantified. There is far more involved than checking that the seller has title to the shares themselves; all aspects of the target company are of concern to a potential buyer and should, ideally, be examined.

Chapter 3 contents
What are the buyer's objectives?
Scope of the investigation
Accountants' investigation and report
Enquiries before contract
Searching the file at the Companies Registry
Internal registers
Credit reports
Checking the solvency of the seller
Property matters
Environmental matters

Business sale

The buyer of a business does not assume the liabilities of the business (except as regards employees, see Chapter 6), which remain with the seller unless he is released from them by the third parties involved. The buyer will, however, often agree to accept responsibility for certain of these liabilities by giving the seller an indemnity in the acquisition agreement. The buyer will, therefore, direct his investigation at the specific assets which he wishes to acquire and the liabilities which he is prepared to accept. It should, however, be appreciated that the goodwill of the business acquired by the buyer may be adversely affected by certain liabilities, even if these remain with the seller (eg a successful claim against the seller for manufacturing defective products). Consequently, it is in the buyer's interest to discover as much about the business generally as is feasible in the circumstances.

3.2.2 Limiting factors

The buyer is not always able to be as painstaking as he would like in his investigation of the target. A number of matters may, in practice, hinder a thorough scrutiny of the target business or company.

Time constraints

Time constraints are often the most significant factor in determining the scope of the buyer's enquiries. It is in the nature of commercial transactions that tight (and sometimes unrealistic) timetables are often agreed upon by the parties. Also, where the seller is in a strong bargaining position (perhaps because there are other interested parties) he may dictate a short timescale for the parties to enter into the contract.

Financial resources and manpower

The buyer may be unable to commit sufficient financial resources or manpower to a full-scale examination of the target. Saving money at this stage of the transaction may prove a false economy in the long term but, nevertheless, the buyer will inevitably be working within the constraints of a budget.

Confidentiality

The seller may be keen to keep the proposed sale a secret, not only from outsiders, such as competitors and suppliers, but also from his own work-force (see **2.2.1**). The practical limitation which this puts on the extent of the searches and enquiries of the buyer and his advisers is obvious. The seller will often insist that all communications are channelled through one person; that a code-name is used for all such contact; and that the true purpose of any visits to the seller's premises by the buyer or his advisers (eg a surveyor) is not disclosed.

It has also been seen that sellers may, understandably, be reluctant to pass on commercially sensitive information to the buyer, such as customer lists, in advance of exchange of contracts. This problem may, in some cases, be mitigated by a confidentiality agreement between the parties.

Link with contractual protection

The extent to which a buyer needs to safeguard himself by including warranties and indemnities in the agreement will depend, at least in part, on the scope of his investigation. The less he knows about the target, the more he will wish to safeguard his position in the contract. This may, in fact, work against a buyer who has conducted a thorough investigation into the target, as it will leave him vulnerable to the argument from the seller that some of the warranties and indemnities are unnecessary. The buyer will, on the other hand, be reluctant to give up contractual protection as a consequence of conducting a full investigation.

3.3 ACCOUNTANTS' INVESTIGATION AND REPORT

3.3.1 Nature and purpose

The buyer may instruct a firm of accountants (if the buyer is a company, its auditors will often be appointed) to investigate the target and produce a report. Normally, this is done when negotiations are far enough advanced for the buyer to feel that the expense is justified.

The accountants' report is often central to the conduct of negotiations between the parties and plays an important role in the framing of the acquisition documentation, particularly the warranties and indemnities (although it is likely that the buyer will have produced the first draft of the main agreement before the report is available). It is important that the buyer's professional advisers liaise with their client and with each other on the precise scope of the various investigations to be carried out. An early meeting between the buyer's solicitor and the reporting accountants should serve to define areas of responsibility, avoid duplication and determine a timetable which ensures that the report is produced early enough to be useful in negotiations.

The buyer should instruct the firm of accountants formally by a letter of engagement, which should set out clearly the matters on which the accountants are required to report (the initial draft of the letter is often produced by the firm of accountants after discussions with their client). The accountant will need to be in direct contact with the proprietors or management of the target and must be informed of the terms of any confidentiality agreement between the parties.

3.3.2 Matters covered by the report

The matters on which the accountants may be asked to report include the commercial activities of the target, management structure and employees, taxation, profitability, balance sheet strength, accounting systems and policies, and premises.

Commercial activities
The report may include the following:

(1) details of the past, present and planned activities of the target;
(2) an analysis of the market in which the target operates and a description of its main customers, geographical coverage, market share and principal competitors;
(3) details of pricing policy, terms of trade (including credit arrangements) and significant agreements with suppliers, customers, agents, etc.

Management structure and employees

The information requested may include the following:

(1) management structure and details of the ages, qualifications and service records of the directors and senior management;
(2) details of the service contracts of the directors and senior management including remuneration, commission, fringe benefits, pensions, profit-sharing and share option schemes, etc;
(3) the number of other employees (broken down into departments and locations) and details of pay structure and staff relations;
(4) staff training schemes and recruitment policies.

Taxation

The buyer will usually want detailed information about the tax affairs of the target (particularly on a share acquisition). The tax due diligence will usually cover the following main areas:

(1) the current tax position of the target – details of current tax liabilities, the adequacy of provisions made for tax in the accounts of the target, VAT and PAYE compliance and whether the target's tax affairs are up to date;
(2) if relevant, what effect the acquisition will have on the tax affairs of the target and of the buyer, for example whether the transaction will itself create any charges to tax;
(3) the likely future tax position of the target;
(4) the warranties and indemnities that should be obtained, including any specific indemnities to cover known problem areas.

Profitability

The accountants will usually conduct a detailed review of the audited results of a target company for the previous three or four accounting periods and any unaudited information which may be available (eg management accounts), with a view to providing a detailed breakdown of turnover, overheads and profit (perhaps in relation to each activity of the target) and analysing relevant trends.

Balance sheet strength

The accountants will report on the assets and liabilities of the target and may include details of (and comments on) the following:

(1) borrowing commitments, both long term and short term, including details of any security provided;
(2) recent capital expenditure, outstanding capital commitments, long-term contracts and contingent liabilities;
(3) debtors and provision for bad debts;
(4) insurance policies (and adequacy of cover).

Accounting systems and policies

A report on the accounting systems and the accounting policies adopted by the target will assist the buyer in understanding the accounts and in determining whether changes will be necessary after completion (eg to integrate with the buyer's systems).

Premises

The buyer will usually be relying on his solicitor to provide detailed information about the properties owned or occupied by the target but the accountant's report will often contain brief details including location, use and tenure of each property.

3.3.3 Use of the report

The final section of the report which usually sets out the accountants' summary of the strengths and weaknesses of the target, any recommendations and his conclusions on the reasonableness of the price is often of greatest interest to the buyer who may use the report as a lever for lowering the price.

Practice on allowing the seller to have a copy of the report is variable (although, if he is given a copy, the summary and conclusion will often be omitted). The seller's disclosure letter may deem matters contained or referred to in the accountant's report to have been disclosed by the seller (thus potentially reducing the seller's exposure under the warranties). In these circumstances the buyer may insist on a warranty by the seller as to the accuracy of the contents of the accountant's report (see **4.4.2**). These are all matters for negotiation between the parties.

The buyer will, of course, have claims against the reporting accountants if the report is negligently prepared (both in contract for breach of the implied duty of reasonable skill and care and in tort for negligent misstatement). It is noted in **4.6.2** that if the buyer does not commission his own report but merely relies on the audited accounts of the target company, he will not normally have any remedy against the company's auditors if they act to his detriment.

3.4 ENQUIRIES BEFORE CONTRACT

3.4.1 The request

The buyer's solicitor will often begin the due diligence process by forwarding a detailed request for information to the seller's solicitor often known as a 'due diligence questionnaire'. This request should not be a pro-forma document but should be tailored to the particular business involved, thus avoiding burdening the seller's solicitor with unnecessary or irrelevant questions. The buyer's solicitor should liaise with the other professional advisers representing the buyer in an attempt to avoid duplicating requests for information; he will often act as 'information controller'.

3.4.2 The replies

On a share sale, if any of the selling shareholders are not also directors, they may have little personal knowledge of the matters raised. Consequently, the seller's solicitor will have to obtain much of the information which is requested about the structure of the company and the running of the business from the management of the target company. Whatever the source of the information, the seller has little to gain from giving evasive replies (particularly if the replies are to be attached to the disclosure letter, thus qualifying the warranties). So, provided he is satisfied as to the confidentiality of any information passing to the buyer, he should give full and frank replies to the pre-contract enquiries.

The buyer's solicitor, in conjunction with his client and the rest of the team, should check the replies carefully and follow up any points which remain outstanding. As with the accountants' report, the replies are likely to have a significant bearing on the warranties and indemnities required by the buyer.

3.4.3 Nature of information required

Contracts fundamental to the business

One of the main advantages of a share acquisition is the lack of disruption which it causes to the target's trade, since outstanding contracts generally remain unaffected by the change in ownership of the company. This contrasts with a business acquisition where the benefit of existing contracts entered into by the seller will not pass to the buyer unless the contracts are assigned or novated. In either case, however, the buyer will require full details (and copies) of all significant contracts which the target has entered into. On a business sale, the buyer should examine those contracts which he considers vital to the well-being of the business to see whether they require consent to assignment or contain other restrictions on assignment. The buyer of shares will need to check that none of these significant contracts will be affected by the change of control of the company.

Contracts which may be fundamental to the business (and which may account for much of its turnover) include long-term contracts for the supply of the target's goods or services, distribution and agency agreements, contracts for the supply of raw materials to the target, etc. The buyer of shares should check which contracts are due to expire in the near future so that he can investigate the chances of renewal, perhaps by contacting third parties directly (subject to confidentiality). Similarly, some of these contracts may be terminable on short notice and the buyer will want to be satisfied that this is not likely to happen as a result of the change of control.

The buyer of shares faces a danger in relation even to long-term contracts entered into by the target company. Such contracts may include a term which entitles the other party to terminate the agreement if control of the target changes hands ('change of control' clauses). Such clauses are sometimes included in, for example, distribution agreements, franchise agreements and joint venture agreements.

The buyer of a target will also need to check that none of these fundamental contracts contains provisions which infringe EC or UK competition laws.

Loans

On a business acquisition, existing banking arrangements in relation to the target will generally cease and the buyer will need to organise his own facilities. The buyer should enquire as to whether any of the assets which are being transferred are the subject of a charge; any such charge will have to be removed on completion or the consent of the chargee obtained for the asset to be transferred subject to the charge.

On a share acquisition, the buyer should request copies of all loan documentation in order to ascertain the nature and extent of the target's borrowing commitments and obligations. He should check whether any loans are repayable on demand (this is common with bank overdraft facilities) or entitle the lender to demand immediate repayment of the balance of the loan on a change of control. In either case, unless he can make satisfactory arrangements with the lender directly, he will need to be confident of securing funds from elsewhere.

A buyer of shares will also be interested in whether the seller has guaranteed any obligations of the target (eg repayment of a fixed-term loan). Although this is the primary concern of the seller, whose liability will continue after completion, the buyer should anticipate that he may be asked to try to procure the release of the seller from such guarantees and to indemnify the seller if the release is not obtained on completion (see **4.7**). Whoever has the benefit of the seller's guarantee is likely to require at least equivalent pledges from the buyer before agreeing to release the seller.

Finally, where the target company is a member of a group, it may have guaranteed various obligations of other members of the group. The buyer will insist that such guarantees do not continue in place after completion.

Intellectual property

Depending on the type of business, the seller or target may own or use on licence trade marks, patents, registered designs, know-how, service marks or copyrights. These intellectual property rights may be crucial to the business and a thorough review of this area is essential to ascertain whether rights are adequately protected, what agreements or licences are in place and, on a share purchase, whether a change in control will affect such arrangements. The buyer will also want details of the computer system and software packages used by the target (he may wish to integrate these with his own systems). On a business transfer, the buyer may have to approach third parties with a view to re-negotiating licences or agreements entered into with the seller. In addition to requiring full details of all intellectual property rights from the seller, the buyer should, in appropriate cases, carry out a search at the Trade Marks Registry and instruct a patent agent to conduct a patent search to establish not only that the target's patents are valid but also that the target is not infringing any patents owned by others.

Rights triggered by a change of control

Some examples of where 'change of control' clauses in contracts may be found have been given above. Clauses conferring rights on parties where a company changes hands may also be found in employment contracts. For example, directors' service contracts might contain a so-called 'golden parachute clause' which entitles the director to a payment if the company changes hands (usually on the basis that the director can treat himself as dismissed in such circumstances). Also in the employment context, the right of employees to exercise rights to buy shares at a favourable price under share option schemes are sometimes triggered by a change of control of the company.

Non-arm's length trading relationships

Where the target is a member of a group, the buyer should ask for information on all goods and services which have been supplied by or to other members of the group (including administrative and management services supplied by a parent company). As it is unlikely that such arrangements will continue once the group relationship is broken, the buyer should assess the impact of their ceasing on completion of the acquisition.

It is also possible that individual sellers of a target company may have been supplying goods or services to the target company (or receiving goods or services from the target company) either directly or through other companies in which they have an interest. The buyer's analysis of the profit figures of the target may be very different in the light of these sort of arrangements. Past profits may be a poor indicator of future performance of the business if these sources of supply (to or from the target) are terminated after completion, or if the terms of supply are changed significantly.

Accounts

Whether or not a full accountants' report has been commissioned, the buyer's solicitor should study the accounts of the target. In the case of a company, he should request copies of the audited accounts for the last 3 years and of any recently produced management accounts. In liaison with the accountants, the buyer's solicitor can then consider whether any warranties or indemnities ought to be included in the agreement as a result of the information revealed in the accounts. A clear understanding of business and company accounts is also necessary in drafting and negotiating other aspects of the acquisition agreement (eg providing for completion accounts to be drawn up or for part of the purchase price to be deferred and linked to post-completion profits, see **8.4.2**).

Other information

The preliminary enquiries of the buyer will cover a number of other matters; some of these are dealt with later in this chapter and others are dealt with in context in later chapters. For completeness, they are listed below:

(1)   details of employees: see Chapter 6 (business) and Chapter 10 (shares);
(2)   details of pension schemes: see Chapter 6 (business) and Chapter 10 (shares);
(3)   environmental matters: see **3.10**;
(4)   property: see **3.9**;
(5)   taxation: see Chapter 7 (business) and Chapter 11 (shares);
(6)   constitutional matters: see **3.5**.

3.5 SEARCHING THE FILE AT THE COMPANIES REGISTRY

3.5.1 The search

Useful information about a target company can be obtained by making a search of the company's file at the Companies Registry. This is a quick and inexpensive method of enquiry which will provide the buyer's solicitor with information long before he receives the accountant's report or replies to pre-contract enquiries. The buyer's solicitor will usually repeat the search shortly before the parties enter into the main agreement.

Where a company is selling a business or shares in a subsidiary, a search should be made against the selling company. Also, a seller is wise to search the file of a corporate buyer to satisfy himself that it is of sufficient substance to effect the acquisition and to fulfil any post-completion obligations (eg the payment of deferred consideration).

The company search does, however, have serious limitations which means that the information which it reveals cannot be wholly relied upon. The obligation to file information at the Companies Registry is placed on the company itself and although the company and its officers are liable to fines on default, there is no provision for compensating a third party who suffers loss as a result of this information being incomplete or inaccurate. Indeed, the buyer of shares is not given any statutory assistance in these circumstances (see **3.5.2**). In addition, even if the target has duly filed its returns on time, the information revealed by the search will in many cases be out of date.

3.5.2 Contents of file

Memorandum and articles of association

Where a business is being acquired from a company, the buyer's solicitor should check that there is power in the memorandum for the company to dispose of the business and that the articles enable the directors to exercise that power. This is advisable even though the CA 1985 (as amended) now protects third parties where the company acts ultra vires or the directors exceed their powers because it is still open to shareholders to challenge such acts in advance of the company entering into them (CA 1985, s 35A).

The buyer's solicitor will also study the memorandum and articles of a target company to check that the company has power to carry on the business and to discover what steps will need to be taken on completion (eg in relation to the completion board meeting of the target, see **9.4.3**). The buyer should also check whether the articles contain any restrictions on the transfer of shares. They may, for example, contain pre-emption provisions obliging shareholders wishing to transfer their shares to offer them pro rata to existing members. In this event, the selling shareholders will usually waive their respective rights as a term of the acquisition agreement (although it may be safer to change the article since pre-emption rights are sometimes triggered by an 'intention' to dispose of the shares). After he has acquired the shares, the buyer may, of course, wish to change provisions of the target company's constitution to suit his own specific needs.

Directors and shareholders

The annual return contains a list of the shareholders, directors and company secretary and details of the nominal, issued and paid-up share capital of the company. This is a useful starting point for the buyer's solicitor in preparing the initial draft of the agreement but he will need to ask the seller's solicitor to provide details of all changes since the return date because the information revealed may be considerably out-of-date. The buyer's solicitor requires accurate information as to the existing shareholders, in order to ensure that the correct persons enter into the agreement, and as to the current directors, so that the buyer can consider what arrangements should be made with them on completion (the buyer may intend that some directors resign on completion and that others enter into new service contracts with the target company). The annual return will also reveal whether the target's directors hold any other directorships. This may be of interest to the buyer, particularly if it transpires that any of the target's directors are also directors of companies which have been trading with the target.

Charges

A search against a company disposing of a business will reveal whether there are any charges over the assets which are being transferred. The buyer will usually insist that these charges are released on completion.

Similarly, the buyer of shares will want to establish the extent to which a target company has charged its assets as security for loans. Once again, the information may not be up to date since the company may have recently created charges which have still to be registered within the statutory period of 21 days from creation. Even if such charges are not registered within the statutory period, they are, nevertheless, valid against the company itself and thus the buyer of shares receives no protection against late registration or non-registration. Indeed, the target company is in a vulnerable position in relation to charges which have not been registered; not only is it the company's duty to register, in default of which it is liable to a fine but, perhaps more significantly, the loan becomes immediately repayable.

Accounts

The accounts filed at the Companies Registry are of limited value because they may not include the latest set of audited accounts (these can be filed up to 10 months after the accounting reference period) and may be in abbreviated form only (the CA 1985 allows 'small' and 'medium sized' companies to file modified accounts). The buyer's solicitor and accountants will want to see any recent management accounts as well as the full version of the audited accounts.

Insolvency procedures

The search may reveal that the target company is in liquidation, receivership or administration.

3.6 INTERNAL REGISTERS

The buyer's solicitor will wish to inspect the internal registers of the target company (statutory books and otherwise). The register of members and the minute books will be of particular interest; the buyer's solicitor should check that allotments and transfers of shares have been carried out in accordance with the CA 1985 (eg ss 80 and 89 on issues of shares) and the articles of the company (eg in compliance with any pre-emption provisions). Copies of charges created by the company and copies of directors' service contracts should also be available for inspection.

3.7 CREDIT REPORTS

A quick and easy method of obtaining general (and up-to-date) financial information about a target company is for the buyer to request a credit report from a reputable credit agency. As well as commenting on the company's creditworthiness in general, such reports will also deal with specific aspects of its performance and financial position (eg average debt collection and payment periods and the company's 'liquidity', ie its ability to pay off short-term liabilities out of realisable assets).

3.8 CHECKING THE SOLVENCY OF THE SELLER

Bankruptcy searches at the Land Charges Department should be carried out against individual sellers of shares or of a business immediately before completion. Similarly, a search of the file at the Companies Registry of a corporate seller of shares or a business should be made prior to completion to ensure that no notice of insolvency procedures has been entered. As this information may not be up to date, a telephone enquiry should also be made to the Central Registry of winding up petitions. Any transactions entered into after the commencement of insolvency procedures may be void.

3.9 PROPERTY MATTERS

3.9.1 Scope of investigation

The buyer's solicitor will not always carry out comprehensive searches and enquiries in relation to all the properties owned and occupied by the target. The timetable agreed by the parties for the acquisition often rules out a full investigation of all the conveyancing aspects. It may also prove impractical for full structural surveys to be carried out, particularly when the seller is keen not to alert his work-force to the proposed sale. The risk to the buyer in these circumstances depends on the importance of the properties. If they are relatively insignificant in the context of the deal as a whole, he may be justified in limiting the scope of his investigation. Also, the buyer may be able to rely on other means of protection against title or other property-related problems. Apart from a full title investigation by the buyer's solicitor, the two main means of protection for the buyer are:

(1)   a certificate of title given by the seller's solicitor;
(2)   property warranties given by the seller in the acquisition agreement.

The buyer may seek to protect his position by using a combination of these methods.

Certificate of title

The seller's solicitor will have to carry out his own title investigation before he is in a position to give a certificate of title. This may be particularly appropriate where the seller's solicitor is already familiar with the target's property portfolio or where he is instructed well in advance of a specific deal being agreed.

The chief certification sought by the buyer is that the properties have good and marketable title. A description of each property, including the title number and class of title of registered property and a summary of the principal terms of any leases, is usually contained in a schedule to the certificate. A statement may also be included that the properties are not subject to any specified encumbrances or defects except as set out in the certificate.

The precise format and wording of the certificate will often be the subject of much negotiation between the parties. The seller's solicitor will be reluctant to extend the scope of the certificate beyond points of pure title to, for example, planning and environmental matters. He will also wish it to be clearly stated on which information the certificate is based (eg searches made, deeds examined and information given by the client).

The certificate is addressed to the buyer, who can sue the seller's solicitor if it has been negligently prepared. However, if a false statement or omission in the certificate is a result of incorrect information supplied by his client, the seller's solicitor will not generally be liable provided the certificate makes it clear that that statement or omission was based on information given by his client. In these circumstances, the buyer will be left without a remedy unless he has obtained a warranty direct from the seller that the information on which the certificate is based is true and accurate.

Property warranties

The following are examples of property warranties which the buyer may seek to include in the agreement:

(1) the company (or seller) has good title to the each of the properties and has possession or control of all deeds and documents necessary to prove title;

(2) each property is free from any mortgage, charge, lien or other encumbrance;

(3) the current use of each property complies with town and country planning legislation and all necessary planning and building regulation consents have been obtained;

(4) all obligations, restrictions, conditions and covenants affecting any of the properties (leasehold or freehold) have been observed and performed and no notice of breach has been received;

(5) the company (or seller) has vacant possession of each of the properties;

(6) there are no outstanding disputes affecting any of the properties and no outstanding orders, notices or demands have been made by local or other authorities;

(7) each of the properties is in good and substantial repair and fit for the purposes for which it is presently used;

(8) each of the properties is free from any notice, inhibition, caution, land charge, or local land charge not of general application to the area.

The seller is free to qualify these warranties by making disclosures in the usual way.

Warranties are, of course, only useful to the extent that the seller is able to compensate the buyer for loss arising from breach. The advantage of a full investigation by the buyer's solicitor is that major problems are more likely to be identified ahead of completion.

3.9.2 Form of investigation

Where a full investigation is to be carried out, the buyer's solicitor will need to make all the usual conveyancing searches and enquiries in relation to the properties being transferred (business acquisition) or owned or occupied by the target company (share acquisition). It is not intended to explore these in detail; however, a number of points may be of particular concern to the buyer of a target business or company.

Inspection/valuation/survey

The practical difficulties of the buyer and his representatives carrying out inspections and surveys of the target's premises have already been discussed. However, physical inspection of properties which are important to the target is advisable as this may disclose obvious problems which ought to be addressed prior to completion or may prompt further enquiry of the seller (eg whether certain uses have planning permission). In the case of leasehold premises, one of the main purposes of making an inspection is to ascertain whether the repairing obligations under the lease have been complied with. Also, by requisitioning a valuation of the properties concerned, the buyer will be able to compare their actual values with the values which appear in the accounts of the target business or company, although this may not be necessary if the buyer has access to a recent valuation carried out on behalf of the seller.

A full structural survey (of leasehold and freehold property) is the ideal, but is often not feasible in the circumstances.

Landlord's consents

On a business transfer, the consent of the landlord will frequently be required for the assignment of any leasehold premises included in the sale, as a term of the lease. Even on a share transfer, where the properties do not change hands, the buyer's solicitor should check the terms of leases carefully. It is not unusual for the landlord's consent to be required on a share acquisition (the lease may, eg, define assignment as including a change in control of the tenant company).

The buyer's solicitor should also ascertain whether the seller has guaranteed the lease obligations. The seller is likely to ask for an undertaking from the buyer (as a term of the main agreement) that the buyer will use his best endeavours to obtain the release of the seller from such guarantees and, in the meantime, to indemnify the seller against any liability (see **4.7**). The buyer's solicitor should ask the landlord (subject to confidentiality) whether he will agree to release the seller and, if so, on what terms (the landlord is likely to insist that the buyer enters into a similar guarantee).

Original tenants of leasehold property

For leases granted before 1 January 1996, the original tenant of leasehold premises is in an invidious position because he remains liable to the landlord for breaches of the terms of the lease even after he has assigned the lease to a third party. Although there is an implied indemnity by the assignee in favour of the original tenant, this will be of little use if the assignee becomes insolvent. Indeed, the present tenant's insolvency is likely to be the reason why the landlord is pursuing the original tenant for breach of covenant.

On a business sale, the seller may, therefore, have a contingent liability after completing the assignment to the buyer of leasehold premises of which he was the original tenant. On a share sale, the buyer's solicitor should ask whether the target company has been granted a lease at any time. Since the target company will remain liable on any such lease, he should ask for a copy of the lease to establish the extent of the potential liability.

For leases granted on or after 1 January 1996, the concept of continuing original tenant liability has been abolished. An original tenant who lawfully assigns his lease is generally released from liability as from the date of assignment, but could be required by the terms of the lease to guarantee performance of the lease obligations by his immediate assignee under an 'authorised guarantee agreement'.

Problems of investigation on a share purchase

A buyer of shares will not obtain protection from searches of official registers in the same way as a buyer of a business. This is because protection is usually afforded to, inter alia, a buyer of an interest in land, whereas on a share acquisition, there is no change in ownership of the target company's properties. It has already been seen that failure to register a charge at the Companies Registry does not render it void against the company itself. The position is similar with searches at HM Land Registry, the Land Charges Department and the Local Land Charges Registry. Although pre-completion searches at HM Land Registry or the Land Charges Department will reveal most registered charges etc, the buyer of shares does not have the benefit of any priority period within which he can safely complete the acquisition without further matters appearing on the register (this follows from the fact that unregistered charges are valid against the company in any case). In addition, the buyer of shares is not entitled to receive compensation from a local authority which fails to register a local land charge (the Local Land Charges Act 1975 provides for the payment of compensation to a person who acquires an interest in the land).

3.10 ENVIRONMENTAL MATTERS

3.10.1 The environmental problem in acquisitions

With both a business acquisition and a share acquisition, the buyer does not know the nature and extent of the environmental liabilities. If the deal is to be undertaken by a share acquisition, then the buyer would be directly liable for the past actions of the company as he is, in effect, taking over the identity of the target company. This situation is of greater concern than the alternative, a business acquisition, but there are still significant concerns even in that situation – the state of the site(s) being the most obvious.

To illustrate the problems, consider the operations of a typical factory. In this case, the environmental problems for a buyer fall into three categories.

First, there is the buyer's requirement that the factory should continue to operate after completion of the deal, otherwise the whole thing is pointless and the solicitor could be sued for negligence! In order that the factory continues to operate, all relevant environmental licences must be in place and must be transferred to the buyer if necessary. ('Licences' would include authorisations, consents and permits; it is just that the terminology varies; see (1) and (2) below.)

Secondly, the buyer will be concerned to know whether the operations of the factory have resulted in pollution of the site, or of anywhere else. The buyer will also need to consider the historical use of the site and whether this may have caused pollution. If the site owned by the target company is polluted, then the target and/or its new owner could be liable for the costs of cleaning it up, whether the pollution was caused by the operations of the factory or by, for example, previous owners of the site.

Thirdly, any pollution caused by the factory may give or have given rise to third party claims against the target, for example claims for nuisance, negligence or trespass, and breaches of environmental legislation may result in criminal sanctions.

3.10.2 The legislation

The Environmental Protection Act 1990 (EPA 1990) as amended by the Environment Act 1995 introduced a wide-ranging system of environmental control which impacts on a large number of businesses. It is inevitable that regulation in this area will become stricter and more comprehensive in the future with the result that certain businesses will be faced with further onerous and costly obligations.

A detailed explanation of the system of environmental regulation is beyond the scope of this book. However, a number of points of particular relevance to a potential buyer of a target business or company are made below.

(1) Licensing

The EPA 1990 introduced a system of integrated pollution control (IPC) which regulates the release into any environmental medium of discharges from processes involving, inter alia, fuel and power, metals, minerals, waste, and chemicals. This net has been widened by the enactment of the Pollution Prevention and Control Act 1999 (PPCA 1999). The PPCA 1999 implements the integrated pollution prevention control (IPPC) regime, which will take account of a far wider range of environmental impacts, including noise, site restoration and energy efficiency. The regulatory body is the Environment Agency. There is also a system of local authority air pollution control.

A central element to the system (as amended by the PPCA 1999) is that a licence is required for a business to conduct a prescribed process (these are listed in the Environmental Protection (Prescribed Processes and Substances) Regulations 1991, as amended) and fall into two categories of process, either Part A or Part B. Therefore, if the business is not involved in prescribed processes, no licences will be needed.

If the prescribed process is a Part A one, a full IPC licence is required. The IPC licence, as its name suggests, regulates all discharges from the process into any environmental medium. This means that any waste, effluents or discharges into waterways will be covered by this licence. If the prescribed process is a Part B one, a licence covering air emissions only will be required from the relevant local authority. This is known as an LAAPC licence. However, depending on the business's operations, a process covered by an LAAPC licence may need further authorisation (eg waste control).

A licence will list conditions to which it is subject. Obviously, the content of such conditions may be important to a buyer. Often, they involve specific restrictions on the operation of the relevant processes and can entail considerable expense. For example, a condition on a full IPC licence may require an update to old machinery. If this is the case, the Environment Agency is obliged, in considering the conditions to attach to an authorisation, to ensure that the 'best available techniques not entailing excessive cost' (BATNEEC) are employed to minimise harm to the environment (EPA 1990, s 7). Even in the absence of express conditions, there is a general condition to the same effect which is implied into every authorisation (s 7(4)). In the case of local authority air pollution control, similar conditions will be imposed, although these will only regulate emissions into the air.

The BATNEEC requirement can have an enormous impact on the viability of a business as it may involve massive investment in new 'environmentally friendly' technology. It is not only the equipment itself which must comply with the standard but also all matters related to the particular process, such as working methods, training, qualification and supervision of staff, design and construction of buildings, and site management. A potential buyer of a business using technology which is outmoded or which may become so in the near future may, therefore, be inheriting a substantial potential liability. The licensing authority is under an obligation to review specific conditions attached to an authorisation every 4 years.

Part II of the EPA 1990 contains a system of regulating waste management. A licence is required to deposit controlled waste on land or to treat, keep or dispose of controlled waste. The Environment Agency is given wide powers to revoke licences (eg where it considers that continuation of the authorised activities would pollute the environment or harm human health, or that the licence holder has ceased to be a fit and proper person). Therefore, if the process involves waste management then the buyer will need to check that the business is properly licensed for this.

A licence holder remains responsible for breaches of the terms of the licence until the Environment Agency accepts the surrender of the licence, which it will only do if it is satisfied as to the condition of the land at the end of the operation of the site. A buyer should ask the seller to produce a certificate of completion issued by the Agency in these circumstances. Licences are transferable but the Agency will consent to a transfer only if it is satisfied that the transferee is a fit and proper person.

(2) Consents

Under the Water Resources Act 1991, a consent is required if the process involves the discharge of any polluting matter into water courses (eg rivers and ground water) and, under the Water Industry Act 1991, a consent is needed from the relevant water company before trade effluents are discharged into public sewers.

(3) Liability for contaminated land and harmful activities

A number of provisions in the EPA 1990 and other statutes give various bodies power to remedy the consequences of pollution and pass on the cost to the person responsible or, in certain circumstances, the current owner of the contaminated land. Some of these are mentioned below.

(A) The Environment Agency is empowered (by s 161 of the Water Resources Act 1991) to carry out certain works and operations if it appears that any poisonous, noxious or polluting matter or any solid waste matter is likely to enter a river (or other 'controlled water') and to recover the expense from any person who, inter alia, 'caused or knowingly permitted' the relevant matter to be present in the water.

(B) On 1 April 2000, Part IIA of the EPA 1990 came into force. The Act (supported by regulations and statutory guidance) creates a contaminated land regime in England and Wales. It is a regime which applies to historic contamination not covered by existing pollution controls, so the regime will not apply when the contamination and clean-up process can be dealt with under IPCs or LAAPC licences.

The legislation requires local authorities to identify contaminated land in their area. If the harm of pollution is serious (as opposed to significant), the site will be categorised as a 'special site' and will be dealt with by the Environment Agency. Once a property is identified as being contaminated land, a remediation notice will be served on the 'appropriate person' for the site. Primarily, this will be the person who caused or knowingly permitted the contamination to be in, on or under the land (a 'Class A' person). If, after reasonable enquiry, no Class A person can be found, then the owner or occupier of the land for the time being will be served instead (a 'Class B' person). If neither a Class A person nor a Class B person can be found, the site will be classified as an orphan site, and the local authority will become primarily responsible for remediation.

In the event of non-compliance with the notice, there are default powers for the enforcing authority to carry out clean-up works with provision for cost recovery, and criminal sanctions may be imposed.

Any remediation required should result in the land being 'suitable for use' and compliance with the notice is likely to result in high costs.

In the context of acquisitions, buyers of contaminated or potentially contaminated land, on the face of it, should be free from liability. However, the statutory guidance includes provisions which shift liability from the seller to the buyer. The two most likely provisons to affect acquisitions are:

(i)   where payment has been made for remediation. This would occur where the seller has reduced the purchase price in order to account for the clean-up of contaminated land which the buyer has undertaken to deal with after completion;

(ii) where (through due diligence) the buyer is aware of the problem and proceeds with the transaction. Here, the local authority is likely to assume that the buyer, knowing of the problem, will have adjusted the price accordingly and, even if he hasn't, accepts responsibility for the clean-up costs.

The sale and purchase agreement should therefore clearly set out where liability will rest, and, if necessary, include warranties and indemnities to cover potential liability.

On the other hand, a seller of contaminated (or potentially contaminated) land may also be at risk when he releases control of the land to the buyer. The acquisition agreement should therefore deal with this possibility and either apportion liability or include a specific indemnity in favour of the seller. The agreement may also provide for the seller to retain control of the clean-up process or, at the very least, provide for the seller to be kept informed as to its progress.

Note that a person who does not have any interest in the capital value of the land, or who occupies a site under licence or other agreement which has no market value, or under a lease where market rent is payable, cannot be a Class B person and is therefore excluded from liability.

(C) Where the land is not designated 'contaminated land' under the EPA 1990, the regulators can take action on the basis of statutory nuisance. The main aim of the statutory nuisance provisions is to provide a quick and easy remedy in respect of nuisances with which the common law is too slow or too expensive to deal. Local authorities can serve abatement notices in respect of statutory nuisances under s 81 of the EPA 1990 and in default can enter land to abate the nuisance. Failure to comply with an abatement notice is a criminal offence. The regulator is entitled to recover the cost of remedying the nuisance from those responsible for causing it.

If land is designated as 'contaminated land', it cannot also constitute a statutory nuisance (ie (B) and (C) are mutually exclusive).

3.10.3 Consequences of non-compliance

Civil liability

In addition to criminal liability, an individual or company may face civil liability in tort for any damage done to other property caused, for example, by chemicals leaking from the land. The torts of nuisance, negligence, trespass and the rule in *Rylands v Fletcher* are all potentially relevant. The remedies available to claimants are damages and injunctions. Depending on the amount of harm done, damages could be considerable.

Criminal penalties, directors' liability and clean-up costs

Breach of various provisions of the EPA 1990 (eg carrying on a prescribed process without a licence) and the Water Resources Act 1991 give rise to criminal liability involving stiff penalties. Some offences, for example, carry a maximum prison term of 6 months or a maximum fine of £20,000 for each offence committed (magistrates' court) and a maximum prison term of 5 years and an unlimited fine (Crown Court).

In addition, where the offence is committed by a company, an offence is committed by any director, manager, secretary or other similar officer who is proved to have consented to or connived in the offence or to whose neglect the offence is shown to have been attributable (EPA 1990, s 157 and Water Resources Act 1991, s 217).

Further, the various regulatory authorities have wide powers to require land to be cleaned up (see **3.10.2**).

3.10.4 What precautions can the buyer take?

Public information

One of the objectives of the EPA 1990 is to make information on environmental matters available to the public by obliging relevant authorities to compile and maintain registers. The buyer of a business or company is, therefore, able to obtain useful information on the environmental background of the target. The EPA 1990 imposes a duty on licensing authorities such as the Environment Agency to maintain public registers of information relating to authorisations. These should include details of the initial application, the grant of authorisation and any conditions attached, statutory notices served, and prosecutions brought. The only restriction on publicity is in relation to matters which are harmful to national security or commercially confidential.

In addition, following the enactment of the Environment Act 1995, local authorities are required to keep registers of any remediation notices served in respect of contaminated land.

Licences

When acting for the buyer, it is important to ask the seller's solicitor for copies of all the relevant licences. An environmental lawyer (or consultant) can advise on the types of licence which a particular target business should have. These will need to be checked to make sure that they:

- cover all the operations of the business;
- are still in force;
- do not contain any requirements regarding future upgrading of pollution control equipment (eg BATNEEC); and
- are not due to expire in the near future, as further upgrading requirements could be imposed as a condition of renewal of the licence.

Transfer of licences is rarely a problem and is often treated by the relevant authorities as merely a bureaucratic exercise. The exception is the transfer of a waste management licence which requires a formal notification to the Environment Agency. It has the power to refuse a transfer if the intended transferee is not a fit and proper person.

The main commercial problem with licences is usually costly upgrading requirements contained in LAAPC or IPC authorisations. However, there is always the problem of the seller who should have an LAAPC/IPC authorisation and does not. It is likely that considerable expenditure on pollution control equipment would be needed before such an authorisation could be obtained.

Other searches and enquiries, etc

The extent of the buyer's enquiries of the seller will depend on the nature of the target business. However, even the most environmentally friendly business may be occupying a site which has a contamination history. The seller should be asked to provide details of any applications for authorisation, any statutory notices served on him or the target and any complaints made by third parties. The seller should also be asked whether an environmental audit has been carried out in relation to the target and, if so, to provide a copy.

Where a target business or company is involved in environmentally sensitive operations or where land sites may have a history of contamination, the buyer should also consider commissioning a full environmental audit prior to entering into the agreement. This is likely to prove expensive and will require the full co-operation of the seller. However, the extent of the buyer's potential liability in these circumstances will often make it a worthwhile investment.

A Phase I audit covers research into old records and maps to find out the history of the site – its historical use. It usually also includes a physical inspection of the site by a consultant to look at the current operations and to see if there are any obvious manifestations of problems.

A Phase II audit follows on from a Phase I audit and is one where the site (and possibly its surroundings) is investigated more thoroughly by sampling the soil and underground waters. Samples are also taken from any streams or rivers, and, where appropriate, air sampling may be undertaken. The consultant uses the results of the sampling to decide whether there is any significant amount of pollution on the site and, if so, whether it is likely to cause harm to man or natural resources, such as rivers.

The Phase III part of this process is to decide on the clean-up technology to be employed, if indeed a clean up is to be undertaken. Factors to be taken into consideration include the cost and the applicability of different clean-up technologies.

Protection by warranty

Environmental warranties in acquisition agreements are becoming more extensive as general awareness of the implications of the legislation in this area (and concern over the possible scope of future regulation) intensifies. As in the case of other warranties, the twin purposes of environmental warranties are to provide contractual protection for the buyer and to elicit relevant information from the seller in the form of disclosures. The buyer may seek to include some or all of the following warranties in a share acquisition agreement:

(1) full particulars of all environmental authorisations (defined) required by the company to carry on its business or to use its property are contained in the disclosure letter and the company has complied with all conditions (express or implied) attaching to such authorisations;

(2) the company has supplied such environmental information to the competent authorities as is required by law;

(3) all environmental information supplied by the company to the competent authorities was correct at the time it was given and, to the seller's knowledge, all information appearing on public registers in relation to environmental matters is correct;

(4) the company has not received any notice amending or revoking such authorisations;

(5) the company has not committed any breach of environmental legislation (defined);

(6) the company has not received any notices alleging breach of or requiring compliance with environmental legislation and no claims (including common law claims) are pending or threatened;

(7) the seller is not aware of any facts which may involve the company in liability for cleaning up or decontaminating any sites now or formerly owned by the company.

Indemnities

As a result of more stringent environmental law, and more effective enforcement of legislative provisions, it is not unusual for a buyer to demand an environmental indemnity as part of the acquisition process, giving him the opportunity to recover costs of environmental liabilities on a pound-for-pound basis from the seller. In addition to allowing the buyer to recover in respect of environmental risks identified in the due diligence process or as a result of an audit, the indemnity should also cover the buyer for costs incurred as a result of, for example, remedying pre-completion contamination of land or non-compliance with environmental legislation, and of third party claims.

The scope of the indemnity will depend on factors such as the bargaining strength of the parties and the likelihood of liability arising, bearing in mind the nature of the business and the history of the site. The buyer should be aware, of course, that an indemnity is only as good as the party giving it so may be of little use if, for example, the seller is no longer in business when a claim is made. The buyer may therefore choose to take out insurance to reinforce his position, though such insurance is often prohibitively expensive. High premiums and a large excess are usually payable. Also, cover under environmental insurance policies is often very limited, and an environmental audit may be required as a pre-condition of the policy being granted.

The seller should ensure that any indemnity given is limited as to duration and the maximum sum recoverable by the buyer. These limits can be set at different levels for each individual site included in the sale. It is also quite common for a 'ratchet' mechanism to be built into an environmental indemnity, whereby the buyer becomes increasingly more liable over time (and the seller therefore less so) for his own environmental losses.

Chapter 4

SELLER'S LIABILITY AND BUYER'S REMEDIES

4.1 INTRODUCTION

Chapter 4 contents
Introduction
Are any protections for the buyer implied into the contract?
Express contractual protection
How may the seller limit his liability?
Criminal liability for false or misleading statements
Negligent statements
Seller's liability under guarantees
Restrictions on the seller

The last chapter dealt with the investigations that a prudent buyer should endeavour to carry out when making an acquisition. What if, however, even after extensive due diligence, the acquisition does not turn out to be what the buyer expected? This chapter deals with the courses of action available to an aggrieved buyer and the extent to which a seller of a business or shares may be liable to the buyer for problems arising out of the acquisition. The protections which buyers may seek to include in the acquisition documentation and the ways in which sellers often try to limit their exposure to liability are also discussed.

4.2 ARE ANY PROTECTIONS FOR THE BUYER IMPLIED INTO THE CONTRACT?

4.2.1 Shares

On a share acquisition, neither common law nor statute protects the buyer by implying terms into the contract; the law is one of caveat emptor. It was noted in Chapter 1 that there is, indeed, every reason for a buyer of shares to beware, because he will be inheriting indirectly all the liabilities of the target company, whether he knows about them or not. In the absence of express provisions, an aggrieved buyer has very little comeback on the seller unless he is able to establish a misrepresentation (discussed at **4.3.1**). In order to protect himself from the many risks involved he must, therefore, make express provision in the acquisition agreement.

4.2.2 Business

The buyer of a business is not in such an exposed position as he does not assume automatically all the liabilities of the business. However, as on a share acquisition, there will be many safeguards which the buyer will wish to incorporate expressly into the acquisition agreement.

4.3 EXPRESS CONTRACTUAL PROTECTION

4.3.1 Warranties

Much of the acquisition agreement is usually taken up with warranties by the seller in favour of the buyer, covering a whole range of aspects of the target business or company, including the accounts, subsisting contracts, employees, pensions, intellectual property rights, etc (see Chapters 5 and 8 for details of typical warranties in business and share acquisitions respectively).

One of the purposes of warranties is to elicit information about the business from the seller (see **4.4.2**) and this process very much ties in with the due diligence investigation discussed in the previous chapter. Another purpose is to provide a means of redress for the buyer if the acquisition turns out to be other than he bargained for. Warranties are terms of the contract and, if they prove to be untrue, the buyer will have a claim for damages against the warrantor for breach of contract.

What damages are recoverable?

Under the rule in *Hadley v Baxendale* (1854) 9 Exch 341, loss will be recoverable if it is not too remote. It must fall within one of the two following categories:

(1) loss which flows naturally from the breach; in other words, it is a natural consequence of the breach, the type and extent of which a reasonable person would expect in the circumstances;

(2) loss which was fairly and reasonably in the contemplation of both parties, at the time they entered into the contract, as the probable result of the breach. This might cover a more unusual type of loss due to special circumstances which were known or should have been known to the parties at the date of the contract.

The aim of contractual damages is to put the buyer in the position he would have been in if the contract had not been breached, subject to the duty to mitigate. This measure of damages allows recovery for loss of bargain.

How are these general principles applied to breach of warranty on a share acquisition?

The buyer's loss in these circumstances is the difference between the value of shares if the warranty had been true and their actual value, ie the difference in the value of the shares with and without the breach. The basis used for valuing the shares will, therefore, be relevant in assessing the loss.

For example, the shares may have been valued on an earnings basis, perhaps by applying a multiplier to a warranted level of profit. If this profit has been overstated, the buyer's loss should be calculated by applying the same multiplier to the deficiency. On the other hand, where there is a breach of warranty which results in the assets of the target being less than expected, this may not have a direct effect on the value of the shares, unless they were valued on an assets-related basis.

Can the parties interfere?

The parties will often seek to reduce the uncertainty involved in assessing loss in this way by specifying in the agreement how the loss should be quantified if certain warranties are broken. For example, where profit levels have been warranted, the parties may agree a formula which specifies an appropriate multiplier to apply to any shortfall. It is also quite common for a clause to be included which obliges the seller to pay for any deficiency in assets or any undisclosed liability arising from a breach of warranty, thus avoiding the need to prove an equivalent diminution in the value of the shares (the seller may resist what is essentially an indemnity basis for breach of warranty, see **4.3.2**).

Is there any restriction on the parties' freedom to agree the measure of damages in advance in this way? The parties to a contract are free to agree in advance a sum payable in damages in the event of a breach of contract, provided it is a genuine pre-estimate of the actual loss which would be suffered by the innocent party ('liquidated damages') as opposed to a fine or penalty in the nature of a threat held over the other party (a 'penalty'). The distinction depends on the intentions of the parties which are to be gathered from the whole of the contract.

What is the link with an action for misrepresentation?

Typically, the signing of the acquisition agreement will be the culmination of extensive contact and correspondence between the parties and their advisers. The buyer and his advisers will have sought replies to a whole range of questions affecting the target and its business. If any statements which have been made by or on behalf of the seller prove to be untrue, will the buyer have an action for misrepresentation? How does this tie in with the buyer's express protections included in the acquisition agreement?

GENERAL PRINCIPLES

A misrepresentation is a false statement of fact made by one party to the contract to the other which induces the other party to enter into the contract. Accordingly, where a buyer has relied on a representation of past or existing fact about the target which turns out to be untrue, he will, prima facie, have a claim for misrepresentation. What are his remedies?

Rescission

Whether the misrepresentation is fraudulent, negligent, or innocent, the buyer has the right to rescind the acquisition agreement. Rescission is a remedy aimed at putting the parties back into the pre-contract position. However, the right to rescind is subject to two important qualifications.

First, s 2(2) of the Misrepresentation Act 1967 enables the court to award damages instead of rescission for 'innocent misrepresentation', that is, a representation which is neither fraudulent nor negligent. The court may exercise this discretion if it feels that rescission is too drastic a remedy in the circumstances (see below for futher discussion on the discretion to award damages under s 2(2)).

Secondly, rescission is an equitable remedy and will not be available if, for example:

(1) it is impossible to restore the parties to their pre-contract position; or
(2) bona fide third party rights have been acquired; or
(3) the innocent party, knowing of the misrepresentation, takes some action affirming the agreement; or
(4) there is undue delay in seeking relief.

These 'bars' to rescission may mean that the remedy will not be available once a share or business acquisition has been completed, because of the difficulties in restoring the parties to their pre-contract position. On the other hand, where exchange and completion are not contemporaneous, rescission should be available if a misrepresentation is discovered between exchange and completion.

Damages

If the misrepresentation is innocent, s 2(2) provides that the court 'may award damages in lieu of rescission'. It should be noted that the court has a discretion to award damages; there is no right to damages. The question arises as to whether the court can still award damages in lieu of rescission if rescission itself has been lost due to one of the equitable bars. In the recent case of *Government of Zanzibar v British Aerospace (Lancaster House) Ltd and Others* [2000] 1 WLR 2333, it was held that, in order for the court to award damages in lieu of rescission, the right to rescind must not have, in fact, been lost. This conflicts with the earlier obiter statement by Jacob J in *Thomas Witter Ltd v TBP Industries Ltd* [1996] 2 All ER 573.

Where the misrepresentation is negligent, ie the maker is unable to show that he had reasonable grounds for believing, and did believe, that the statement was true, the innocent party is entitled to damages under s 2(1) of the Misrepresentation Act 1967.

Damages are also available in the tort of deceit for a fraudulent misrepresentation. However, for this, it is necessary to show that the maker had no genuine belief in the truth of the statement. Usually, there is little point trying to prove fraud as damages are assessed on a very similar basis to negligent misrepresentation. In both cases, damages are measured on the tortious basis, which aims to put the innocent party in the position he would have been in if the tort had not been committed. In the context of an acquisition, this involves restoring the innocent party to the position he would have been in if he had not entered into the acquisition agreement; in other words, the court must try to assess to what extent he has lost out by entering into it.

REPRESENTATIONS AND WARRANTIES

The nature of an acquisition agreement renders it likely that any representations made by the seller in pre-contract discussions and negotiations, which induce the buyer to enter into the agreement, will be included as warranties in the agreement. It is rare, therefore, for an action for misrepresentation to be founded on a matter which is not included in the contract. Indeed, it is common for the agreement to incorporate an acknowledgment by the buyer that he has not relied on any representations which are not contained in the contract and that the contract sets out the entire agreement and understanding between the parties (known as an 'entire agreement clause'). Any attempt to exclude liability for misrepresentation must be reasonable in order to be effective (s 3 of the Misrepresentation Act 1967 as substituted by s 8 of the Unfair Contract Terms Act 1977 (UCTA 1977)).

An entire agreement clause was considered in the case of *Thomas Witter Ltd v TBP Industries Ltd* [1996] 2 All ER 573. Jacob J concluded (obiter) that the clause in question was ineffective. Whilst doubting whether the wording of the clause was sufficiently explicit to exclude liability for misrepresentation, he ruled that it would, in any event, be unreasonable because it did not distinguish between different types of misrepresentation. He felt that it would never be reasonable to exclude liability for fraudulent misrepresentation. Following the judge's reasoning, the seller should ensure that the buyer expressly agrees to waive his right to damages or rescission for non-fraudulent misrepresentation in relation to representations not included in the contract.

Even where a clause of this nature is included in the agreement, this does not render misrepresentation redundant. Many of the representations which the seller makes to the buyer in the lead up to the signing of the agreement will be included as express warranties in the agreement itself. If any of these warranties are broken, the buyer will be able to claim damages for breach of contract as explained above. Section 1 of the Misrepresentation Act 1967 makes it clear, however, that where a misrepresentation has become a term of the contract, this will not affect the innocent party's right to rescind (provided none of the equitable bars operate). In contra[...] breach of warranty does not enable the buyer to discharge the contract. This may n[...] be significant where the misrepresentation is only discovered after completion if by then it is too late to rescind. However, it would be important if the buyer becomes aware of the falsity of the representation after exchange but before completion.

Where there is an interval between exchange and completion, the buyer will usually seek to negotiate a contractual right to withdraw from the contract if he becomes aware of any breach of warranty. This will often be backed up by obliging the seller to inform the buyer if the seller becomes aware of anything which is inconsistent with the warranties or makes them inaccurate.

Such a provision is of advantage to the buyer as it will enable him to 'rescind' the agreement whether or not the breach of warranty is also a misrepresentation (avoiding argument as to whether the warranty repeated statements made pre-contract which the buyer relied upon, etc).

Where the remedy sought is damages, the difference in the measure of damages for breach of contract and misrepresentation may also be significant. It has been seen that the contractual measure allows for loss of bargain and, on a share purchase, involves assessing the difference between the actual value of the shares and their value if the warranty had been true. On the other hand, the aim of tortious damages is to put the buyer in the position he would have been in if he had not entered into the agreement; this will involve calculating the difference between the price paid for the shares and their actual market value. The contractual measure will often lead to higher damages because of the ability to recover for loss of bargain. However, this will not always be the result, particularly where the bargain is not a good one (eg in a share acquisition, where a buyer has paid more than market value for the shares). In these circumstances, the buyer may be better off with the restitutionary approach.

Seller's rights against the management of the target

On a share sale, where the shareholders of the target company are not also directors, it will be the latter who will provide much of the information about the business which is requested by the buyer. Where this information is inaccurate or incomplete, this may lead to the selling shareholders becoming liable to the buyer for breach of warranty or misrepresentation; they may in turn be inclined to shift responsibility to the directors of the target by bringing a claim against them.

The buyer will wish to avoid the sellers' responsibility for breach of warranty effectively being shifted back onto the directors of the target who may well still be employed by the target. This is usually achieved by the selling shareholders waiving any right they may have to bring a claim against the management or the target itself in these circumstances (except in the case of any directors of the target who are also sellers).

4.3.2 Indemnities

The buyer may seek further contractual protection in the form of indemnities included in the acquisition agreement or, occasionally, incorporated in a separate deed.

What is the difference between a warranty and an indemnity?

A warranty is an undertaking by the seller that a particular state of affairs exists. On a breach of warranty, the buyer must establish his loss under normal contractual principles. For example, on a share sale, he will have to establish the reduction (if any) in the value of the shares (see **4.3.1**).

An indemnity, on the other hand, is essentially a promise to reimburse the buyer in respect of a designated type of liability which may arise in the future. On a share sale, there is no need to assess any reduction in the value of the shares; the recipient of the indemnity simply receives an amount equal to the actual liability (the indemnity clause will usually provide for costs and expenses relating to it to be recovered as well). For example, if the buyer is worried about an outstanding debt owed to the target, he could seek an indemnity against the possibility of the debt becoming bad. If this happens, the buyer will receive the amount of the outstanding debt and, possibly, incidental costs in seeking to recover it.

Another difference between a warranty and an indemnity is that, in the case of the latter, there is no duty to mitigate the loss; such a duty may, however, be incorporated in the contract.

Taxation indemnities

It is common for buyers of shares to seek protection from tax liabilities in the form of both warranties and indemnities. On a business acquisition, extensive safeguards are unnecessary because almost all tax liabilities remain with the seller.

The warranties usually deal with the target's compliance with tax and VAT requirements, such as the proper submission of returns and the correct implementation of the pay as you earn (PAYE) system, etc as well as other areas where the buyer is mainly concerned with prompting disclosures from the seller (eg whether there are any existing disputes with the Inland Revenue). The indemnities, on the other hand, will cover specific tax charges which may arise over and above those provided for in the accounts and which are referable to the seller's period of ownership.

Dealing with most tax matters by way of indemnity has the advantage to the buyer that he does not need to prove the link between the unexpected tax liability and the value of the shares. However, warranties are often appropriate for many matters in respect of which buyers seek indemnities and the seller should consider arguing this point.

Tax consequences of payments under warranties and indemnities

The following discussion applies to payments made by the seller under **any** warranty or indemnity brought by the buyer following completion of the acquisition, not merely to payments in respect of taxation warranties and indemnities.

WARRANTIES

Warranties are always given in favour of the buyer.

On the sale of the business or shares, the seller may have made a chargeable capital gain on the disposal, based on the consideration that he received. Let us assume that the seller later has to make a payment to the buyer under a warranty contained in the acquisition agreement. What are the tax consequences for the seller and the buyer of such a payment?

Section 49 of the TCGA 1992 provides that no tax allowance will be made in the first instance for any contingent liability in respect of a warranty or representation. However, if the liability crystallises, an adjustment will be made to the price of the target for capital gains purposes. If, therefore, the seller makes a payment under a warranty to the buyer, then the capital tax computation would be adjusted as follows.

(1) The consideration which the seller is treated as having received on completion will be reduced by the amount paid out under the warranty claim thus reducing any gain. If the seller has already paid the tax, he will be entitled to a refund.

(2) The buyer's acquisition cost is reduced by the same amount: his potential gain on a subsequent disposal of the target is therefore increased because his acquisition cost reduces.

INDEMNITIES

The position is not as straightforward when it comes to payments under indemnities. Consider the example of a standard tax indemnity in a sale of shares. The buyer will be keen to ensure that the target company has accounted for all outstanding taxes and has no hidden tax liability. The sale agreement will contain an indemnity in the event of the target company being called upon to pay additional tax. It used to be the practice that indemnities were often given in favour of the target company itself, not the buyer, as it is the target company upon whom the tax liability would fall. The case of *Zim Properties Ltd v Procter (Inspector of Taxes)*; *Procter (Inspector of Taxes) v Zim Properties Ltd* [1985] STC 90, however, threw considerable doubt on the tax efficiency of this practice.

In *Zim*, a firm of solicitors acting for a taxpayer in a conveyancing transaction were allegedly negligent, with the result that a sale of three properties owned by the taxpayer fell through. The action for negligence was settled with the taxpayer receiving compensation of £69,000. Undoubtedly, this was a capital sum but the question arose as to whether it derived from the disposal of a capital asset.

Warner J in *Zim* held that the right to sue the solicitors was an asset for CGT purposes (since it could be turned into a capital sum by negotiation of a compromise). Thus, the settlement of the action was the disposal of a *chose in action* (a personal right to property which can only be claimed or enforced through legal action) giving rise to CGT. Furthermore, the case also established that this *chose in action* would normally have a nil acquisition cost; accordingly, the amount received in settlement would be liable to tax in full.

It is considered that this principle could apply to an indemnity *in favour of the target company*. In order to indemnify the target fully, it would be necessary to gross up any sum paid to take account of this tax liability (the relevant indemnity clauses should contain a *grossing-up clause*).

Example

The buyers purchase from the sellers the entire share capital of Target Limited.

In the acquisition agreement the sellers give a tax indemnity in favour of Target Limited.

Target Limited is later required to pay £50,000 in unpaid tax and claims under the indemnity.

Assume that Target Limited receives from the sellers the sum of £50,000.

If the *Zim* principle applies to indemnities, Target Limited is treated as having disposed of a chargeable asset and will be liable to tax on the amount of consideration less the acquisition cost. There is a nil acquisition cost. Target Limited is treated as having made a chargeable gain of £50,000 upon which it has to pay corporation tax.

The indemnity should contain an appropriate grossing-up clause, so that Target Limited will receive from the sellers a sum, which, after tax, leaves Target Limited with £50,000 (eg assuming Target Ltd pays corporation tax at 30%, it would need to receive approximately £71,429).

Many sellers will be unwilling to agree to a grossing-up clause (perhaps for obvious reasons!). The Inland Revenue sought to clear up the alarm through the issue of an extra statutory concession (ESC D33) on 19 December 1988.

EXTRA STATUTORY CONCESSION (ESC D33)

In ESC D33, the Inland Revenue has made it clear that it will not regard the principle in *Zim* as applicable where payments are made to the buyer under warranties. The Concession also states that indemnity payments 'by the vendor *to the purchaser*' will be treated the same way as warranties, ie the seller's sale proceeds are adjusted and the buyer's cost of acquisition in the event of a further disposal is reduced by the sum received. The Concession does not deal with payments made to the target company itself. Therefore, the safe approach is that indemnities should be expressed to be *in favour of the buyer*, and not in favour of the target company.

The practice of providing that payments under indemnities are made to the buyer has been widely adopted and relevant provisions are now normally contained in the main acquisition agreement. Although they are not always described as indemnities (eg they may be described as 'taxation covenants'), they are invariably still drafted like indemnities, ie to compensate the buyer for an amount equal to the liability imposed on the target.

4.3.3 Who gives the warranties and indemnities?

The sellers of the target and those giving the warranties and indemnities are not always one and the same. Some sellers may be unwilling to accept any liability or, at least, may try to limit their share of liability. The buyer, on the other hand, will usually want all the sellers to give the warranties and indemnities and to do so on the basis that they are jointly and severally liable for any breaches.

Joint and several liability

Where there is more than one warrantor the buyer will invariably insist that they accept joint and several liability; this will enable him to sue any one of the warrantors for the full amount of the liability. Although this will not be of concern to the buyer, s 1 of the Civil Liability (Contribution) Act 1978 gives the party called upon to discharge the liability the right to recover a contribution from the other warrantors who are liable in respect of the same damage.

In an action under s 1, the court determines the amount of the contribution recoverable from the others on the basis of what it considers just and equitable having regard to the extent of their responsibility for the particular damage (s 2). It is likely that these contributions would reflect the amount of the purchase price which each warrantor received, although there is nothing to prevent the court from also taking into account other factors connected with the acquisition. As a result of this uncertainty, it is common practice for the warrantors to agree how any liability should be borne between them. This is permitted by the 1978 Act and will usually be on the basis that liability is shared in proportion to the allocation of the purchase consideration. Such an agreement may be in a separate document ('a deed of contribution') or it may be incorporated in the main acquisition agreement. In the latter case, the clause allocating liability will usually be expressed to be: 'as between the warrantors'. It is important to appreciate that the buyer will not be affected by an agreement in these terms and will still be able to sue any warrantor for the full amount. In other words, the risk of a warrantor being unable or unwilling to pay his share falls on his fellow warrantors and not the buyer, whose concern is simply that he should be able to recover compensation from someone.

Who may be unwilling to give warranties?

On a share sale involving a large number of shareholders, the buyer will not always insist that all of them give the warranties and indemnities. This is particularly so in relation to minor shareholders who may, often justifiably, not wish to be exposed to the risk which joint and several liability entails.

Problems often arise where some of the shares of a company are held in trust. Trustees will wish to avoid personal liability and may refuse to give any warranties or undertakings, except that they have unencumbered title to the shares. If the trust holds a significant number of shares, this puts both the buyer and the other shareholders in a dilemma; the buyer has less security in the event of a breach and the other shareholders may feel aggrieved at undertaking a contingent liability disproportionate to the benefit they are receiving.

A solution which may be acceptable to all concerned is for the buyer to acknowledge in the acquisition agreement that the trustees' liability is limited to the net value (ie after tax) for the time being of the capital of the trust. The danger to the buyer of the capital being distributed shortly after completion may be met by obliging the trustees to require any beneficiary receiving capital to give appropriate warranties to the buyer. However, the terms of the particular trust may preclude the trustees from committing themselves to doing this.

Finally, even relatively substantial shareholders will sometimes try to avoid giving warranties and indemnities on the grounds that they have had no involvement with the management of the target company and, therefore, cannot be expected to give promises in relation to matters they know nothing about. It is true that one of the purposes of warranties is to extract information about the target and that this information will generally come from the target's management. Nevertheless, the other (and probably more important) role of warranties is to allocate risk between seller and buyer. The price will be negotiated on the assumption that the warranties are true and this is the basis on which all the shareholders (whether executive directors or not) receive their share of the consideration. If a breach of warranty means that the shares are not as valuable as the parties envisaged when entering into the deal, then it seems reasonable that there is an adjustment to the amount received by each shareholder; otherwise those shareholders who are not also warrantors effectively receive a windfall benefit.

4.3.4 Assignment of warranties/indemnities

If the buyer decides to sell the target soon after acquiring it, will he be able to assign the benefit of the warranties and indemnities which he received from the seller to the 'new' buyer? It is generally considered that the benefit of warranties are personal to the buyer and cannot be assigned, at least without the consent of the warrantor. This is also likely to be true in relation to indemnities given to the buyer (this problem will not arise if the indemnity is in favour of a target company).

If the buyer foresees the possibility of selling the target, he may try to negotiate with the seller an express right to assign the benefit of the warranties and indemnities. His own buyer will certainly want the benefit of the usual protections, and an assignment of the existing warranties is a more attractive proposition than providing these warranties himself.

However, prior to May 2000, even where such provision has been made, there was some doubt as to whether the assignee could recover substantial damages, due to the rules of privity of contract (ie the rights assigned are those of the immediate buyer, but, on assignment, the immediate buyer is unlikely to have suffered loss). The third party assignee therefore does not gain any benefit.

The position of an assignee has perhaps become clearer with the introduction of the Contracts (Rights of Third Parties) Act 1999 (in force from 11 May 2000). Under the 1999 Act, a person who is not a party to a contract may, nevertheless, have a right to enforce a term of the contract. This would occur where the contract either expressly confers a right in favour of a third party or the terms of the contract purport to confer such a right. Being a statutory right, a buyer of shares should be advised to structure the acquisition agreement to take advantage of the 1999 Act, so that the seller expressly agrees to confer the benefit of the warranties directly on subsequent buyers. If the seller has agreed to this, an assignee should not encounter problems recovering loss from the seller (see previous paragraph).

However, a seller is likely to oppose such express provision, as he would have no control over the identity of the assignee of the warranties. This is particularly the case where a buyer is an individual. In the case of a corporate buyer, the seller may agree to the buyer assigning the benefit of the warranties to members of the buyer's group. If assignment is agreed, the seller should ensure that the agreement provides that the assignee will be bound by the procedural provisions set out in the agreement (eg notification of claims and limitation periods) in the same way that the immediate buyer would have been.

4.3.5 Buyer's security for breach of warranty etc

The potential liability of the seller in relation to the warranties and indemnities is usually substantial and may not come to light until some time after completion. The buyer is in an exposed position in relation to contingent liabilities which are the subject of warranties and indemnities. He or the target itself may be directly liable to third parties, for example, but may be unable to recover the loss if the seller is in financial difficulties. The buyer should consider reducing the risk by insisting on some form of security from the seller.

Guarantees

Where the sellers of a business or shares are individuals, the buyer will want to be satisfied as to the seller's financial status and ability to cover any claims, so may insist on taking a charge over their assets or receiving a guarantee from a third party.

Where the seller of a business or shares is a company which is part of a group, the seller's parent company may be prepared to guarantee the seller's obligations. However, where a company owned by individuals is selling its business, it is likely to be a mere shell after completion which may be wound up shortly afterwards as a way of remitting the proceeds to the shareholders. In these circumstances, the financial security of the seller is clearly in doubt and the buyer should seek guarantees from its shareholders at the very least.

Retentions from the purchase price

Another method of securing the buyer's position is for the acquisition agreement to provide for the buyer to retain part of the purchase price of the target for a certain period after completion and for this sum to be used to pay any successful claims under the warranties or indemnities. Such provision may be made in the following terms:

(1) payment of the retention into a joint account in the names of the seller's and buyer's solicitors;

(2) the retention to be remitted to the seller on a certain date after completion (eg 12 months after completion) unless the buyer makes a claim under the warranties or indemnities before that date;

(3) where the buyer does make such a claim, only the balance of the retention, after deducting the amount of the claim, to be paid to the seller on the specified date;

(4) the buyer to be paid the amount of the claim within a short period (eg 14 days) of this being determined and any balance remitted to the seller;

(5) payment of accrued interest on the fund to the parties in the same proportion that they receive the retention;

(6) an obligation on the buyer to pursue any claims against the seller which may delay the remittance of the fund promptly and diligently.

The seller may also insist that any claim which delays payment of the retention must be properly made. For example, the buyer may be obliged to provide full details of the claim, perhaps backed up with an opinion of counsel.

The retention will not affect the CGT position of the parties (see **11.4**). Only if it is used to pay warranty claims will there be an adjustment to the consideration for CGT purposes as explained at **4.3.2**.

4.4 HOW MAY THE SELLER LIMIT HIS LIABILITY?

The seller will seek to limit his potential exposure to liability by negotiating specific provisions in the acquisition agreement, making appropriate disclosures in the disclosure letter and, perhaps, by taking out insurance. Each of these methods is considered in turn.

4.4.1 Limitations in the agreement

The first draft of the acquisition agreement prepared by the buyer will invariably include extensive warranties and indemnities with no specific limitations on the seller's liability. In most cases, there is considerable scope for negotiating the agreement and it is the warranties and indemnities which usually take up most of the time and energies of the parties' solicitors. Indeed, the final agreed version often bears little resemblance to the original draft.

The seller may be able to limit his liability by arguing successfully for the deletion of certain of the warranties and indemnities. Even if he is unable to achieve this, negotiating changes to the wording of a clause which effectively 'water it down' may make a significant difference to the seller's exposure. There is considerable merit in analysing carefully the wording of each warranty and indemnity. For example, the initial draft of a warranty may state: 'no customer of the company will cease to deal with it as a result of the acquisition'. The seller's solicitor may try to amend this by requiring knowledge of the seller and restricting the warranty to substantial customers; thus the agreed version may read: 'the seller has no knowledge, information or belief that any substantial customer of the company will cease to deal with it as a result of the acquisition'. Similarly, the seller may be asked to warrant that the company is not in breach of a particular agreement. The seller's solicitor may be able to limit the scope of the warranty by again requiring knowledge of the seller and by restricting it to breach of 'material terms' of the agreement.

Where warranties are given by reference to the 'knowledge, information or belief' of the seller in this way, the buyer may insist on the seller acknowledging that in giving the warranties he has made all due enquiries and taken all reasonable steps to ensure their accuracy.

In addition to negotiating the terms of each warranty, the seller will also seek to restrict his liability in relation to the warranties and indemnities generally by including a set of standard limitation clauses in the agreement. Such limitations on the seller's liability for breach of warranty contained in a share sale agreement are not controlled by the UCTA 1977 (Sch 1, para 1(e) precludes the operation of its relevant provisions to any contract so far as it relates to the 'creation or transfer of securities or of any right or interest in securities'). Business sale agreements are not the subject of a similar specific exclusion. However, s 3 of the UCTA 1977, which invalidates attempts to exclude liability unless they satisfy the requirement of reasonableness, only applies where one party deals on the other's written standard terms of business or 'as a consumer' (ie he neither makes the contract in the course of a business nor holds himself out as doing so and the other party does make the contract in the course of a business: s 12). In any event, freely negotiated warranty limitations contained in an acquisition agreement are unlikely to be the subject of a successful challenge.

Limits on the amount of claims

The concept of joint and several liability and attempts by sellers to limit their share of liability have already been discussed (see **4.3.3**). In addition, it is usual to include maximum and minimum limitations.

MAXIMUM LIMITS

The seller will negotiate for a maximum liability under the warranties and indemnities. The limit which is often agreed upon is the price which the buyer paid for the target. It is possible, particularly on a share sale, that the buyer's loss, recoverable under the rules of *Hadley v Baxendale* (see **4.3.1**), may exceed the amount which he paid for the target. Few sellers, however, are prepared to risk being sued for more than they receive for the shares or assets and most buyers will accept this limitation. The buyer must take care in agreeing to such a clause, however, if the actual purchase price is relatively low but he is obliged as part of the deal to inject money into the target to discharge certain liabilities, such as outstanding loans owed by the target to the sellers. The amount of such liabilities should be treated as part of the consideration for this purpose.

MINIMUM LIMITS

The parties will often agree a minimum threshold for claims. This will typically be about 1% of the consideration. In other words, the buyer is prevented from making any claim unless the aggregate of all claims exceeds the threshold. This is really on the basis that it is virtually impossible to gauge precisely the value of a business or a company and the parties accept that there is margin for error. The effect of warranty claims is to adjust retrospectively the purchase price and it seems reasonable for the parties to take the view that relatively minor adjustments do not justify the expense and inconvenience involved in pursuing warranty claims. The buyer is, however, wise to insist that once the threshold is exceeded, he can recover the full amount, rather than just the amount by which the threshold is exceeded. So, for example, on a £5 million sale, where the threshold is £50,000 and the loss suffered is £60,000, the buyer will be entitled to recover £60,000 rather than £10,000.

The seller may also seek to set a 'de minimis' limit on individual claims, to apply even where the aggregate threshold has been exceeded. For example, the buyer may be prevented from bringing any claim worth less than £5,000. Difficulties can arise, however, in respect of continuing breaches and claims which are similar in nature or arise from the same default. Where, for example, the seller has warranted that all book debts will be fully recoverable, claims relating to debts from different sources should not be treated as separate for this purpose. As so often with acquisition documentation, careful attention to detail in drafting such a clause is necessary.

Time-limits

The limitation period for bringing a claim for breach of contract is normally 6 years from the date of the contract. Where the share or asset sale is by deed, the limitation period is 12 years (or if there is a separate deed of tax indemnity, the period will be 12 years in relation to the tax matters covered).

Most sellers will wish to be 'off the hook' well before the limitation periods expire. It is common to restrict the period in which the buyer can make claims relating to tax matters to 6 years from the date of the contract. This is related to the Inland Revenue's time-limit for making an assessment to tax (6 years from the end of the relevant tax year except to recover tax lost through fraudulent or negligent conduct). To be safe, the buyer may insist on the period being 7 years.

For non-tax matters, the period negotiated is usually much shorter and, on a share sale, tends to be linked to the target company's audit (on the basis that the audit may 'flush out' breaches of warranty). A period allowing for two full audits to be carried out and their results digested is commonly agreed.

The agreement may allow the buyer to bring claims outside these time-limits provided he has notified the details to the seller (ie sufficient information to identify the nature and substance of the claim). In these circumstances, there should be a long-stop time-limit for instituting proceedings, so that the buyer is not able to extend the limitation period 'by the back door'!

Insurance cover

The seller will invariably seek to prevent the buyer from bringing a claim where the loss is covered by insurance taken out in relation to the target. The main argument between the parties often centres around whether this should extend to insurance cover that the buyer could reasonably be expected to take out (perhaps related to the level of cover in place before the acquisition).

Recovery from third parties

The buyer may also be required to give credit for any sums received from third parties in relation to the subject matter of the claim. This will usually be expressed widely enough to cover tax reductions (eg an undisclosed liability may be a deductible expense for tax purposes, resulting in a saving of tax).

Assets understated in the accounts

The seller may want to include a provision that any claim will be reduced by the amount by which the seller can show that the net assets of the target were understated in the accounts drawn up before completion, for example, by demonstrating either of the following:

(1)   that assets have been realised for more than their value in the accounts; or
(2)   that liabilities have been satisfied for less than is specified in the accounts.

The buyer should be wary of accepting this, particularly where the valuation of the target was not assets-based.

Conduct of claims

Claims made by third parties against the target may result in the seller becoming liable to the buyer under a warranty. The seller may, for example, have warranted that the target company has not manufactured any products which are faulty in any material respect. A successful action against the target under the Consumer Protection Act 1987 in respect of damage caused by a defect in a product manufactured by the target prior to completion would amount to a breach of this warranty. The buyer will seek to reclaim the amount of any judgment entered against the target and costs incurred in connection with the claim.

The seller may argue that, since he will ultimately bear the liability, he should have the right to have conduct of the claim. He may be worried that, if the buyer has control over the dispute, the buyer may be less than vigorous in defending a claim when he knows that he will be able to sue under a warranty if it succeeds. The buyer is under a duty to mitigate his loss but it may be difficult for the seller to prove a failure to mitigate in these circumstances.

The buyer, on the other hand, may have reservations about allowing the seller to have control, on the basis of the possible damage to the reputation and goodwill of the target which may ensue as a consequence. For example, he may feel that the seller's main concern will be to protract the matter rather than come to a settlement which leaves the target's reputation intact.

Whichever party it is decided should have control of claims, the agreement will often provide for the other party to have some influence over his conduct (eg requiring consent to settle the claim). If the seller is given control, the buyer may reserve the right to require him to provide security and/or an indemnity in respect of costs and expenses which the target or buyer may incur in relation to the claim. The buyer, for his part, will be obliged to notify the seller promptly of any circumstances which may give rise to a claim.

4.4.2 Disclosures

Nature and purpose of the disclosure letter

One of the aims of including a long list of warranties in the acquisition agreement is to elicit information about the target from the seller. Warranties can be seen as providing a checklist for the buyer of all the matters which may be of concern to him in relation to the acquisition. Much of the information requested by the buyer is produced in the form of disclosures by the seller, which have the effect of qualifying the warranties. The incentive for the seller in making disclosures is that they avoid him being in breach of warranty in relation to those matters disclosed. This can be illustrated by considering a few examples in the context of some standard warranties.

Example 1

The agreement includes a warranty that the target is not engaged in any litigation as claimant or defendant. The target is, however, being sued for breach of copyright.

The seller can avoid liability for breach of warranty by disclosing full details of the copyright action. This is easier than negotiating an alteration to the terms of the warranty to exclude the copyright action from its scope (the buyer would not agree to the deletion of the warranty as he would be left without any protection against undisclosed claims). The buyer must take a view on the significance of the disclosure to the deal which he has negotiated. It may prompt him to withdraw from the acquisition, renegotiate the price, or ask the seller for an indemnity for any damages awarded against the target and any costs incurred in relation to the claim.

Example 2

The agreement includes a warranty that the target company is not party to any contract or agreement which cannot be terminated by the company on 3 months' notice or less. The company is, however, party to a distribution agreement which either party can bring to an end by giving 12 months' notice and two of the directors have 9 months of their fixed-term service contracts to run.

Once again, the simplest way for the seller to avoid liability is to disclose the existence and main terms of the three agreements and attach copies to the disclosure letter.

Example 3

The agreement includes a warranty that the disclosure letter contains full particulars of the pension scheme for the target's employees.

This is a different type of warranty which obliges the seller to give full and accurate details of the pension scheme (the seller will normally provide copies of the trust deed and rules).

The disclosure letter has such an important role in determining the potential liability of the seller and, correspondingly, the risk undertaken by the buyer, that it will be the subject of the same careful scrutiny by the parties as the acquisition agreement itself. The specific disclosures which are made will depend entirely on the position of the particular target. However, there are also a number of more general matters which the parties will need to consider.

Full disclosure

The acquisition agreement will provide that the warranties are given subject to matters disclosed in the disclosure letter. The buyer may insist that the disclosures are properly made, ie that they are accurate and fully disclose the matters to which they relate. It is understandable that the buyer will not want to accept limitations on the seller's potential liability under the warranties unless he has full details of the relevant circumstances. From the seller's point of view it will also be advisable to make any disclosures to the buyer as specific as possible. Following the case of *Levison and Others v Farin and Others* [1978] 2 All ER 1149, it is clear that in order for a disclosure to be effective the buyer must be given specific notice of it. In this case, the buyers were generally aware of the run-down condition of the business but this did not preclude them from successfully claiming for breach of a warranty which said that 'there will have been no material adverse change in the overall value of the net assets of the Company'.

The seller (or his advisers) will normally have passed a great deal of information to the buyer in the pre-contract period and may wish the buyer to acknowledge that the disclosure letter is deemed to include all this information. The buyer will usually prefer that copies of all information and documentation which he or his advisers have received in this way and which are to be taken to be disclosed are attached to the disclosure letter. Although the buyer's solicitor will have the task of working through the attached bundle of documents, there is less chance of the buyer inadvertently accepting disclosures. Indeed, the buyer will usually insist on limiting disclosure specifically to matters revealed in the disclosure letter and bundle and there will be a clause in the acquisition agreement saying that the warranties are only qualified by matters contained in these documents and not the buyer's own knowledge. The buyer should, however, be aware of the fact that he may not be able to rely on such a clause. In the case of *Eurocopy plc v Teesdale and Others* [1992] BCLC 1067, the general rule that the buyer's own knowledge will not provide a defence to breach of warranty was brought into question. In this case, the sellers had warranted that all material facts had been disclosed to the buyer. The buyer brought a breach of warranty claim on the grounds that the sellers had failed to disclose certain material facts (relating to maintenance contracts for photocopiers). The sellers claimed that the buyer had actual knowledge of those facts from their due diligence. The buyer moved to strike out this aspect of the defence, on the basis that the agreement stated that the warranties were subject only to the disclosure letter and that no other information relevant to the target of which the buyer had knowledge affected any warranty claims. The Court of Appeal refused to strike out this aspect of the defence partly on the basis that the price they paid 'must have been influenced by their knowledge of material facts and circumstances'.

Whilst it accepted that this case was only an interlocutory application, it must still be borne in mind when advising a buyer who has information on the target which may lead to a warranty claim. In practice, the door has now been left open for a warrantor to argue that the buyer might be prejudiced by actual knowledge of the facts.

Overlap between warranties

For ease of reference, the disclosures made will usually refer to specific clauses (or sub-clauses) of the acquisition agreement. However, there is often a significant degree of overlap between the warranties contained in an acquisition agreement. The disclosure letter invariably provides, therefore, that each disclosure is deemed to be in respect of all the warranties and not merely the warranty referred to in it.

Deemed disclosures

The disclosure letter will state that a number of matters are deemed to have been disclosed to the buyer. These relate to publicly available information, which the buyer can be expected to find out for himself and may include the following:

(1) information on a target company's file at the Companies Registry;

(2) matters apparent from the deeds of properties owned or occupied by the target and any information available from HM Land Registry, the Land Charges Department or which would be revealed by appropriate searches and enquiries of local authorities. This extensive disclosure is likely to qualify a number of property warranties (eg that the target has good title to the properties, that they are free from mortgages and charges and that the use of each property is a permitted use for planning purposes);

(3) matters which would be disclosed by physical inspection of each property. The buyer should only be prepared to accept this if he has commissioned a survey of all the target's properties (time constraints will often prevent this);

(4) matters which are in the public domain. This is very wide ranging and the buyer may try to restrict its scope to matters which the buyer could reasonably be expected to be aware of as affecting the target;

(5) matters disclosed or referred to in the audited accounts of a target company (eg for the last 3 years);

(6) matters included or referred to in the accountant's report prepared on behalf of the buyer. The nature and purpose of the accountant's report is discussed in Chapter 3. There is often considerable disagreement between the parties as to how the report should be treated for this purpose. Reports are often very comprehensive, covering a great deal of ground; accordingly, a disclosure in these terms may reduce considerably the buyer's scope for suing for breach of warranty (eg where the inaccuracy of certain warranties could have been ascertained from the contents of the report). The buyer may, however, be prepared to accept this deemed disclosure in return for the seller warranting the accuracy of the report.

4.4.3 Insuring against liability

Increasingly, buyers and/or sellers are seeking to cover the risk of potential warranty claims by taking out warranty and indemnity insurance. The price of securing the seller's peace of mind in this way can be high (premiums being between 1% and 5% of the limit of liability) and will often involve the insurers in picking through the acquisition documentation (usually via their own solicitors and at the seller's expense). The insurers will not agree cover until they have analysed the scope of each warranty, the effect of the disclosures and the extent of the general limitations on the seller's liability. Any policy is likely to contain a number of general exclusions (eg excluding liability in respect of matters within the knowledge of the seller at the date of the contract).

The sale and purchase agreement should incorporate a clause which obliges the buyer to claim from an insurer before commencing an action against the seller.

4.5 CRIMINAL LIABILITY FOR FALSE OR MISLEADING STATEMENTS

Section 397(1) and (2) of the FSMA 2000 makes it a criminal offence for a person knowingly or recklessly to make a statement, promise or forecast which is misleading, false or deceptive. It is also an offence under the section for a person with the requisite intent to conceal dishonestly any material facts. The person will be guilty of the offence if he makes the statement, etc or conceals the facts for the purpose of inducing, or is reckless as to whether it may induce, another person to, inter alia, enter into an investment agreement. A person guilty of an offence is liable to a fine, or imprisonment for a maximum term of 7 years for conviction on indictment, or to both. The following points in relation to this offence should be noted:

(1) the term 'investment agreement' includes a share sale agreement but not a business sale agreement;
(2) the offence is committed if a person recklessly makes a false or misleading statement 'dishonestly or otherwise';
(3) the statement need not be made to the person whom the maker intends to induce (or in respect of whom he is reckless as to whether he is induced) to enter into the agreement.

The lack of a requirement for dishonesty in making statements, etc means that the seller and his professional advisers must be careful not to make statements in relation to a possible share acquisition (eg relating to the past performance of the target) unless these are fully justified by the facts.

There is a separate offence in s 397(3) of deliberately creating a false or misleading impression as to the market in or the price or value of any investments for the purpose of inducing another person to, inter alia, acquire those investments. This provision is most likely to be used in relation to practices aimed at manipulating the share price of listed companies, but is wide enough to catch private company deals as well. For example, a seller who 'talks up' the value of the company by 'inventing' interested potential buyers might be liable under this provision.

For further details on the effect of the FSMA 2000, see LPC Resource Book *Corporate Finance: Public Companies and the City* (Jordans).

4.6 NEGLIGENT STATEMENTS

If the buyer enters into the acquisition agreement relying on information from the seller or third parties, does he have a claim in tort for negligent misstatement if that information turns out to be incorrect? If so, how does this interrelate with the other remedies available to the buyer which are described above?

4.6.1 Statements by the seller

The House of Lords' decision in *Hedley Byrne and Co Ltd v Heller and Partners Ltd* [1964] AC 465 established the principle that an action might lie in tort for negligent misstatement where a person relies to his detriment on advice, information or opinion given by someone who holds himself out as having special knowledge or skill. It was emphasised that a vital ingredient was the existence of a 'special relationship between the parties', although this did not mean that they must have been in direct contact. In *Hedley Byrne*, the defendant bankers gave a favourable reference when asked about the financial stability of one of their customers and this was relayed to the plaintiffs' bankers who passed the information to the plaintiffs (claimants). It was clear to the defendants from the circumstances of the request that the party on whose behalf the inquiry was made wanted the information to judge whether it was safe to extend substantial credit to the bank's customer. The House of Lords was satisfied that a special relationship existed, although on the facts the action failed because of an effective disclaimer given by the defendants.

The development of the law since *Hedley Byrne* confirms that the principle can apply to negligent pre-contractual statements made by one party to a contract to the other. It is also clear that potential liability is not restricted to professionals, such as solicitors and accountants, whose business it is to give advice. Liability could, therefore, extend to the seller of shares or a business in relation to pre-contractual statements made to the buyer about the target, since the seller has special knowledge of the target and the parties are in a 'special relationship'.

If there has been a negligent misstatement upon which a buyer is basing his claim, it is likely that he will also still bring a claim for negligent misrepresentation under s 2(1) of the Misrepresentation Act 1967. Negligent misrepresentation may also be easier to prove because s 2(1) places the onus on the maker of the statement to prove that he had reasonable grounds to believe and did believe in the truth of the statement. However, an action for misrepresentation can only be founded on statements of fact, whereas the scope of negligent misstatement extends to advice and opinion. In any action, it is likely that both claims are made, together with an action for breach of contract.

4.6.2 Statements by third parties

The buyer of shares or a business may have relied on statements, forecasts and opinions (in relation to financial matters, in particular) made by parties other than the seller. Will he have a remedy against these third parties if the information turns out to be false or misleading? The scope of negligent misstatement generally and its application to acquisitions in particular have been considered in several important decisions.

Caparo Industries plc v Dickman [1990] 2 WLR 358

Caparo, which was a shareholder in Fidelity plc, acquired control of the company relying on the audited accounts. Caparo claimed that the accounts were inaccurate and misleading in showing a pre-tax profit when, in fact, the company had made a loss. It sued the company's auditors for negligence in auditing the accounts (and certifying them as 'true and accurate'). Caparo alleged that the auditors owed it a duty of care either as a potential investor or as an existing shareholder. The Court of Appeal held that the auditors owed Caparo a duty of care as shareholders but not as potential investors.

The House of Lords emphasised that the imposition of a duty of care in economic loss cases required 'proximity' of relationship as well as foreseeability of loss (a third criterion being that it must not be unreasonable to impose a duty of care). In determining the question of proximity, there was no single general principle and the court should be guided by established categories of negligence. A review of previous cases in this area led the House of Lords to identify three conditions for proximity to exist. It must be shown that the maker of the statement knew the following:

(1) that the statement would be communicated to the person relying on it or to a clearly defined class of person to whom that person belonged; and
(2) this would be done specifically in connection with a particular transaction or a particular type of transaction; and
(3) the person would be very likely to rely on it in deciding whether to enter into the transaction.

The House of Lords decided that the auditors owed no duty of care to Caparo as investors or shareholders; it was not prepared to find a duty of care on auditors to members of the public at large as potential investors (or bidders). As for shareholders, it considered that the auditor's duty in relation to the accounts was owed to the shareholders as a body to enable them to exercise collective control of the company, and not to individual shareholders to assist in their decision whether to buy more shares.

Morgan Crucible Co plc v Hill Samuel and Co Ltd [1991] 2 WLR 665

Caparo was distinguished in the *Morgan Crucible* case. Following a takeover bid for a listed company by the plaintiffs (claimants), the chairman of the listed company incorporated various statements and profit forecasts in documents issued to shareholders and to the press as a defence to the bid. The plaintiffs increased their bid and successfully acquired control of the company. Some of the financial statements and forecasts were misleading and the company was not as valuable as this information had led the plaintiffs to believe. They sued the chairman, the auditors, and the merchant bank advising the board in negligence.

On an application to amend the statement of claim after the decision in *Caparo* (the original claim had also been based on financial statements made prior to the bid and the plaintiffs wished to restrict it to statements etc made after the bid), the Court of Appeal granted leave on the grounds that the amended claim disclosed a reasonable cause of action. The court was of the view that it was arguable that there was a sufficient degree of proximity since the defendants intended the plaintiffs to rely on the representations in deciding whether to make an increased bid (the case settled before reaching trial).

4.7 SELLER'S LIABILITY UNDER GUARANTEES

On a share sale, the liabilities of the target company remain with it and become the indirect responsibility of the buyer. The seller need not concern himself with these liabilities except in so far as they may result in a claim against him by the buyer for breach of warranty. An exception to this (when the seller may continue to have responsibility after completion of the sale) is where he has guaranteed obligations of the target company.

The nature of limited liability makes it likely that the principal shareholders of a target company will have been required to provide personal guarantees to third parties, which may be backed up by charges over their personal assets. Where the target company is a subsidiary, the parent company or, possibly, some of the parent company's shareholders or directors may have given guarantees. Individual or corporate sellers of shares will, accordingly, have continuing liability after completion for those obligations which they have guaranteed unless they are able to negotiate a release. Guarantees may have been provided in relation to the following:

(1) bank borrowings, including overdraft facilities;
(2) non-bank borrowings (eg a fixed-term loan for the purchase of plant and machinery);
(3) leases of premises: the landlord will often require the lease obligations (in particular to pay rent) of a corporate tenant to be guaranteed;
(4) commercial contracts: these may include hire purchase and conditional sale agreements, equipment leases etc. In addition, contracts such as supply agreements and distribution agreements entered into by a subsidiary may have been guaranteed by the parent company.

The seller will seek to obtain a release from such guarantees which is effective from completion of the acquisition. Those who have the benefit of the seller's guarantees may be unwilling to agree to a release unless the buyer is willing to undertake equivalent obligations and is of no less financial status. In any event, arrangements for release are often not in place by the time completion takes place. In these circumstances, the parties should make suitable provision in the acquisition agreement to deal with the contingent liability of the seller.

The buyer will commonly be obliged to use his best endeavours to secure the release of the seller from the guarantees (he should be careful not to make an absolute promise to achieve this) and, in the meantime, to indemnify the seller against any liability which may arise under them. This is not entirely satisfactory for the seller but he will be left with little alternative unless he is prepared to delay completion (perhaps by means of a contract conditional on release).

4.8 RESTRICTIONS ON THE SELLER

Whether it is a business acquisition or a share acquisition, the value of the buyer's investment could be reduced substantially by the post-completion activities of the seller, whose detailed knowledge of the target would enable him to cause it considerable harm. It is in the buyer's interests to protect his investment by making express provision in the acquisition agreement to curtail any such activities of the seller. This section deals with the position where no express agreement is made, the type of restrictions which the buyer may seek to impose and whether the validity of such provisions can be challenged.

4.8.1 What can the buyer do if there are no express restraints?

The case of *Trego v Hunt* [1896] AC 7 established that, on the sale of the goodwill of a business, the courts will refuse to imply a covenant by the seller not to set up in competition. In the absence of express provision, very limited protections for the buyer of goodwill (the position of a buyer of shares was not considered) will be implied into the agreement. The only implied undertakings of the seller are as follows:

(1) not to use or disclose confidential information relating to the business;
(2) not to represent himself as successor to the business, or as carrying on the same business;
(3) not to solicit customers of the business (ie those who were customers prior to the sale).

4.8.2 Express restrictions

The buyer of a business or shares will usually value the target on the assumption that its goodwill will be preserved. Indeed, on the acquisition of a business, a specific value will be attributed to goodwill. The buyer is, in effect, paying for the benefit of the good name of the target and the expectation that existing customers (and suppliers) will continue to deal with it (and, indeed, that new customers will be attracted to it).

As the seller is being paid for goodwill, the buyer is justified in seeking ways of preventing the seller from damaging it by, for example, taking away customers of the business. The buyer does not, however, have unlimited scope to restrain the activities of the seller after completion since the law is reluctant, on public policy grounds, to restrict competition in general and a person's ability to earn his livelihood in particular. The buyer must go no further than is reasonably necessary to protect the goodwill of the target.

The buyer commonly seeks to include in the agreement some or all of the following undertakings by the seller:

(1) a covenant not to be engaged or concerned in any competing business for a specified period after completion;
(2) a covenant not to try to solicit or entice away from the target customers or suppliers who have recently dealt with the target for a specified period after completion;
(3) a covenant not to try to solicit or entice away from the target employees of the target for a specified period after completion;
(4) an undertaking not to use or disclose any confidential information about the target or its customers;
(5) a covenant not to use the name of the target (where a business is acquired from a company, the selling company may be required to change its corporate name).

4.8.3 Will these restrictions be valid at common law?

All covenants in restraint of trade are prima facie void at common law. However, the court will not strike down restrictive covenants which it considers to be reasonable to protect a legitimate interest of the buyer. The preservation of goodwill, which is reflected in the value of the business or shares, and the protection of business secrets are the interests which the buyer is concerned to protect; the restraints must, therefore, go no further than is strictly necessary to achieve this. The factors which the court considers relevant are the same on a business sale as on a share sale. It should also be noted that the courts are not as strict in striking down clauses in acquisition contracts, which are freely negotiable, as they are in employment contracts. The following factors are relevant:

(1) the duration of the restraint;
(2) the geographical area of the restraint;
(3) the activities restricted.

Duration

The buyer will usually seek to prevent the seller from competing and soliciting customers etc for between one year and 5 years after completion. Where the seller is prevented from using or disclosing confidential information, it will not generally be necessary to stipulate a time-limit on this restriction.

Area

The geographical area in which a covenant preventing the seller from setting up a business of the same type is intended to operate must be closely related to the area in which the target operates. What is permissible, therefore, varies considerably and depends on whether the business is locally or nationally based. If the covenant is appropriately worded, it may not be necessary to stipulate a geographical limit. For example, if the clause disallows the seller from setting up a 'competing business', this has the effect of limiting the restraint to the area in which the target carries on business (otherwise it would not be competing for the same clientele). If, on the other hand, the clause restricts the seller from carrying on a defined business, it will be necessary to specify a reasonable area of restriction to prevent it from being considered too wide.

Activities

Any attempt to extend the restrictions to activities which are not carried on by the target itself will fail, on the grounds that they are excessive in order to protect the goodwill of the target. Accordingly, the buyer will not be able to prevent the seller from competing with other businesses that the buyer owns or intends to acquire in the future. Indeed, in *Ronbar Enterprises Ltd v Green* [1954] 2 All ER 266, the court considered a clause preventing the seller carrying on a business 'similar to' that of the target to be too wide.

Another relevant factor is the extent to which the parties being asked to give the covenants have been actively involved in the business. It may be difficult, for example, to enforce a non-competition covenant against a minority shareholder who has taken no part in managing a target company and has never been involved in the same industry.

A non-solicitation clause should not be so wide as to include those who have had no recent dealings with the target prior to completion. It may, for example, be unreasonable to restrict the seller from contacting 'customers' or 'suppliers' who have not dealt with the target for more than one year before completion.

4.8.4 Enforcement

If the restrictive covenants are reasonable, the buyer will be able to claim damages for breach of contract and may be granted an injunction. But what if only some of the restrictions are reasonable?

If each restraint is contained in a different clause or sub-clause and they are expressed to be separate and independent restrictions, even if the court considers one restraint to be too wide, the others will remain enforceable. Also, the court will not always strike out the whole of a clause or sub-clause. It is sometimes prepared to 'blue pencil' certain parts of a clause (ie to draw a line through certain words) leaving the remaining parts enforceable, but will not re-write a clause to make it reasonable. It is quite common to find a clause in the acquisition agreement where the parties agree that, if any of the restrictions are found to be invalid, but would be valid if, for example, the period or area of the restriction were reduced, such restriction shall apply with such amendments as are required to make it valid. Such a clause is unlikely to be effective.

4.8.5 The Competition Act 1998

The Competition Act 1998 (which came into force on 1 March 2000) introduces provisions into UK law which are very similar to the regime which applies under Articles 81 EC and 82 EC. Section 60 sets out the governing principle, directing that questions relating to competition are to be:

> 'So far as is possible ... dealt with in a manner which is consistent with the treatment of corresponding questions arising in Community law in relation to competition within the Community.'

There is therefore a general prohibition of anti-competitive agreements and a prohibition of abuse of a dominant position.

The Competition Act 1998 has repealed the Restrictive Trade Practices Act 1976 (RTPA 1976), the Resale Prices Act 1976 and the provisions of the Competition Act 1980 relating to anti-competitive practices.

If an agreement is found to breach s 2 or s 18 of the Competition Act 1998 (see below), the agreement or (subject to severance) the anti-competitive terms will be unenforceable.

The impact of the Competition Act 1998 on acquisition agreements is not clear. However, legal advisers are wise to consider its possible effect and to take action where appropriate. This may result in re-negotiation of the agreement, or notification to the Competition Commission either for guidance or a decision.

Anti-competitive agreements

The wording of s 2 of the 1998 Act follows closely that of Article 81 EC. There is a prohibition on agreements and other business arrangements between two or more undertakings which may affect trade in the UK and which have as their object or effect the prevention, restriction or distortion of competition within the UK. Section 2(2) provides a non-exhaustive list of agreements which infringe the prohibition, similar to that found in Article 81(2) EC.

As with Article 81 EC, there will be block and general exemptions. These will be drafted by the OFT. The exemptions will cover similar ground to that covered by the Article 81 EC exemptions, with block exemptions dealing with common agreements such as exclusive distribution agreements, franchise agreements and distribution agreements. In any event, parallel exemptions apply to agreements which are covered by a European Commission exemption under Article 81(3) EC or would be covered if the agreement had an effect on trade between Member States. There are also de minimis provisions similar to those contained in the Notice on Agreements of Minor Importance. Significantly, any agreement which is exempt under EC law will also be exempt under UK legislation.

Abuse of a dominant position

The wording of s 18 of the 1998 Act concerning abuse of a dominant position is similar to that of Article 82 EC. There is a prohibition on the activities of one or more undertakings which amount to the abuse of a dominant position within the UK or a substantial part of it.

In the context of an acquisition agreement, a buyer should be aware that, in particular, restrictive covenants could fall foul of UK competition law.

Consequences of infringement

Restrictions in breach of the new Act will be void. The DGFT is empowered to impose fines of up to 10% of an undertaking's turnover. The parties may be ordered to cease or modify the agreement. As with EC law, notification of an agreement will bring an exemption from fines until the DGFT makes a decision. The DGFT has substantial investigative powers, including the right to raid premises unannounced (the so-called 'dawn raid') provided a search warrant has been obtained from a High Court judge. There is the possibility of an appeal from the decisions of the DGFT to the Competition Commission.

4.8.6 EC v UK competition law

Restrictive covenants in acquisition agreements may breach Articles 81 and 82 EC (particularly Article 81 EC). Trade between Member States must be affected for either Article to apply. If Article 81 EC applies, the acquisition agreement may come within the scope of the Notice on Agreements of Minor Importance. These Articles are considered in the LPC Resource Book *Business Law and Practice* (Jordans).

If there is a community dimension, compliance with EC competition law will also satisfy UK competition law.

The Competition Act 1998 is considered in more detail in the LPC Resource Book *Commercial Law and Practice* (Jordans).

PART II

ACQUIRING A BUSINESS

Chapter 5

THE ACQUISITION AGREEMENT

5.1 INTRODUCTION

Chapter 5 contents
Introduction
**Structure of the
agreement**
Assets and liabilities
Consideration
Conditional contracts
Completion
Insurance
Employees and pensions
Warranties
**Some procedural
requirements for
corporate sellers and
buyers**

In this chapter the main elements of a typical agreement for the acquisition of a business are discussed. It is assumed for the most part that the business is being sold as a going concern as opposed to there being a mere asset sale. Most of the general principles discussed below apply whether it is a sole trader or partnership which is selling up or a company which is disposing of its business. In either case, the buyer may be an individual, a partnership or a company. It is also assumed that the acquisition is an arm's length transaction rather than the conversion of an unincorporated business (sole trade or partnership) into a company.

5.2 STRUCTURE OF THE AGREEMENT

The order of the agreement will usually be as follows:

(1) date;
(2) parties;
(3) operative provisions;
(4) schedules;
(5) execution by the parties.

5.2.1 Parties

The obligations of either the seller or the buyer may be guaranteed by a third party who joins in the agreement. It will be seen below that the seller is likely to have obligations which continue after completion and the buyer may insist on their performance being guaranteed, particularly where the seller is a company. The selling company may be a mere shell after disposing of its business and the buyer may look to the individual owners of the company (or the parent company if it is a subsidiary) to provide a guarantee. On the other hand, where any part of the purchase price of the business is to be left outstanding on completion (see **5.4.3**) the seller may demand that the buyer's obligation to pay the balance is guaranteed (eg by the owners of a corporate buyer – whether individuals or a parent company).

5.2.2 Operative provisions

As a matter of good drafting, the operative provisions should commence with a definitions and interpretations clause. This defines terms which are used throughout the agreement (including the schedules) and, consequently, avoids repetition and the need for cumbersome cross-references.

An aspect of interpretation clauses which sometimes proves controversial concerns references to statutory provisions. The buyer will usually want it to be expressly provided that references to statutory provisions are to be interpreted as including subsequent amendments to those provisions. This is dangerous for the seller, particularly in relation to his potential liability under the warranties because, by agreeing to such a clause, he would take the risk of those liabilities increasing as a result of legislation enacted after completion which has retrospective effect. For example, this could be a significant factor in the context of environmental protection legislation which it is foreseeable will become very much stricter in the future.

5.2.3 Schedules

Much of the bulk of acquisition agreements is usually attributable to schedules. Warranties given to the buyer by the seller, the transfer of pension rights and details of the freehold and leasehold properties included in the sale are just some of the matters which are invariably consigned to schedules. The advantage of drafting the agreement in this way is that the main body of the agreement is not broken up with long lists of detailed information, which makes the agreement as a whole easier to follow.

5.3 ASSETS AND LIABILITIES

The buyer will acquire only those assets and liabilities which the agreement specifies as being included in the sale; consequently, it is important that these are accurately defined. Although it is not strictly necessary, some agreements contain a list of assets which are excluded from the transfer. There is usually little point, for example, in including cash in hand or on deposit in the sale since this would simply involve the buyer paying an equivalent sum as part of the purchase price. Debtors and creditors are also commonly left with the seller. In addition, the seller may wish to retain certain assets which he will continue to have use for after completion. Some assets may, on the other hand, be surplus to the buyer's requirements.

5.3.1 Land and premises

General considerations

Freehold and leasehold premises which are to be transferred will normally be listed in a schedule. The buyer will obtain the benefit of the appropriate implied covenants for title if the seller sells with full or limited title guarantee. The buyer will assume risk on the premises as from exchange of the agreement and should take out insurance from this date or, in the case of leasehold property where the lease obliges the landlord to insure, have his interest noted on the landlord's policy.

Licence to assign

REQUESTING CONSENT

Where the terms of a lease require the consent of the landlord to assignment, there is often considerable delay in obtaining a formal licence to assign. The seller should, therefore, request consent from the landlord as early as possible in the hope that the licence will be available in good time for exchange of contracts. The buyer is also advised to give the seller details of referees so that these can be passed on to the landlord immediately (the provision and taking up of references is commonly a chief cause of delay).

The seller, as the existing tenant, does have some redress if the landlord acts unreasonably. Section 19 of the Landlord and Tenant Act 1927 provides that, where the lease contains a covenant not to assign without the landlord's consent (such qualified covenants against assignment are standard in commercial leases), the landlord cannot unreasonably withhold his consent. The landlord is also under a duty to give his decision within a reasonable time and to give reasons for a refusal (Landlord and Tenant Act 1988, which entitles tenants to damages if the landlord unreasonably refuses or delays the granting of a licence to assign).

For leases granted on or after 1 January 1996, landlords are able to exercise greater control by stipulating in the lease any conditions which they will require the tenant to fulfil in order to assign the lease.

GUARANTEES

The position regarding guarantees was discussed in Chapter 4 (see **4.7**). The landlord will not normally be willing to grant a licence to assign and to release guarantors of the seller's obligations under the lease unless he is provided with equivalent guarantees of the buyer's obligations (eg from the directors of a corporate buyer). Indeed, the lease may stipulate that the landlord is not obliged to consent to the assignment unless this is done.

CONDITIONAL CONTRACT

If the licence to assign is not ready by the time the parties are in a position to sign the acquisition agreement, they may decide to make the agreement conditional on the consent of the landlord to the assignment and incorporate a right for the parties to rescind if this is not obtained within a specified time-limit (conditional contracts are discussed further in **5.5**).

COSTS OF LICENCE

The terms of the licence to assign will oblige the tenant to pay the costs of the landlord's solicitor in dealing with the matter. It is rare for the seller of a business to pass this cost to the buyer (although it is common practice for the assignee to bear these costs on the assignment of a lease by itself).

5.3.2 Plant and machinery

Schedule

A schedule of the items of plant and machinery (including vehicles) which are part of the sale should be attached to the acquisition agreement. A buyer who wishes to purchase all of these assets of the business may seek to safeguard himself by providing that plant and machinery 'used in the business' are to be transferred, including those items listed in the schedule. Thus items omitted from the schedule by mistake (it may be difficult for the buyer to check the accuracy of the schedule) will, nevertheless, be included in the sale.

Risk

The buyer will assume risk on the plant and machinery when the acquisition agreement is exchanged (or, if it is a conditional contract, when the condition is satisfied) and should effect insurance cover from this date, even if completion is delayed.

Warranties

The buyer will often seek to include the following warranties as to the state of the items of plant and machinery listed in the schedule:

(1) they are in a proper state of repair and condition and in satisfactory working order;

(2) they are not dangerous, obsolete or in need of replacement;

(3) they have been properly and regularly maintained;

(4) they are adequate for (and not surplus to) the needs of the business.

The seller should think twice before accepting these warranties and consider trying to restrict any liability to major defects. Also, in relation to (4), as he will have no control over how the buyer carries on the business after completion, he may wish to add the words 'as carried on by the seller prior to the agreement'.

5.3.3 Intellectual property

Ideally, all trade marks, service marks, registered designs, copyrights and patents which are to be included in the transfer should be listed in a schedule or appendix to the agreement. The buyer may seek warranties in relation to the following matters:

(1) that the seller is the beneficial owner or registered proprietor of the intellectual property rights (as defined in the interpretation clause);

(2) that to the best of the seller's knowledge and belief those rights are valid and enforceable;

(3) that the seller has not granted any person a right to do anything which would otherwise be an infringement of those rights;

(4) that no licences for the use of intellectual property have been granted to the seller or are required to run the business;

(5) that the operation of the business does not infringe the intellectual property rights of any other person.

The buyer may also insist on a warranty that the seller has not disclosed trade secrets, know-how or confidential information (eg customer price lists) except in the normal course of business.

5.3.4 Leasing, hire-purchase and other finance contracts

Equipment employed by the seller in the business which is subject to hire-purchase, contract hire or leasing arrangements does not belong to the seller and cannot, therefore, be included in the transfer without the consent of the true owner. The owner may be prepared to consent to the assignment or novation of the agreement to the buyer or may prefer to enter into a fresh agreement with him.

Since these arrangements may not be in place on completion, the acquisition contract should make it clear that, as between the parties, the seller is responsible for discharging the obligations under the agreements until completion, after which liability shifts to the buyer.

5.3.5 Stock and work in progress

Stock will usually be defined as including raw materials, work in progress and finished goods. Since it is impossible to determine the level of completion stock in advance, it is unusual for the parties to agree a value for the stock prior to completion. They will often provide in the agreement for the stock to be valued at or shortly after completion and for the price of the stock to be left outstanding until they have agreed the valuation.

Stock and work in progress will often be a significant element in the overall consideration for the business and the agreement should, therefore, specify who is to carry out the valuation, the basis on which the stock is to be valued, and the procedure to be followed if the parties dispute the valuation.

The parties may agree to carry out a joint stock-take, with the actual valuation to be prepared by the seller or may provide for specified professional valuers to undertake the valuation.

The agreement may provide for the stock to be valued on the same basis as in the audited accounts (eg this will often be on the basis of the lower of cost or net realisable value); on some other general basis, such as market value; or in accordance with a detailed formula which, for example, takes account of slow-moving or obsolete stock.

Where the seller prepares the valuation, provision will usually be made for any dispute to be referred to an independent expert. The buyer may be obliged to pay a percentage of the valuation (eg 50%) immediately, with any balance payable within a specified time-limit of its final determination – this should avoid the procedure being employed by the buyer simply as a method of delaying payment.

The buyer may wish to set a limit on the amount of stock he is obliged to purchase on completion and, in order to guard against the seller reducing stock to a level which will make it difficult for the buyer to meet orders, he may also stipulate a minimum amount of stock. The buyer may also seek warranties that the stocks are of satisfactory quality and that none of the items are obsolete or unmarketable.

5.3.6 Contracts

Passing the benefit and burden

The buyer will want to ensure that he receives the benefit of all contracts entered into between the seller and third parties which are important to the business, such as agency or distribution agreements, contracts with suppliers or customers, licensing agreements, etc. One way to achieve this is to assign the benefit of contract and, if legal assignment is required, notice must be given to the other contracting party under s 136 of the Law of Property Act 1925. The buyer should, however, check whether or not the terms of the contract prohibit assignment or require the consent of the other party. With this method, only the benefit will be transferred and the seller will still be liable to the third party to fulfill any outstanding obligations, for example, in an exclusive distribution agreement, if the seller is the distributor, the benefit under the agreement is the receipt of goods for resale in a given territory; the burden is payment for the goods.

To get around this, the existing contract may be novated. This involves the other party to the contract agreeing to release the seller from the contract and allowing the buyer to take over the benefit and burden of the contract. Alternatively, the other contracting party may agree to enter into a fresh agreement with the buyer. This gives the buyer scope to negotiate new terms and conditions if the existing ones are commercially unacceptable in their present form.

As the co-operation of the other party to a contract is usually required, it is a time-consuming process to put all the necessary arrangements in place and this may not coincide with the timetable agreed between the buyer and seller for the transfer of the business.

What if consents etc are delayed?

ROUTINE CONTRACTS

With some agreements (eg small or routine contracts) the parties will often be happy to proceed to completion without having obtained the required consents. They may agree between themselves that the buyer will take over the contracts on completion and that each will use his best endeavours to obtain the consents of third parties to assign or novate existing contracts or to enter into new contracts. Remember, the seller will remain liable on such contracts unless and until specifically released by the third parties. The buyer will, therefore, normally undertake to perform the contracts on behalf of the seller and to indemnify the seller against any liability arising under the contracts.

FUNDAMENTAL CONTRACTS

In relation to contracts which the buyer considers fundamental to the business, ideally, the buyer should defer entering into the acquisition agreement until all necessary consents have been obtained. Alternatively, the parties may agree to the agreement being made conditional on the assignment or novation of specified contracts. The buyer should, in these circumstances, seek an undertaking from the seller not to vary the terms of the contracts during the period between exchange and completion without his consent.

5.3.7 Debtors and creditors

Sums owed to the seller by third parties (debtors) are an asset of the business; sums owed by the seller to third parties (creditors) are a liability of the business. There are a number of ways that trade debtors and creditors can be dealt with in the agreement.

Transfer to buyer

The debtors and creditors may be transferred to the buyer. In this case, full details should be included in a schedule or an appendix to the acquisition agreement. In order for the assignment of debts to be a legal assignment (as opposed to an equitable one), s 136 of the Law of Property Act 1925 requires, inter alia, written notice of the assignment to be given to each debtor. The seller will, however, remain liable after completion to his creditors unless they agree to release him. Accordingly, where the parties have agreed to transfer the creditors, he should seek an indemnity from the buyer against such liability. If a buyer agrees to buy both the debtors and creditors, he will pay the agreed market value of the business assets, less the value of the creditors. For example, if the agreed value of the assets is £500,000, and the creditors amount to £150,000, the buyer will pay £350,000 in total for the business.

Currently, a disadvantage to the buyer of acquiring the debtors and creditors is that he is liable for stamp duty on both the book debts and on the amount of the liability to creditors.

With reference to the example above, this simply means that stamp duty will be charged on the full value of the assets (£500,000 if all the assets are dutiable), not on the actual sum paid. However, this position is shortly to be remedied. Plans to revise the stamp duty regime, which should come fully into effect in late 2003, include an exemption from duty for the transfer of debts.

There are also several other drawbacks to transferring debtors and creditors to the buyer. Apart from the complication of defining accurately the debts and liabilities involved and of giving notice to all debtors, there is the difficulty of valuing the book debts. If these are transferred at their face value the buyer will not only suffer a cash flow disadvantage but will also bear the risk of some of the debts proving irrecoverable. The amount of any discount on book value to reflect these uncertainties is likely to be the subject of much negotiation between the parties. Alternatively, the seller may be prepared to warrant that the debts are fully recoverable. The buyer should, however, be wary of any 'de minimis' limit which applies to the warranties generally (see **4.4.1**).

Retention by seller

It is common for debtors and creditors to remain with the seller, although this can also give rise to a number of difficulties. The buyer will, for example, be keen to preserve the goodwill of the business by maintaining good relations with suppliers and creditors of the business and will, therefore, wish to ensure that the seller pays off his creditors promptly and is not too exuberant in chasing his debtors. The buyer may, therefore, insist on a retention from the purchase price which is only to be released once the creditors have been paid. He should also consider extracting an undertaking from the seller not to issue proceedings to recover debts for a specified period after completion and to give the buyer the option to buy the debts from the seller at the end of this period (at least in relation to those debtors who continue to be customers of the business after the change in ownership).

A difficulty of this arrangement from the seller's point of view is that he may no longer have the means to collect the debts after completion, particularly where those employees responsible for debt collection have been transferred to the buyer. A solution to this problem, which often suits both parties, is for the buyer to agree to collect the debts as agent for the seller. The buyer will often be happy to assume this responsibility (usually on payment of a collection fee) as there will be less danger of the goodwill of the business being damaged if the process of collection of debts is undertaken by the buyer. The buyer will usually be required to use his best endeavours to collect the debts but without being obliged to commence legal proceedings. As an incentive to the buyer, the collection fee may be based on a percentage of debts successfully recovered.

A complication which arises where debtors continue to deal with the business after its change in ownership is the application of sums received by the buyer after completion. For example, should such sums received reduce the debtor's original liability to the seller, or any liability of the debtor to the buyer incurred since completion? The acquisition agreement should specify the order in which the buyer should apply sums which he receives in these circumstances.

Who takes responsibility for on-going service and repair obligations?

Depending on the type of business, the seller may have entered into commitments to customers to provide an after-sales service in relation to products or services supplied prior to completion. It is in the interests of the buyer that these obligations are met in full since a failure to do so may have a detrimental effect on goodwill and may reflect badly on the buyer. However, once he has disposed of the business, the seller is unlikely to be in a position to carry out repairs or provide an after-sales service. A solution to this problem is for the buyer to agree to perform the seller's obligations and to be reimbursed the cost of doing so by the seller (the buyer may also be able to negotiate a mark-up on the direct costs which he incurs).

Apportionment of outgoings and payments

The seller will have incurred various liabilities to, for example, utility companies for the use of gas, electricity, telephones, etc which have not been billed at the date of completion. Similarly, the seller may have made payments in advance which relate to periods after completion, for example, rental payments or payments due under continuing contracts. Whichever method the parties choose to deal with the creditors and debtors, it will be necessary to apportion the outgoings and payments to the date of completion (or such other date agreed upon by the parties). The seller will usually be responsible for making the apportionments and providing full details with supporting documentation. As with the valuation of stock, the agreement may incorporate a system for resolving disputes between the parties. In any event, it is normally impractical for the apportionments to be made and agreed by completion and, consequently, provision is usually made for the buyer to draw up a completion statement after completion and for adjustments to be made to the consideration when the parties have agreed the statement.

5.3.8 Goodwill, name and restrictions on the seller

Goodwill

Goodwill is an intangible asset of the business which is as difficult to define as it is to value. Where a business is sold as a going concern, a value is usually placed on the good name and reputation of the business and the likelihood that customers and suppliers will continue to deal with it in the future. In other words, the value of goodwill reflects the fact that the business is 'up and running', has traded successfully in the past and should continue to do so in the future.

A crude method of valuing goodwill is to apply a multiplier (usually between one and three) to the net profits of the business. In the case of a partnership, the net profit figure before any salaries or interest on capital payable to partners are deducted should be used for the calculation as these items are merely allocations of the profit. However, the amount attributable to goodwill is extremely variable and, to a large extent, depends on buyer's assessment of the potential of the business; the buyer may, for example, be prepared to pay a sum for the business which is well above its net asset value because he feels that it will fit in well with his existing businesses. Also, goodwill tends to be more of a factor in 'employee orientated' businesses, ie those that rely on the flair and imagination of the employees, than in 'asset orientated' businesses, such as property investment businesses, for example. The state of the market is one of the most influential factors in determining how much the buyer is prepared to pay for goodwill. In the sellers' market of the late 1980s, astronomical sums over and above net asset values were paid by buyers caught up in the euphoria caused by the spate of commercial activity. In times of recession, however, buyers are more inclined to study the balance sheet values closely and to base their valuation of the business on the tangible benefits which they are acquiring.

The buyer may try to negotiate the inclusion of a warranty that the seller is not aware of any matter arising since the date of the latest accounts which might adversely affect the trading prospects of the business and that the seller has not done anything (or omitted to do anything) which might adversely affect goodwill.

Name

The goodwill to be acquired by the buyer will usually be defined to include the exclusive right of the buyer (or any assignee) to represent himself as carrying on the business in succession to the seller and to use the name of the business and all trade names associated with it. The seller will normally be required to undertake that he will not use the name or any other name intended or likely to be confused with it, or to hold himself out as being connected with the business, at any time after completion. The seller may even agree to covenant that he will endeavour to ensure that the buyer obtains full benefit of the goodwill and that customers, etc deal with the buyer instead of the seller.

On the acquisition of the whole of its business from a company, the agreement should provide that the seller changes its registered name to one that is acceptable to the buyer and does not suggest any connection with the business. As part of the completion arrangements, the buyer may require the seller to hand over the special resolution changing the name (and appropriate fee) and agree with the seller to file this at the Companies Registry.

Restrictive covenants

The buyer will seek to protect the goodwill of the business by restricting the activities of the seller after completion, thereby preventing him from damaging goodwill. The seller will be prevented from competing with the business, soliciting customers, suppliers and employees of the business and from disclosing confidential information. The nature, extent and validity of such restrictions on the seller are dealt with in **4.8**.

5.4 CONSIDERATION

5.4.1 Amount

The acquisition agreement will usually provide for the total purchase price for all the assets, with the exception of stock (and, perhaps, debtors), to be paid on completion. The value of stock may not be ascertained until after completion (see **5.3.5**). Also, a completion statement may have to be drawn up after completion in relation to creditors and debtors (see **5.3.7**).

The amount of the consideration which is attributable to each separate asset must be specified in the agreement (the apportionment is often contained in a schedule). The parties have some flexibility in making this apportionment and are usually influenced heavily by taxation and stamp duty implications (see Chapter 7).

5.4.2 Form

In an arm's length transaction, the price will normally be payable in cash. Where the buyer is a company, all or part of the consideration may, however, be satisfied by the company issuing shares or debentures to the seller (this form of consideration is dealt with further in the context of share acquisitions, see **8.4.1**).

5.4.3 Deferred payment

It has been seen that payment for stock may be delayed until after completion. In certain circumstances, the seller may be prepared to allow other sums to remain outstanding on completion. Where, for example, it is agreed that the sellers (or some of them) will continue to manage the business after completion, as a means of providing them with an incentive to perform effectively, part of the purchase price may be determined by future profits of the business. Such an arrangement is called an 'earn-out' and this and other schemes involving deferred consideration are considered in more detail in the context of share acquisitions, where they are more widely used (see **8.4.2**).

Where part of the purchase price does remain outstanding on completion, the seller may seek security for the outstanding sums in one of the following ways:

(1) by taking a charge over some or all of the assets transferred to the buyer;
(2) by requiring a guarantor of the buyer's obligation to pay the balance of the price, for example individual shareholders, directors or the parent company of a corporate buyer;
(3) by providing in the agreement that title to specified assets is to remain in the seller until the purchase price is paid in full;
(4) by obliging the buyer to place a specified sum in a joint deposit account on completion and defining the circumstances in which this (and accrued interest) can be released to the parties (this will not be appropriate if the seller is simply allowing the buyer time to finance the acquisition).

5.5 CONDITIONAL CONTRACTS

5.5.1 Causes of delay

Unlike a typical conveyancing transaction, completion of a business acquisition is normally simultaneous with exchange of contracts. The parties usually try to avoid any gap between exchange and completion and the consequent problems connected with the running of the business during this period; however, it is not always possible to achieve this.

Delay often arises in obtaining the consent of the landlord to the assignment of leasehold premises and in entering into satisfactory arrangements with third parties in relation to fundamental contracts (ie the novation or assignment of existing agreements or negotiation of fresh agreements). Delay may also be caused, for example, in effecting the removal of charges over assets being transferred, obtaining consent of the holder of a charge for an asset to be transferred subject to the charge, or receiving confirmation from the holder of a floating charge that it has not crystallised (a letter of non-crystallisation).

5.5.2 Conditions precedent

As an alternative to delaying exchange until all these matters have been resolved and thus leaving open the possibility that either party may simply walk away from the deal for any reason, the parties may agree to enter into a contract which is conditional on, for example, specified consents being obtained. This commits both parties to the acquisition except in the event of the condition not being satisfied. It is usual to include the following provisions in relation to conditional contracts:

(1) an obligation on one party to take all reasonable steps to try to procure the satisfaction of the condition as early as possible (or, where appropriate, an undertaking by both parties to co-operate in taking such steps);

(2) a long-stop date by which the conditions have to be satisfied (or, possibly, waived by the party for whose benefit they were included) and, in default, provision for the agreement to terminate automatically without any liability attaching to either party;

(3) if the conditions are satisfied prior to the long-stop date, provision for completion to take place within a specified period of this happening.

5.5.3 Seller's undertakings pending completion

Management of the business

In the period between exchange and completion the buyer will wish to ensure that the seller carries on the business in the normal way and does not do anything to prejudice the position and prospects of the business. The buyer may be able to insist on being given some managerial control during this period. For example, the seller may agree not to enter into contracts or other commitments involving expenditure exceeding a specified amount or borrow over a certain limit without first obtaining the written consent of the buyer. Otherwise, the buyer may have to be satisfied with undertakings by the seller not to enter into any commitments unless they are routine and in the ordinary course of business.

Whatever provisions are included in the agreement, it is never entirely satisfactory to have a gap between exchange and completion as there is always a risk of lack of business direction during this period which may have a lasting effect on the goodwill of the business.

Right to withdraw

The buyer usually seeks to negotiate a contractual right to withdraw from the agreement in the event of any warranty being incorrect or becoming incorrect prior to completion (the seller should try to restrict this right to breaches of material warranties or specified warranties only): see **4.3.1**. The seller may also be obliged to notify the buyer if he becomes aware of anything which makes the warranties inaccurate.

5.6 COMPLETION

5.6.1 Transferring title

The following formalities are required to transfer the legal interest in the assets of the business to the buyer:

(1) conveyances, transfers or assignments of land and premises;

(2) assignments of goodwill, certain intellectual property rights (including copyrights, patents and trade marks) and the benefit of contracts.

Stock and movable assets, such as loose plant and machinery, are transferable by delivery; it is sufficient if the acquisition agreement requires delivery to be given on completion.

5.6.2 Documents to be handed over on completion

The seller will usually be required to hand over or make available to the buyer on completion the following:

(1) documents transferring title to the assets. Drafts should have been agreed by the parties prior to completion and the agreed form may be annexed to the acquisition agreement (see **5.6.1**);

(2) deeds and documents of title to the assets, including freehold and leasehold properties (see **5.6.1**);

(3) financial records and books of account, customer lists, computer programs, designs, drawings, plans, sales and promotional materials, national insurance, PAYE and VAT records, employee records, and other documents required by the buyer to run the business. The seller is advised to reserve the right for a certain period after completion to inspect and take copies of the records, etc which are handed to the buyer in case these are needed in relation to the seller's affairs (eg by the tax authorities);

(4) duly executed releases of charges over the assets and confirmation of non-crystallisation of floating charges;

(5) originals, counterparts or certified copies as appropriate of licences to assign leasehold property, novation agreements and consents from third parties to assignment of contracts, etc;

(6) certified copy of special resolution of selling company resolving to change its name (see **5.3.8**);

(7) where the seller is a company, a board resolution authorising a representative to sign the documentation.

The buyer will be required to pay the amount of the purchase price due on completion, usually by banker's draft or telegraphic transfer to the seller's bank account. A corporate buyer will also be required to produce a board resolution authorising a representative to sign the transaction documentation.

5.7 INSURANCE

Risk in the assets which are being sold passes to the buyer, subject to contrary agreement, on exchange of contracts or, if the contract is conditional, on the fulfilment of the condition. The buyer should arrange for his own insurance to be in place as soon as the risk passes (see also **5.3.2**).

5.8 EMPLOYEES AND PENSIONS

These topics are dealt with in Chapter 6.

5.9 WARRANTIES

5.9.1 Scope

The nature and purpose of warranties, the liability of the warrantor and methods available to him of limiting his exposure (eg by disclosures and specific limitations in the agreement) were considered in Chapter 4. The scope of warranties on a business acquisition does not need to be as extensive as on a share acquisition. As there is less risk of unexpected liabilities arising than on a share purchase, the buyer is mainly concerned with the specific assets and liabilities which he has agreed to acquire. Taxation liabilities, for example, remain with the seller and, consequently, there is little need for extensive tax warranties and indemnities; these will normally be limited to warranties designed to elicit information, such as the proper operation of the PAYE scheme. An exception to the general principle that liabilities do not transfer automatically to the buyer of a business is in relation to employees (see Chapter 6).

The buyer of a business as a going concern will usually assume responsibility for the performance of outstanding contracts, etc. Also, in acquiring the goodwill of the business, the buyer has a legitimate interest in the way that the seller has conducted the business prior to completion. In practice, therefore, warranties on a business sale are often extensive and, depending on the bargaining power of the parties, may in fact range beyond the specific assets and liabilities transferred.

5.9.2 Some areas covered by warranties

Assets

OWNERSHIP

The buyer will seek warranties that the seller owns the assets absolutely; that they are not subject to any charge, encumbrance, lien, option or retention of title provision; and that the seller has not agreed to dispose of them or grant security or any other encumbrance in respect of them.

CONDITION AND ADEQUACY

It will usually be a matter of much negotiation between the parties as to whether the seller should give warranties as to the condition of, for example, fixed assets and stock and as to the adequacy of the assets for the requirements of the business (see **5.3.2**).

Trading and conduct of the business

The buyer will seek assurances (or disclosures) in relation to, inter alia, the following matters:

(1) that the business has been carried on in the ordinary course since the date of the last accounts, and that its turnover, financial or trading position has not deteriorated;

(2) that the seller has obtained all licences and consents required to carry on the business properly and is not in breach of their terms;

(3) that the seller is not aware of any suppliers or customers who will cease to deal with the business (or substantially alter their trading relationship with it) after completion;

(4) that the seller has not been a party to any agreement, practice or arrangement relating to the business which contravenes, for example, the Trade Descriptions Acts 1968 and 1972, the Fair Trading Act 1973, the Consumer Credit Act 1974 or the European Community Treaty 1957;

(5) that the seller is not a party to any litigation proceedings in relation to the business and no such proceedings are pending, threatened or, to the seller's knowledge, likely to arise.

Accounts

The buyer may have used the accounts as a basis for agreeing a valuation of the business, in which case, he will normally seek a warranty that the latest accounts (including, possibly, management accounts) give a true and fair view of the financial position of the business and are not affected by extraordinary or non-recurring items. The buyer will also wish to ensure that the financial books and records which the seller is obliged to deliver to him on completion are complete and accurate in all material respects.

Contracts

The buyer may require assurances (or disclosures) in relation to the contracts which he is taking over as follows:

(1) that none of the contracts is of an unusual or onerous nature or was entered into otherwise than in the ordinary course of business;

(2) that the seller is not in breach of any of the terms of the contracts and has not waived any rights under the contracts;

(3) that no event has occurred which entitles the other party to the contract to terminate or rescind the contract;

(4) that the seller has not sold or manufactured products which, in any material respect, are defective or do not comply with warranties or representations made by the seller.

Intellectual property rights

Examples of warranties which the buyer may wish to include in relation to intellectual property rights are given at **5.3.3**.

Properties and environmental matters

The pre-contract investigations and enquiries which the buyer is advised to carry out in relation to properties and environmental matters and the protections that he may seek in the form of warranties were considered in Chapter 3.

Employees and pensions

Warranties covering employees and pensions are considered in Chapter 6.

5.9.3 Corporate seller

Where the seller of the business is a company, the buyer may be unwise to rely on warranties given by the company itself, unless the company is simply disposing of one of several businesses and is to remain a substantial concern after the disposal (see **5.2.1**). If the company is divesting itself of its main business and is likely to be wound up after completion the buyer should require its individual owners (or, if it is a subsidiary, its parent company) to join in as warrantors or as guarantors.

5.9.4 Management buy-outs

A management buy-out is a transaction by which the target is acquired by some or all of its management, usually through the vehicle of a new company established for this purpose. Management buy-outs may proceed as share or business acquisitions and may involve a hive-down arrangement (see **1.3.8**). In the context of warranties, the seller is likely to resist extensive warranties being included in the acquisition agreement on the basis that the managers who are buying the target are likely to have more knowledge about the business than the seller. On the other hand, warranties are designed to allocate risk between seller and buyer as well as to elicit information about the business. The seller will, of course, be receiving full consideration whether or not the buyers are part of the management team and should, arguably, be prepared to give full warranties.

5.9.5 Insolvent seller

If the corporate seller of the business is in liquidation, receivership or administration or an individual seller has been made bankrupt, the buyer will invariably not receive the benefit of any significant warranties. The insolvency practitioner will argue that he is unable to wind up the seller's affairs while there is a continuing potential liability in relation to warranties, etc. He will usually agree only to a warranty that he has not personally encumbered the assets.

5.10 SOME PROCEDURAL REQUIREMENTS FOR CORPORATE SELLERS AND BUYERS

5.10.1 Compliance with the constitution

Where the seller of the business is a company, the objects clause in the company's memorandum must permit the sale of the business. The seller's solicitor should ensure that requirements as to notice, quorum and conduct of the meetings contained in the company's articles are complied with. The disposal of the business may just require a decision of the directors (under their general management powers in Table A, Art 70) or the articles may require the directors to obtain the prior consent of the members.

Similarly, the solicitor acting for a company which is acquiring a business should ensure that the provisions of its articles and memorandum are observed.

5.10.2 Company law requirements

Interests of employees

Not only do the directors of a company have a fiduciary duty to act in the interests of the company as a whole (ie the members as a body) but they are also obliged by s 309 of the CA 1985 to have regard to the interests of the company's employees. This duty is, therefore, relevant on business transfers, which invariably have a significant practical impact on the employees. However, the effectiveness of this provision is limited because the duty is owed to the company and not to the employees, who are unable to take action to enforce it.

Directors' interests in the acquisition agreement

A director of a company which is buying or selling a business may have a personal interest in the transaction over and above that of managing the buying company. The business which is acquired by a company may, for example, be owned by one of its directors (or a director may be a partner in the business). In a management buy-out (see **5.9.4**), those directors of the selling company who are acquiring the business clearly have a personal interest in the acquisition. The following provisions of the CA 1985 must be considered in these circumstances:

(1) Section 317 requires a director who is directly or indirectly interested in a contract or proposed contract with the company to declare the nature of his interest at the first board meeting at which the proposed transaction is discussed (the company's articles may also contain provisions relating to directors' rights to count in the quorum and vote and to retain benefits, eg Table A, Arts 94 and 95).

(2) Section 320 applies to an arrangement whereby a director of a company (or its holding company) or a person connected with such a director acquires a non-cash asset from the company or disposes of such an asset to the company and the asset is of the 'requisite value', ie worth more than £100,000 or 10% of the company's net assets (subject to a minimum of £2,000). An arrangement which comes within s 320 must first be approved by an ordinary resolution of the members in general meeting and, if the director is a director of its holding company, by an ordinary resolution of the holding company. No approval is required, however, by any company which is a wholly owned subsidiary (see Chapter 12 for this definition). Breach of the section renders the arrangement or any transaction entered into in pursuance of it voidable at the instance of the company except in specified circumstances (s 322).

Example

Tony and John, two directors of Basilica Ltd, have agreed to buy the retail part of Basilica's business for £500,000. They will buy the business through Newco Ltd, a ready-made company. They are the first directors of Newco and own one share each. They are not shareholders of Basilica Ltd.

The board of Basilica will have to call an EGM to seek authorisation for the sale by way of ordinary resolution from its shareholders. Why? The transaction is a substantial property transaction: Basilica is selling a non-cash asset of requisite value (over £100,000) to a person connected with its directors. CA 1985, s 346 defines a 'person connected' with a director as including a body corporate with whom he is associated if the director owns at least 20% of the shares in the company (here, Newco).

On the other hand, Newco need not pass an ordinary resolution authorising the purchase because although it is purchasing a non-cash asset from Basilica, Basilica is not connected to Tony and John.

The above provisions are dealt with in the LPC Resource Book *Business Law and Practice* (Jordans).

Payments to directors in connection with the transfer

Section 313 of the CA 1985 provides that if, in connection with the transfer of the whole or any part of the undertaking or property of a company, any payment is made to a director of the company by way of compensation for loss of office, or as consideration for or in connection with his retirement from office, particulars of the proposed payment (including the amount) must be disclosed to the members of the company and approved by ordinary resolution of the members. A director receiving payment in breach of this requirement is liable to repay it and the directors responsible for it being made are also liable. The section does not apply to bona fide payments by way of damages for breach of contract or by way of pension in respect of past services (s 316(3)).

Directors' service contracts

Where a company acquires an unincorporated business as a going concern it may wish to take advantage of the managerial expertise of some or all of the former owners of the business by appointing them as directors of the company. Similarly, if the business is purchased from a company, the deal agreed between the parties may involve the acquiring company appointing employees of the business (including, perhaps, directors of the selling company) to its board of directors.

If new directors are appointed and given service contracts for more than 5 years (although this is unusual), consent of the members by ordinary resolution is required by s 319 of the CA 1985. If consent is not obtained, the service contract is terminable by the company at any time on reasonable notice. A written memorandum of a proposed contract requiring consent must be made available at the registered office of the company for at least 15 days prior to the meeting and at the meeting itself (or if the written resolution procedure for private companies is used, the written memorandum must be supplied to each member at or before the time at which the resolution is supplied to him for signature) (CA 1985, s 381A and Sch 15A).

Chapter 6

EMPLOYEES AND PENSIONS ON A BUSINESS ACQUISITION

6.1 INTRODUCTION

The parties must consider the impact of the acquisition on the employees of the target business. How does the transfer affect their contracts of employment? Can the buyer choose not to take on employees who are surplus to his requirements? What are the implications if the buyer wishes to integrate the terms and conditions of the target's employees with those of his existing work-force? What claims can employees bring against the seller or buyer if they are dismissed before or after the transfer? Can the employees object to working for the buyer? The buyer will often have a clear idea of which employees he wishes to retain and how he intends to integrate them with his current work-force. However, the employment consequences of the transfer of a business do not always coincide with the expectations of the parties; this is an area which may impact significantly on the value of the business and, consequently, the purchase price.

This chapter considers the rights of employees on the termination of their employment (in outline); the effect of the transfer of the target business on their contracts of employment; liabilities of the seller and buyer in relation to the acquisition; and specific provisions which the parties may include in the acquisition agreement. There is also a brief discussion of pension aspects of business acquisitions.

6.2 WHAT ARE AN EMPLOYEE'S RIGHTS ON THE TERMINATION OF HIS EMPLOYMENT?

The main obligations which an employer owes to his employees were dealt with in the LPC Resource Book *Business Law and Practice* (Jordans), including the duty imposed by s 1 of the Employment Rights Act 1996 (ERA 1996) to provide a written statement of the terms of employment within 2 months of the commencement of employment. Some employees may, of course, have a formal contract of service which includes, inter alia, these terms. It is important to appreciate that, whatever the contractual position, there is a significant element of statutory interference in the relationship between employer and employee. There follows a brief description of the rights of employees, both contractual and statutory, on the termination of their employment which is intended to give only outline coverage of the topic.

6.2.1 The contractual claim: wrongful dismissal

The claim

An employee whose employment is terminated in breach of contract is entitled to claim damages for wrongful dismissal. This will usually occur where the employer

Chapter 6 contents
Introduction
What are an employee's rights on the termination of his employment?
The Transfer of Undertakings (Protection of Employment) Regulations 1981 (implementing the Acquired Rights Directive)
Effect of a relevant transfer – Regulation 5
What the transferee acquires
Dismissal of an employee resulting from a relevant transfer – Regulation 8
Transfer-connected dismissals and post-transfer variations to terms and conditions
Due diligence and protection in the acquisition agreement
Pensions
Flowchart

dismisses the employee before the end of a fixed-term contract or, in the case of an indefinite term contract, without giving the employee the correct period of notice. If there is no contractual notice period, the employee is entitled to receive 'reasonable' notice; what is reasonable depends on factors such as the age, length of service and position of the employee. The contractual or reasonable notice period cannot be less than the statutory minimum laid down by s 86 of the ERA 1996 which requires one week's notice to be given to an employee employed for at least one month but less than 2 years, and one week's notice for each complete year worked to be given to an employee employed for 2 years and over (subject to a maximum of 12 weeks). The employer may, however, be justified in dismissing without notice where the employee has been involved in gross misconduct, ie a serious breach of the express or implied terms of the contract, in which event the employer will not be liable for wrongful dismissal.

A successful claim will also arise if the employee is prompted to leave as a result of a repudiatory breach of contract by the employer, ie where the employer commits a serious breach of the express or implied terms of the contract. For example, if the employer makes a unilateral change to an important term or condition of employment, such as the pay structure, an employee who is affected to his detriment is entitled to accept the employer's repudiatory breach as discharging the contract and walk out without notice (this is called 'constructive dismissal').

The remedy

All claims for breach of contract can be brought before the civil courts. Employment tribunals also have jurisdiction to deal with most breach of contract claims by employees of up to £25,000 in aggregate value, provided that the claim is brought within 3 months of dismissal. The employee is entitled to damages calculated on the normal contractual basis. The starting point is net salary (ie after deduction of tax and national insurance) for the notice period or, in the case of a fixed-term contract, for the remainder of the term. The award will be increased to compensate for loss of fringe benefits, commission and pension rights. The court or tribunal may, however, reduce the award to take account of accelerated receipt, ie to reflect the fact that the employee effectively receives his salary early, in the form of a lump sum which he will be able to invest (this is only likely to be a significant factor in the case of a long fixed-term contract). The damages will also be reduced by any salary or benefits which the employee receives from alternative employment. If the employee remains unemployed, the court or tribunal may, nevertheless, reduce the award if it feels that he has failed to mitigate his loss by, for example, not making a genuine attempt to secure another position. In order to compensate for the employee's actual loss, the award is increased to take account of any tax which he will suffer on the damages: the first £30,000 is tax free (ss 148 and 188 of the ICTA 1988) but any amount in excess of £30,000 is taxable as earned income.

6.2.2 The statutory claims

Dismissed employees may also have claims before an employment tribunal for unfair dismissal and redundancy under provisions contained in the ERA 1996. In order to bring a claim, however, an employee must be eligible and must have been dismissed within the statutory definition. He must also bring the claim within short time-limits: 3 and 6 months from dismissal for unfair dismissal and redundancy respectively.

Matters common to redundancy and unfair dismissal

ELIGIBILITY

To be eligible, an employee must be under such age as is the normal retiring age in that undertaking for employees of both sexes (provided that, in the case of redundancy only, that age is lower than 65) or, if there is no normal retiring age, 65; have, in the case of unfair dismissal, one year's continuous employment, and, in the case of redundancy, 2 years of continuous employment and, with both types of claim, not ordinarily work outside Great Britain.

'DISMISSAL'

In addition to the more obvious forms of dismissal, employees who have been constructively dismissed (see **6.2.1**) or who have fixed-term contracts which have expired without being renewed are treated as 'dismissed' for the purposes of the statutory claims.

Redundancy

DEFINITION

An eligible employee who is dismissed by reason of redundancy is entitled to a redundancy payment. An employee is taken to be dismissed by reason of redundancy if:

'the dismissal is attributable wholly or mainly to –

(a) the fact that his employer has ceased, or intends to cease, to carry on the business for the purposes of which the employee was employed by him, or has ceased, or intends to cease, to carry on that business in the place where the employee was so employed; or

(b) the fact that the requirements of that business for employees to carry out work of a particular kind, or for employees to carry out work of a particular kind where he was so employed, have ceased or diminished or are expected to cease or diminish' (ERA 1996, s 139).

The two redundancy situations can be summarised as follows:

(1) where the employer closes down either the business or the employee's place of work;

(2) where the employer cuts down the number of employees employed in the business or at the employee's place of work.

It is important, therefore, to determine the place of work of the employee. This may be defined in the contract of service, and it is one of the terms required by s 1 of the ERA 1996 to be included in the written statement of terms. Also, if the employee is asked to move to another place of work because, for example, his place of work is closing down, he will be unable to claim redundancy if his contract contains an express or implied 'mobility clause', ie a provision enabling the employer to move the employee. If he refuses to move and leaves, he will not be able to establish a constructive dismissal as there is no breach of contract by the employer. If the employer dismisses him, the dismissal will not be by reason of redundancy; it will be attributable to the employee's failure to obey a lawful order.

The ceasing of or reduction in the requirements for employees to carry out work of a particular kind may arise in a number of ways. It may, for example, be a result of initial overmanning, the introduction of new technology, a fall off in orders, or a reorganisation of the business producing more efficient working practices.

OFFER TO RENEW OR RE-ENGAGE

The employer can in some circumstances avoid liability for redundancy if he or an associated employer makes a suitable offer to renew the employee's contract or to re-engage him under a new contract and the employee unreasonably refuses the offer (s 138). Two employers are treated as associated if one is a company of which the other has control or if both are companies of which a third party has control. In determining whether an offer to re-engage is suitable, the tribunal will assess whether the new post is substantially the equivalent of the old. The employee's personal circumstances are relevant in determining whether any refusal is reasonable. Subject to certain conditions, an employee is usually allowed a trial period of 4 weeks in order to decide whether to accept an offer to re-engage.

THE AMOUNT OF THE AWARD

The calculation of the redundancy payment is based on the employee's age, week's pay and length of service (subject to a maximum).

DUTY TO CONSULT TRADE UNIONS

Regulations on the duty to consult trade unions are contained in the Collective Redundancies and Transfer of Undertakings (Protection of Employment) (Amendment) Regulations 1999, SI 1999/1925. These Regulations affect large-scale redundancies (ie where 20 or more employees are being made redundant) and transfers of businesses (see later).

The main provisions implemented by the Regulations are that employers who recognise a trade union must consult with that union and cannot just consult other representatives of the employees, and specific requirements are laid down for electing employee representatives to be consulted in cases where the employer does not recognise a union. The Regulations also deal with the remedies that employees and their representatives may obtain in cases where employers fail to comply with the duty to consult.

Unfair dismissal

An eligible employee who is dismissed will have a successful claim for unfair dismissal unless the employer can show that the only or principal reason for the dismissal was one of five specified reasons set out in the statute and the tribunal considers that the employer acted reasonably in treating that reason as a sufficient reason for dismissing the employee (s 98).

THE FIVE 'FAIR' REASONS

The reason or principal reason must be one which:

(1) related to the capability or qualifications of the employee for performing work of the kind which he was employed to do; or
(2) related to the conduct of the employee; or
(3) was that the employee was redundant; or
(4) was that the employee could not continue to work in the position which he held without contravention of a duty or restriction imposed by or under an enactment; or

(5) was some other substantial reason of a kind such as to justify the dismissal of an employee holding the position which that employee held.

Although redundancy is a fair reason for dismissal, this does not prejudice the employee's right to a redundancy payment.

Dismissals which are attributable to the employer carrying out a genuine business reorganisation may come within the 'some other substantial reason' ground.

DID THE EMPLOYER ACT REASONABLY?

Even if the employer establishes one of the five 'fair' reasons, the dismissal is still unfair unless he acted reasonably. In determining whether the employer acted reasonably, the tribunal is directed to have regard to the size and administrative resources of the employer's undertaking and the equity and substantial merits of the case. If the employer puts forward conduct as the reason, the tribunal will have particular regard to whether he followed the procedure recommended by the Advisory, Conciliation and Arbitration Service (ACAS) in its Code of Practice on Disciplinary and Grievance Procedures. This recommends, inter alia, a series of warnings except in cases of gross misconduct. Where the reason for the dismissal is redundancy, the tribunal will consider factors such as whether the employer had fair selection criteria and whether he consulted the employees affected and any trade union. Proper consultation and adequate notice are also important factors if the employer is carrying out a genuine business reorganisation and relying on 'some other substantial reason'.

SPECIAL RULES

The normal rules on unfair dismissal are modified in certain situations. For example, special rules apply on the transfer of a business (see **6.3.2**).

ORDERS AVAILABLE

The employee can ask to be reinstated or re-engaged by the employer but the tribunal will not make an order if it considers that it is not practicable to do so. The vast majority of employees, however, claim compensation which comprises two elements: a basic award and a compensatory award.

The basic award is calculated in the same way as a redundancy payment. The aim of the compensatory award, which is subject to a maximum, is to compensate for financial loss sustained by the employee in consequence of the dismissal. Heads of loss include loss of net pay from the date of dismissal to the date of the hearing, future loss of pay, and loss of fringe benefits and pension rights. In order to assess future loss, the tribunal must make a judgement as to how long it will take the employee to obtain alternative employment. The employee is under a duty to mitigate his loss by attempting to obtain suitable alternative employment. Any contributory fault on the part of the employee will also reduce the award.

6.2.3 Overlapping claims

A dismissed employee may have more than one potential claim against his employer. For example, all three claims of wrongful dismissal, redundancy and unfair dismissal would be available to the employee unfairly dismissed without proper notice by reason of redundancy.

Wrongful and unfair dismissal

For many employees, the statutory claims (despite being subject to maxima) will be more valuable than the contractual claim. However, for employees, such as directors, who have long-term service contracts at lucrative salaries, a claim for wrongful dismissal is likely to yield the highest sum. If the employee is successful in both claims, he will not be entitled to compensation for the same loss twice. Thus, damages for wrongful dismissal can be reduced by the unfair dismissal compensatory award.

Redundancy and unfair dismissal

The redundancy payment will be set against the unfair dismissal award.

Redundancy and wrongful dismissal

Although there are conflicting authorities on the point, it is generally accepted that a redundancy payment should not be taken into account in awarding damages for wrongful dismissal.

6.3 THE TRANSFER OF UNDERTAKINGS (PROTECTION OF EMPLOYMENT) REGULATIONS 1981 (IMPLEMENTING THE ACQUIRED RIGHTS DIRECTIVE)

At common law, the transfer of a business operates to terminate contracts of employment, which cannot be assigned because they are personal to the employer and employee. The seller of the business may, therefore, be liable to the employees for wrongful dismissal, redundancy and unfair dismissal. Where the Transfer Regulations apply, however, the common law position is reversed. Contracts of employment are transferred automatically to the buyer (referred to in the Transfer Regulations as the 'transferee') and the contracts continue as if originally made between the employees and the buyer; the transfer of the business does not, therefore, operate as a 'dismissal'. The Transfer Regulations also modify the normal rules on unfair dismissal described above. If any dismissals take place which are 'connected with the transfer', they will be automatically unfair unless, effectively, there is a genuine redundancy situation.

6.3.1 When do the Transfer Regulations apply?

The Transfer Regulations have a number of exclusions and limitations. The most important ones are as follows.

(1) The Transfer Regulations do not apply where there is a sale of assets only. For example, on insolvency the receiver may break up the business and sell off its assets to various buyers, the plant to one buyer and the premises to another. Only an economic entity retaining its identity after the transfer (see **6.3.2**) will be covered by the Transfer Regulations.

(2) Regulation 5 (automatic transfer of contract of employment (see **6.4**)) does not apply to rights under or in connection with an occupational pension scheme. For this purpose, any provisions of an occupational scheme which do not relate to benefits for old age, invalidity or survivors are treated as not being part of the pension scheme, with the result that these benefits will be transferred. However,

the exclusion is limited to occupational pension schemes. It does not, therefore, cover contributions into private pension schemes.

(3) Regulation 5 also does not transfer any liability of any person to be prosecuted for, convicted of and sentenced for any offence. So, for example, if the transferor is liable to be prosecuted for breach of the Health and Safety at Work Act, that liability cannot pass to the transferee on the transfer of a business.

(4) The Transfer Regulations only apply to employees who satisfy the usual qualifying conditions for unfair dismissal protection (ie one year's continuous employment).

(5) The Transfer Regulations do not apply where a purchaser buys a majority shareholding in a company, thereby gaining control. This is because there is no change in the identity of the employer. The transfer must be 'from one person to another' (see **6.3.2**) (see also *Brookes and Others v Borough Care Services and CLS Care Services Ltd* [1998] IRLR 636).

(6) The decision of the ECJ in *Allen and Others v Amalgamated Construction Co Ltd* (Case C-234/98) [2000] IRLR 19 confirmed that the Transfer Regulations can apply to transfers between two companies belonging to the same group. Subsidiaries within a group of companies are all separate legal entities, therefore when employees are moved around from one company to another within the same group, the Transfer Regulations apply in so far as there is a transfer of an economic entity which retains its identity (see **6.3.2**).

6.3.2 A relevant transfer – Regulation 3

The Transfer Regulations only apply to 'a relevant transfer', which under reg 3(1) is 'a transfer from one person to another of an undertaking situated immediately before the transfer in the United Kingdom or a part of one which is so situated'.

This definition is, and has proved, nebulous. Over the last few years there has been much case-law relating to the meaning of 'a relevant transfer'. The most typical situation where the Transfer Regulations apply is the sale of a business as a going concern. However, the Transfer Regulations have not been restricted to such a typical transaction, and have been applied to a variety of situations such as contracting out and the granting of franchises.

The European Court of Justice has propounded various tests and guidelines as to the existence of a relevant transfer. The two key cases outlining the general tests to be applied are *Spijkers v Gebroeders Benedik Abattoir CV* [1986] ECR 1119, ECJ, and *Dr Sophie Redmond Stichting v Bartol and Others* [1992] IRLR 366, ECJ.

From the judgments of these two cases, it is clear that the decisive criterion for establishing the existence of a transfer within the meaning of the Directive is whether the entity in question retains its identity.

Dr Sophie Redmond Stichting v Bartol and Others also confirmed the principle that the Acquired Rights Directive was not confined to commercial ventures. The Transfer Regulations, which originally related to commercial ventures only, were therefore amended from 30 August 1993.

Examples of 'atypical transfers' include the contracting out of certain service functions, for example, cleaning, catering and maintenance. The law on these types of transfer is fairly complex and beyond the scope of the course.

The parties cannot agree to exclude the operation of the Transfer Regulations (reg 12). Whether a transfer is a 'relevant transfer' is a question of fact. The court or tribunal will look behind the label which the parties put on the transfer and will instead examine the substance of the transaction.

If it is not a relevant transfer, any rights which the employees have (eg to claim wrongful dismissal, redundancy, or unfair dismissal) must be enforced against the seller. If the seller is insolvent, certain claims, such as redundancy and the basic award for unfair dismissal, will be met by the Secretary of State for Employment (ERA 1996, s 182). However, the employees will be unable to recover the compensatory award for unfair dismissal in these circumstances.

6.4 EFFECT OF A RELEVANT TRANSFER – REGULATION 5

6.4.1 Automatic transfer of contracts of employment

Regulation 5(1) provides that:

> 'a relevant transfer shall not operate so as to terminate the contract of employment of any person employed by the transferor in the undertaking or part transferred but any such contract which would otherwise have been terminated by the transfer shall have effect after the transfer as if originally made between the person so employed and the transferee.'

Employees do, however, have the right to object to the transfer of their contracts (see later).

Regulation 5(2) states that:

> 'on the completion of a relevant transfer, all the transferor's rights, powers, duties and liabilities under or in connection with any such contract shall be transferred by virtue of this Regulation to the transferee and anything done before the transfer is completed by or in relation to the transferor in respect of that contract or a person employed in that undertaking or part shall be deemed to have been done by or in relation to the transferee.'

The employees, in other words, have the same rights against the transferee as they had against the transferor and their continuity of employment is not affected by the transfer.

6.4.2 Which employees are affected?

Regulation 5(3) states that any reference:

> '... to a person employed in an undertaking or part of one transferred by a relevant transfer is a reference to a person so employed immediately before the transfer, including, where the transfer is effected by a series of two or more transactions, a person so employed immediately before any of those transactions.'

Employees whose contracts would 'otherwise have been terminated by the transfer'

Those employees whose contracts would not be terminated by the transfer do not come within reg 5. This may, for example, apply to an employee who is retained by the transferor and redeployed in some other part of his operation within the terms of the employee's contract or with his consent. Such redeployment should take place before the transfer.

Where part of a business is transferred, employees will not be affected by reg 5 if they did not work in the part transferred. Even employees who perform duties in relation to the part transferred (eg administrative duties performed by a retained department) will not be covered unless they are assigned to the part transferred.

Regard should be had to the test laid down in *Botzen v Rotterdamsche Droogdok Maatschappij BV* (No 186/83) [1986] 2 CMLR 50, ECJ. In summary, the test is whether there is a transfer of the part of the undertaking to which the employees:

> 'were assigned and which formed the organisational framework within which their employment relationship took effect.'

Useful guidance on the *Botzen* test was given by the EAT in *Duncan Webb Offset (Maidstone) Ltd v Cooper and Others* [1995] IRLR 633. In determining to which part of the employer's business the employee was assigned, a tribunal may consider matters such as:

(1) the amount of time spent on one part of the business or the other;
(2) the amount of value given to each part by the employee;
(3) the terms of the contract of employment showing what the employee could be required to do; and
(4) how the cost to the employer of the employee's services was allocated between different parts of the business.

In essence then, the correct test is simply whether a person was assigned to an undertaking or a part. Note, however, that in *Carisway Cleaning Contracts Ltd v Richards and Another* (EAT/629/97) (1998) unreported, 19 June, the EAT held that an employer could not 'off-load' an unwanted employee by deliberately moving him to a part of the undertaking that the employer knew was about to be transferred. They held that such an act was fraudulent and, accordingly, void. The employee was not 'employed in the part of the undertaking' being transferred.

'Immediately before the transfer'

If the transfer is the sale of a business and there is a gap between exchange of contracts and completion, it is the date of completion which is the date of transfer for the purposes of reg 5. What is the position, then, if the employees are dismissed shortly before completion? On a strict interpretation of reg 5, they are not employed immediately before the transfer and, consequently, would not come within the Regulation, ie their contracts would not be transferred to the transferee and they would have to pursue claims for the termination of their contracts against the transferor. This was the approach which the Court of Appeal took in *Secretary of State for Employment v Spence* [1987] QB 179 when it held that the contract must subsist at the moment of transfer; the contracts of employees who were dismissed several hours before completion were held not to be transferred to the transferee.

On this interpretation, a transferee would be able to circumvent reg 5 by insisting that the transferor dismisses some or all of the workforce prior to completion. The House of Lords, however, has added a significant gloss to the wording of reg 5. It decided in *Litster v Forth Dry Dock and Engineering Co Ltd* [1989] IRLR 161, that reg 5 applies not only to a person who is employed immediately before the transfer but also to a person who would have been so employed if he had not been unfairly dismissed in the circumstances described in reg 8(1). Regulation 8(1) provides that the dismissal is automatically unfair unless the employer can show that the dismissal was for an economic, technical or organisational reason ('ETO reason') entailing a change in the workforce.

As a result of the *Litster* decision, reg 5 now applies to two groups of employees:

(1) to those employees actually employed by the transferor at the time of the transfer. Their contracts of employment transfer to the transferee and they will work for the transferee under the terms of those contracts; and

(2) to those employees who were dismissed for a reason connected with the transfer where no ETO reason exists. Any rights they may have had with regard to unfair or wrongful dismissal, together with any claim for a redundancy payment, will transfer with the business to the transferee.

The employee's right of objection

The transfer of the contract of employment and rights, powers, duties and liabilities under and in connection with it will not occur if the employee informs the transferor or the transferee that he objects to becoming employed by the transferee. In that event, the transfer will terminate the employee's contract of employment with the transferor, but he will not be treated for any purpose as having been dismissed by the transferor (reg 4A) (*Senior Heat Treatment Ltd v Bell* [1997] IRLR 614).

From recent case-law, it is now clear that neither the general application of the automatic transfer principle nor the existence of the employee's right to object is subject to a precondition that employees have knowledge of both the fact of a transfer and the identity of the transferee (*Secretary of State for Trade and Industry v Cook and Others* [1997] ICR 288, EAT).

6.5 WHAT THE TRANSFEREE ACQUIRES

The transferee inherits those employees employed by the vendor immediately before the transfer on their existing terms and conditions, assuming that they do not object.

The transferee has no power to impose any different terms and conditions from those he has inherited from the transferor, however commercially convenient this may be.

Equally, the transferred employee has no right to insist that he be given the benefit of any superior terms and conditions enjoyed by the transferee's existing staff.

6.5.1 Rights transferring

The transferee inherits all accrued rights and liabilities connected with the contract of employment of the transferred employee. If, for example, the transferor was in arrears with wages at the time of the transfer, the employee can sue the transferee as if the original liability had been the transferee's. The transferor is relieved of his former obligations without any need for the employee's consent.

Equally, the transferee can sue an employee for a breach of contract committed against the transferor prior to transfer.

The transferee will also inherit all the statutory rights and liabilities which are connected with the individual contract of employment, for example unfair dismissal, redundancy and discrimination.

The transferred employee's period of continuous employment will date from the beginning of his period of employment with the transferor, and the statutory particulars of terms and conditions of employment, which every employer is obliged to issue, must take account of any continuity enjoyed by virtue of the Transfer Regulations.

Restrictive covenants

In the case of restrictive covenants, these will normally be expressed in terms of protecting customers of the transferor. In essence, following the transfer of an undertaking a restrictive covenant should be read as being enforceable by the transferee but only in respect of customers of the transferor who fall within the protection. (Great care needs to be taken if restrictive covenants are re-drafted, post-transfer; see **6.7.2**.)

Collective agreements

Under the Transfer Regulations, any collective agreements made with a trade union by the transferor are deemed to have been made by the transferee (reg 6). Further, the transferee is deemed to recognise the trade union to the same extent as did the transferor (reg 9). In effect, the transferee steps into the shoes of the transferor. Neither the Transfer Regulations nor the general law prevents the employer from seeking to derecognise the union entirely or from amending the basis of the recognition. This lack of an effective remedy undermines the protection given to trade unions on a Transfer Regulations transfer.

Individually, however, there may be 'hangovers' from previous union recognition. Of course, all terms of the individuals' contracts including those pursuant to any collective agreements will be deemed to have been made between the transferee and the employee. It follows that, notwithstanding withdrawal from collective bargaining by the transferee, the right to have pay determined by collective bargaining can persist.

This was considered in *Whent and Others v T. Cartledge Limited* [1997] IRLR 153 where not only the rate of pay and general terms which existed at the time of the transfer, but also the terms providing for the collective bargaining mechanism itself transferred as a result of the transfer. The fact that the employer had derecognised the union was irrelevant.

6.5.2 Rights and liabilities which are not assigned under the Regulations

The Regulations do not have the effect of assigning:

(a) criminal liabilities; or
(b) rights and liabilities relating to provisions of occupational pension schemes which relate to benefits for old age, invalidity or survivors (although changes to this in accordance with the new Acquired Rights Directive (98/50/EC) are expected); or
(c) liability for failure to consult in advance of a transfer (*Transport and General Workers' Union v James McKinnon Jr (Haulage) Ltd and Others* [2001] IRLR 597).

6.6 DISMISSAL OF AN EMPLOYEE RESULTING FROM A RELEVANT TRANSFER – REGULATION 8

If the dismissal is for a reason connected with the transfer then, by reg 8 of the Transfer Regulations, the dismissal is automatically unfair (reg 8(1)) unless the employer can show an 'economic, technical or organisational reason' (an ETO reason) entailing a change in the workforce (reg 8(2)).

6.6.1 When is a dismissal for a reason connected with the transfer?

It is a question of fact whether or not a dismissal is for a reason connected with the transfer. Although dismissals which occur shortly before or after the transfer are likely to be found to be connected with it, an employee may have difficulty convincing the tribunal that a dismissal which took place weeks or even months before the transfer was for a reason connected with the transfer. An employee dismissed prior to the transfer will come under reg 8 if he can prove that, at the time the dismissal took place, a transferee had been found and that the dismissal was connected to the transfer under negotiation.

Less clear is whether it is sufficient for the employee to show that his dismissal was in connection with transfers generally. There is a conflict of EAT decisions on this point.

In *Ibex Trading Co Ltd (in administration) v Walton and Others* [1994] IRLR 564, the EAT held that the actual transferee had to be identified. Dismissal in respect of transfers generally was not sufficient. The employees were held to be dismissed by reason of 'a' transfer, rather than 'the' transfer.

However, in *Harrison Bowden Ltd v Bowden* [1994] ICR 186, and more recently in *Morris v John Grose Group Ltd* [1998] IRLR 499, the EAT has held that the words 'the transfer' in reg 8(1) did not necessarily have to refer to the particular transfer that had actually occurred.

The decision in *Morris* is to be preferred because the ECJ has stated that the proper approach to the issue of whether dismissals were made in connection with a transfer was to look back in time and consider what had happened. On the basis of this method of analysis, the fact that no transferee can be identified at the moment of dismissal does not prevent employee's rights from being protected by the Acquired Rights Directive.

Where there is clear evidence of pre-transfer 'collusion' between the transferor and the transferee with regard to dismissals, ie the transferee had been involved in some way in the decision to dismiss, this may lead to a finding that the dismissals were connected with the transfer. In *Wheeler v Patel and Another* [1987] IRLR 211, Mrs Wheeler was employed by the vendor of a shop in his business which he proposed to sell. Before transferring the shop to a prospective purchaser, Mrs Wheeler was dismissed in order to achieve an agreement for sale. The EAT held that the dismissal was connected with the transfer and fell to be considered for an ETO reason.

6.6.2 Establishing an ETO reason

If the employer can show an ETO reason, he will be deemed to have dismissed for 'some other substantial reason' under s 98(1) of the ERA 1996. Even where the employer can show such a reason, the employment tribunal must still be satisfied that the employer has acted reasonably within s 98(4) of the ERA 1996.

The employer must show an ETO reason entailing a change in the workforce, otherwise the dismissal will be unfair. The scope of the defence has been limited by a number of decisions.

(1) To be an ETO reason within reg 8(2), an 'economic' reason must relate to the conduct of the business as such and does not include dismissing employees simply to obtain an enhanced price or to achieve an agreement for sale (*Wheeler v Patel*). In *Wheeler*, the EAT held that the tribunal had erred in dismissing Mrs Wheeler's unfair dismissal claim against the vendor on grounds that the reason for the dismissal was an 'economic' reason within reg 8(2). Mrs Wheeler's unfair dismissal claim against the vendor succeeded.

(2) To come within reg 8(2), the ETO reason must entail a 'change in the workforce'. For a change in the workforce there has to be a change in the composition of the workforce or possibly a substantial change in job descriptions: *Berriman v Delabole Slate Ltd* [1985] IRLR 305, CA. Effectively, therefore, an ETO reason entailing a change in the workforce will have to be a genuine redundancy situation. Although a real change in the functions of the workforce can satisfy the ETO requirement (*Green v Elan Care Ltd* [2002] All ER (D) 17, Mar), a mere change in the terms and conditions enjoyed by the workforce will not suffice. Consequently, a transferee who provokes an actual or constructive dismissal by attempting to change the terms and conditions of the transferred employees to harmonise with those of his existing workforce would be unable to rely on the defence.

6.6.3 The relationship between reg 8(1) and reg 8(2)

The courts have found it difficult to decide if reg 8(1) and (2) are mutually exclusive; ie if a dismissal falls within reg 8(1), in that it is a dismissal connected with a transfer, then it cannot also be for an ETO reason within reg 8(2). The Court of Appeal, in *Warner v Adnet Ltd* [1998] IRLR 394, held that such an approach was erroneous and that reg 8(1) and (2) should be read together. The Court of Appeal stated that the correct approach is for the tribunal to make a provisional finding as to whether the dismissal falls within reg 8(1) and, if it does, to then go on to consider whether there is an ETO reason.

6.7 TRANSFER-CONNECTED DISMISSALS AND POST-TRANSFER VARIATIONS TO TERMS AND CONDITIONS

On Thursday, 29 October 1998, the House of Lords delivered the long-awaited judgment in *British Fuels Ltd v Baxendale and Another; Wilson and Others v St Helens Borough Council* [1999] 2 AC 52.

The cases of *Wilson* and *Baxendale* raised the following issues:

(1) whether a pre-transfer dismissal by the transferor and re-engagement by the transferee post-transfer on different terms and conditions is effective;

(2) whether a post-transfer dismissal by the transferee and re-engagement on different terms and conditions is effective; and

(3) whether agreed variations to terms and conditions without dismissal post-transfer by the transferee are effective.

It is the third question which raises the most concerns for business and, unfortunately, remains unanswered by the House of Lords.

6.7.1 Transfer-connected dismissals

The House of Lords held that the dismissals in each case were effective. The Transfer Regulations do not prevent dismissals associated with transfers of undertakings. A pre-transfer dismissal is effective to terminate the working relationship so that there is nothing of it to pass to the transferee. The contract of employment is kept alive only for the purpose of enforcing rights for breach of it or for enforcing statutory rights dependent on the contract of employment but not for the purpose of creating an obligation which did not exist under domestic law to continue with the working relationship.

As a result, we are now left in the following position.

6.7.2 Post-transfer variations to terms and conditions

Unfortunately, since the House of Lords held the dismissals to be effective, it was not necessary for the question of post-transfer variations to terms and conditions (even by agreement) to be dealt with. This is obviously because the dismissals 'wiped the slate clean' with respect to rights under the Transfer Regulations.

However, in two cases decided before *Wilson* and *Baxendale*, the Court of Appeal considered the impact of post-transfer contractual variations. In *Credit Suisse First Boston (Europe) Ltd v Padiachy and Others* [1998] IRLR 504, the court refused to enforce a non-competition covenant which had been agreed to by an employee post-transfer as part of an overall package of contractual changes, notwithstanding that the employees were said to be in a better overall position as a result of the changes. In *Credit Suisse First Boston (Europe) Ltd v Lister* [1998] IRLR 700, the Court stated that a restrictive covenant entered into by an employee post-transfer was unenforceable because the variation was made by reason of the transfer.

It seems, then, that post-transfer variations (even those made with consent) will not be enforceable if the variations are due to the transfer.

6.7.3 Summary of effect of the Transfer Regulations on pre- and post-transfer dismissals

Pre-transfer dismissals

Reason unconnected with the transfer

Where the dismissal is not for a reason connected with the transfer (eg for misconduct or redundancy), the normal rules of unfair dismissal apply. In this situation, *Litster* does not apply (because the dismissal is not within the circumstances described in reg 8), and therefore liability remains with the transferor.

The transferee will only be liable to the dismissed employee if that employee was employed immediately before the transfer (ie at the moment of the transfer): *Secretary of State for Employment v Spence* (see **6.4.2**).

Reason connected with the transfer

The effect of *Litster* is that a pre-transfer dismissal, however long before the transfer, which is automatically unfair under reg 8, will result in liability passing to the transferee (but this does not alter the fact that the dismissal remains effective to terminate the contract). Only where an ETO reason exists may the transferee escape liability. Where the transferee does escape liability, liability will obviously fall on the transferor, who will have to make a redundancy payment and, if the dismissal was not handled fairly, an unfair dismissal payment.

So, in the context of a pre-transfer dismissal connected with the transfer, the existence of an ETO reason is essential to determine whether liability rests with the transferor or the transferee.

A genuine redundancy dismissal before the transfer should be for an ETO reason entailing a change in the workforce and should not involve the transferee in liability. However, where the transferee is identified and gets involved in the dismissal, then the dismissal is collusive and may attract the principle in *Litster*.

Post-transfer dismissals

The liability for a post-transfer dismissal will obviously only fall on the transferee.

After the transfer, the transferee may wish to bring the contracts of the transferred employees into line with those of his existing workforce. An employer who expressly or constructively dismisses employees who refuse to accept new terms may encounter difficulty with reg 8. This is because, according to *Berriman v Delabole Slate Ltd* [1985] IRLR 305, CA, a mere change in the terms and conditions enjoyed by the workforce will not satisfy the definition of an ETO reason and will therefore be automatically unfair.

Position as between transferor and transferee

It is not possible for the transferor and the transferee to be jointly liable: *Stirling District Council v Allan and Others* [1995] IRLR 301. In view of the risk that under *Litster* the transferee can be liable for pre-transfer dismissals, the transferee should attempt to obtain indemnities from the transferor to cover this risk.

6.7.4 Practical advice

When acting for a transferee it is imperative to carry out full due diligence of all transferring employees' terms and conditions, since the transferee will inherit those terms and conditions and may not be able to vary them even with the employees' consent.

The transferee should seek an indemnity from the transferor in the event of there being any difference between the terms and conditions detailed in the due diligence process by the transferor, and the actual terms and conditions on which employees transfer across.

A transferee who wishes to be sure that old terms and conditions do not apply, and/or to harmonise terms and conditions with the existing workforce, may dismiss or get the transferor to dismiss. Such dismissals will be effective, but will give rise to the risk of unfair dismissal claims. Such dismissals will be 'automatically' unfair, unless there is an ETO reason. In *Berriman* (see **6.6.2**), the Court of Appeal held that an ETO reason entailing changes in the workforce involves more than a mere change in terms and conditions. If transferees wish to have contractually binding and harmonious terms, they will have to bear in mind the potential costs of any consequential unfair dismissal claims. Alternatively, they will have to try to ensure that changes are not connected with the transfer. Finally, if harmonising terms and conditions of employment is essential to the transaction, the buyer may consider buying the business through a share sale, for example, via a hive-down. Although, on a share sale, the employees can still object to a change in their employment contracts and bring the usual claims for constructive and unfair dismissal, if the employees do accept the new terms and conditions, then the uncertainty created by *Wilson* and *Baxendale* as to whether or not they are effective may be removed. However, this route is not without uncertainty itself. It is always open to the employees to argue that the share acquisition was a 'sham' and that, therefore, the Transfer Regulations do apply.

6.7.5 The duty to inform and consult trade unions

Regulation 10 obliges the seller and buyer to provide information to recognised trade unions or elected employee representatives in respect of any 'affected employee', ie any employee of the seller or buyer who may be affected by the transfer or measures taken in relation to it. The employer must supply specified information long enough before the transfer to enable consultation to take place. The information to be given includes the legal, social and economic implications for the employees and the measures which the employer is proposing to take in relation to them (if there are no measures proposed, this should be stated). The seller must also inform the union or elected representative of any measures which he understands the buyer intends to take in relation to affected employees. 'Measures' in this context would appear to include proposed changes in the work-force or in their terms and conditions.

The employer is under an obligation to consult where he envisages taking measures in relation to the affected employees with a view to reaching agreement to measures to be taken. The employer must consider any representations made, respond to them and indicate the reasons for rejecting any of them.

Failure to comply with reg 10 may lead to the tribunal, on the application of the union or elected representative, awarding up to 13 weeks' pay in respect of each affected employee (reg 11). The employer has a defence if he can show that it was not reasonably practicable to perform the duties, for example because he was bound by obligations of confidentiality.

Collective agreements and union recognition agreements will generally be transferred to the buyer (regs 6 and 9).

6.8 DUE DILIGENCE AND PROTECTION IN THE ACQUISITION AGREEMENT

The parties cannot contract out of the Transfer Regulations. Since *Litster,* the scope for the buyer avoiding the automatic transfer of the employees of the target business is extremely limited. It has been noted, for example, that the practice of requiring the seller to dismiss employees prior to the transfer will rarely be effective to prevent liability passing to the buyer. Often, the safest course for the buyer is to take on all the employees of the target and to carry out any dismissals or changes to their terms and conditions after the acquisition (perhaps after a suitable interval to avoid any dismissal being seen as connected with the transfer within reg 8(1)). When negotiating the purchase price for the business, the buyer should take into account the liability which he will incur in dismissing surplus employees. This is clearly preferable to agreeing an enhanced price on the basis that the seller effects the dismissals but, nevertheless, becoming liable for those dismissals because of the decision in *Litster*.

The buyer should also seek to protect himself by making pre-contract enquiries about the target work-force and negotiating suitable warranties and indemnities in the acquisition agreement itself.

6.8.1 Pre-contract enquiries

Since the buyer will be inheriting all liabilities in relation to the target's employees arising under their contracts or otherwise, he will require full details of all employment matters. The requested information will include the following:

(1) details of each employee including age and length of service;
(2) notice required to terminate contracts of employment;
(3) salary, commission and fringe benefits of each employee;
(4) details of trade unions, recognition agreements, collective agreements, etc;
(5) details of any disputes with employees, litigation threatened or pending (whether in the ordinary courts or the employment tribunal), or employment tribunal awards or court judgments;
(6) copies of contracts of employment (including directors' service contracts) and written statements under s 1 of the ERA 1996;
(7) details of employees who have given notices in relation to maternity rights;
(8) details of recent changes to any employee's terms and conditions of employment.

6.8.2 Warranties and indemnities

Much of the information revealed by the above enquiries may be included in a schedule to the acquisition agreement or, perhaps, in the disclosure letter. The buyer will seek a warranty that this information is complete and accurate. He may also include specific warranties, for example, that there are no employment claims pending and that no event has occurred which may give rise to a claim for constructive dismissal.

The parties may acknowledge in the agreement that the acquisition of the business is a 'relevant transfer' within the meaning of the Transfer Regulations. The buyer will then usually seek various indemnities from the seller. He may, for example, require an indemnity against any costs or liabilities arising out of all outgoings in respect of the employees (eg salary, commissions, bonuses and holiday pay) up to the date of completion (an apportionment will be made to the date of completion).

The buyer may also insist on an indemnity against any claims which are attributable to any breach by the seller of his employment obligations prior to completion (including claims arising on termination of any employee's employment) for which the buyer becomes liable through the operation of the Transfer Regulations.

6.9 PENSIONS

Where the employees of the target business are members of a pension scheme, the parties will need to give careful thought to the pension aspects of the acquisition. This is a complex area which often gives rise to more discussion and negotiation between the parties and their advisers than any other aspect of the transaction; this is understandable since the value of the pension fund may even exceed the consideration for the business itself. The specialist pensions lawyer is often an invaluable member of the legal team involved in an acquisition. It is not intended to deal with pension considerations in detail but merely to highlight a number of general points which may be relevant on a business acquisition.

6.9.1 Money purchase or final salary scheme?

The buyer will require full details of any pension scheme benefiting the employees of the target business; in particular, pre-contract enquiries will include requests for copies of the trust deed and rules under which the pension fund is administered, a list of the members of the scheme, and confirmation that the scheme is 'exempt approved', ie that it enjoys a privileged tax status. There are two main types of pension scheme: money purchase schemes and final salary schemes.

Money purchase

In a money purchase scheme, the employer and employee make fixed contributions into the fund which are invested and used to purchase benefits for the employee on his retirement. Employees are not guaranteed any particular level of benefit on retirement; the amount they receive will depend entirely on the return on the contributions made by them and by the employer on their behalf.

Final salary

In a final salary scheme, the members are guaranteed a particular level of benefit on retirement; this will usually be on the basis of a fraction of their salary at the date of retirement for each year of completed service with the employer. Unlike money purchase schemes, there is no direct correlation between the contributions made to the fund (by employer and employee) and the benefits received by the employee. A final salary scheme may, consequently, be in surplus or deficit at the time of the acquisition; much will depend on the prevailing economic conditions which, of course, have an effect on investment performance. Whether the fund is in surplus or deficit and the amounts involved can only be ascertained by making a host of assumptions about future events. Such an exercise should be carried out by an actuary.

6.9.2 Does the target business have a discrete pension scheme or does it participate in a group scheme?

The pension implications of an acquisition are simplified if the employees of the target business are members of a separate, self-contained pension scheme (a discrete scheme). However, it is often the case that they are members of a larger scheme involving other employees. For example, on a business sale by a company, the selling company may be part of a group pension scheme.

6.9.3 Transferring the pension benefits

Discrete scheme

The assets in the pension fund do not form part of the business which is being acquired; the pension fund is a separate entity administered by the trustees. Where the employees of the business are members of a discrete pension scheme, they will remain in the scheme following the acquisition (usually, at least initially, even if the buyer has an existing scheme covering his own employees). If it is a final salary scheme, it is important for the parties to determine whether it is adequately funded or over-funded at the date of completion. The buyer will often commission an actuary to value the fund for this purpose.

If the scheme is revealed to be in surplus, the seller may seek an increase in the purchase price to reflect this. Although the buyer does not benefit directly from the surplus, it may enable him to take a 'contributions holiday', ie a period in which he does not make any contributions. If, on the other hand, there is a deficit, the buyer may seek a reduction in the price or require the seller to 'top up' the fund. If the actuarial valuation is not ready on completion, the agreement may provide for an adjustment of the price when it is to hand.

The acquisition agreement will usually contain a schedule setting out details of the scheme. Warranties relating to the scheme will include confirmation by the seller that all contributions have been paid to the date of completion and that there are no outstanding claims against the trustees.

Group scheme

Where the target business is a member of a group scheme, a transfer payment must be made from the group scheme to the buyer's scheme (whether an existing scheme or one established for the purpose). The amount of this payment is usually the subject of much argument and negotiation between the parties and their respective actuaries. The discussion often centres around who should have the benefit of any surplus in a final salary scheme. The different bases for calculating the transfer payment can produce vastly differing results. The calculation may, for example, be based on the benefits which the employees would receive on leaving employment or on an apportionment of the fund between those leaving the scheme and those remaining (if the scheme is in surplus, the latter method will be more beneficial for the target's employees).

The provisions relating to the transfer payment are normally contained in a pension schedule to the acquisition agreement. The parties' actuaries may not have agreed the amount of the payment by the date of completion but the basis for calculating the payment is usually included in an 'actuary's letter' attached to the schedule.

It is important to appreciate that the trustees of the scheme will not be parties to the acquisition agreement and can only act in accordance with the trust deed and rules. Since the seller cannot, therefore, force the trustees to make the transfer, the buyer is wise to insist on a guarantee by the seller to make up any shortfall if he is unable to procure the transfer of the full amount. Finally, if the buyer needs to establish a new scheme, the parties may agree that the target's employees should remain with the group scheme for a specified period after completion.

6.10 FLOWCHART

UNFAIR DISMISSAL CLAIMS ON TRANSFER OF AN UNDERTAKING

1. <u>Is there a relevant transfer of an undertaking? – reg 3</u>

    YES   NO →   Normal rules apply
    ↓

2. Is the employee eligible?
    (NB In particular, does employee have 1 year's continuous employment?)

    YES   NO →   No claim
    ↓

3. <u>Has there been a dismissal, actual or constructive?</u>
    (NB The dismissal can occur before or after the transfer)

    YES   NO →   No claim
    ↓

4. <u>Is the dismissal for a reason connected with the transfer? – reg 8</u>

    YES   NO →   Apply usual unfair dismissal rules –
    ↓   if employee's dismissal takes effect
                                               on or after transfer, claim against
                                               transferee, otherwise against
                                               transferor.

5. <u>Can an ETO reason entailing a change in the workforce be established?</u>
    (Note *Berriman v Delabole* on meaning of 'change in the workforce')

    YES   NO →   **Dismissal is automatically unfair** –
    ↓   claim is **against transferee** whether
                                               dismissed on or after transfer
                                               (*Spence*) or before (*Litster*).

    Dismissal deemed to be
    for some other
    substantial reason for
    purposes of ERA 1996.
    Claim is against
    transferee if on or after
    transfer, otherwise
    against transferor.
    ↓

    Does tribunal
    consider that the
    <u>employer has acted</u>
    <u>fairly (s 98(4))?</u>

    YES   NO →   Dismissal is unfair.
    ↓

    Dismissal fair.

Note: Redundancy payment (if employee is eligible) or wrongful dismissal claims could also be appropriate. Claim will be against the same party, transferor or transferee, that the dismissal claim would be against.

Chapter 7

TAXATION ON A BUSINESS ACQUISITION

7.1 INTRODUCTION

This chapter outlines the tax consequences (including VAT and stamp duty) of the transfer of a business. It deals with the implications for a sole trader or partnership disposing of an unincorporated business and for a company selling a business. The tax position of the buyer is also considered.

It is not intended to explain in detail basic tax principles which have been fully explored in the LPC Resource Books *Business Law and Practice* and *Pervasive and Core Topics* (Jordans), such as the nature of the charges to income tax, CGT and corporation tax, and the main relieving provisions, but to deal with these in the context of a business acquisition.

Chapter 7 contents
Introduction
Implications for the seller of an unincorporated business
Implications on the sale of a business by a company
Implications for the buyer of a business
Warranties

7.2 IMPLICATIONS FOR THE SELLER OF AN UNINCORPORATED BUSINESS

This section assumes that a sole trader or partnership is selling the whole of his or its business to an unconnected person at full market value; the buyer may be an individual, a partnership or a company. It is not concerned with the gift of a business or, indeed, the incorporation of a business, ie where the proprietors sell their business to a company which they have formed or acquired specifically for this purpose.

7.2.1 Sales for cash

A sole trader or partnership disposing of the business in an arm's length deal must consider the income tax and CGT implications of the transaction.

Income tax

THE CLOSING YEAR RULES

The sale results in the discontinuance of the business carried on by the seller, so he will be assessed to income tax on the profits made from the end of the latest accounting period to be assessed until the date of the sale, less a deduction for overlap profit (ie any profit that has been charged to tax in two successive tax years).

STOCK

The value at which trading stock is sold will affect the final profits of the business assessable to income tax. It will be seen at **7.4.5** that the parties have some flexibility in apportioning the global consideration for the business between individual assets. Clearly, the higher the value attributed to stock, the higher the final income tax assessment.

BALANCING CHARGES

The sale of the business may result in balancing charges arising in relation to assets on which capital allowances have been claimed (ie items of plant and machinery or industrial buildings). Most items of plant and machinery are 'pooled' together for the purpose of obtaining capital allowances and it is only when the business is sold that the Inland Revenue calculates whether too much or too little income tax relief has been given on all the assets in the 'pool'. On the basis of the sale price attributable to those assets qualifying for capital allowances, the Inland Revenue will either make an income tax balancing allowance (where the pool is sold for less than its tax written down value) or an income tax balancing charge (where the pool is sold for more than its tax written down value). Once again, the apportionment of the global purchase price of the business between individual assets may have a significant effect on the tax position of the seller (and also the buyer, see **7.4.5**).

RELIEF FOR LOSSES

The sale of the business will prevent any unrelieved losses from being carried forward under s 385 of the ICTA 1988. However, terminal loss relief under s 388 can be claimed if the taxpayer suffers a trading loss in the final 12 months in which he carries on the trade; unrelieved capital allowances in this period may be included for this purpose. The loss can be carried back and deducted from profits of the same trade for the 3 years prior to the final tax year, taking the most recent years first. This may generate a repayment of tax.

The seller can also set a trading loss made in the year in which the sale takes place against any income or chargeable gains which he has in that year or the previous year under s 380. A loss relieved under s 380 cannot form part of the terminal loss claim under s 388.

CGT

The seller will be liable to CGT at his marginal rate of income tax on any gain which arises on the disposal of chargeable assets of the business, such as land, buildings and goodwill. On a sale of the business by a partnership, each partner is separately assessed to CGT and is treated as disposing of his fractional share of each chargeable asset (this is determined by the partner's capital profit sharing ratio).

The gain on the sale of a business may be considerable, particularly where the seller has built up the goodwill of the business. For a long-established business, re-basing to 31 March 1982 (ie substituting market value on this date for actual cost in calculating the gain) and the indexation allowance may reduce the gain significantly. However, it should be noted that for a business established since 31 March 1982, the goodwill will have no base cost to which the indexation allowance can attach, resulting in virtually the whole of its value becoming chargeable.

For gains made by individuals on disposals made after 5 April 1998, indexation allowance will be given for the period up to 5 April 1998 but not thereafter. For assets acquired after 31 March 1998, no indexation allowance will be given.

TAPER RELIEF

On the disposal of a business asset after 5 April 1998, taper relief will reduce the gain, depending on the number of complete years the asset has been held. The maximum rate of business asset taper relief is available after assets have been held for two complete years. For example, consider a business asset acquired in January

1996 and disposed of in May 2002. The gain will be subject to indexation allowance for the period up to April 1998. The asset then will qualify for maximum taper relief based on the individual having held the asset for at least 2 complete years. Losses will be set against the gain before applying the taper relief.

The taper relief for gains on business assets is greater than for gains on non-business assets.

A 'business asset' is one used for the purposes of a trade carried on by an individual, his partnership or his 'qualifying company'. To qualify, the company must be a **trading** company which is:

(1) unlisted (eg private companies and unlisted plcs, including those traded on the Alternative Investment Market); or
(2) listed on the Stock Exchange and the individual is either:
    (a) an employee or officer of the company (there is no requirement for full-time involvement); or
    (b) able to exercise at least 5% of the voting rights.

Shares held by an individual in a qualifying company are also classed as business assets, and are eligible for the enhanced business taper.

Shares in a **non-trading** company (ie not a 'qualifying company') which are owned by employees of that company may also attract business asset taper relief if the employee does not have a material interest of more than 10% in the company.

Any asset which fails the test for a 'business asset' is classed as a 'non-business asset' (eg a private investor's small holding of quoted shares). Taper relief on business and non-business assets operates as shown in the table below.

Gains on business assets		Gains on non-business assets	
Whole years held	Percentage of gain chargeable	Whole years held	Percentage of gain chargeable
1	50	1	100
2 or more	25	2	100
		3	95
		4	90
		5	85
		6	80
		7	75
		8	70
		9	65
		10 or more	60

The result is to produce the 'percentage of gain chargeable' to CGT; ie taper relief wipes out part of the chargeable gain.

ANNUAL EXEMPTION

A sole trader, or in the case of a partnership each partner, will have the benefit of the CGT annual exemption (£7,700 for tax year 2002/03) if this has not otherwise been used up in the tax year.

ROLL-OVER RELIEF ON REPLACEMENT OF BUSINESS ASSETS (TCGA 1992, ss 152–158)

A sole trader or partner who reinvests the proceeds of sale of his business or partnership share in another business venture may be able to defer the charge to CGT if he fulfils the conditions for roll-over relief. This relief is considered in the LPC Resource Book *Business Law and Practice* (Jordans). The main features of the relief are outlined as follows.

(1) Where the business or partnership share comprises qualifying assets (or an interest in such assets), the sole trader or partner can elect to roll any gain on such assets into replacement qualifying assets acquired within one year before or 3 years after the sale of the business or partnership share (it is sufficient that an unconditional contract is entered into within these time-limits). CGT is deferred until the replacement assets are disposed of (without themselves being replaced).

(2) It is not necessary for the replacement asset to be of the same kind as the original asset. It is sufficient if both the 'old' and the 'new' assets come within the list of qualifying assets, which includes land or buildings occupied and used for the trade, goodwill and fixed plant and machinery. Thus, an individual who sells one unincorporated business and then invests in another will be able to take advantage of this relief. However, shares are not qualifying assets for the purposes of this relief.

(3) Relief is restricted if the old assets have not been used in the seller's trade (or trades which he carried on successively) throughout his period of ownership or if the whole of the proceeds of sale are not reinvested in new assets.

(4) A partner who allows his firm to use the asset can claim relief on selling the asset if he reinvests in replacement assets.

(5) Note that the seller cannot use his annual exemption to reduce the gain rolled over.

DEFERRAL RELIEF ON REINVESTMENT IN EIS AND VCT SHARES

An individual will be able to claim unlimited deferral of capital gains arising on the disposal, by sale or gift, of any asset when he invests the chargeable gain by subscribing for shares which qualify under the EIS. The individual's chargeable gain on the disposal of the asset (up to the subscription cost) is deferred until he disposes of the shares. The relief is available where the EIS shares are acquired within 1 year before or 3 years after the disposal. Furthermore, the individual can claim income tax relief at 20% on qualifying investments (ie in unquoted companies) of up to £150,000 in any tax year.

A similar deferral relief is available where the individual invests in VCT shares. A VCT is, essentially, a type of company quoted on the Stock Exchange. Furthermore, the individual can claim income tax relief at 20%, but the relief is limited to investments in new ordinary shares of up to £100,000 in any tax year and requires the shares to be retained for 3 years. In this case the shares must be acquired one year before or one year after the disposal.

7.2.2 Sales in consideration for shares

On an arm's length sale of an unincorporated business (whether a sole trade or a partnership) to an existing company, the proprietors of the business may agree to take shares in the buyer company as consideration for the sale. Two special reliefs may be available to the sellers in these circumstances.

Carry forward of unrelieved trading losses

Where a business is sold to a company wholly or mainly for shares, s 386 of the ICTA 1988 allows the seller to carry forward any unrelieved trading losses and deduct them from income received from the company. Initially, the deduction is from any salary paid to him as an employee of the company and then from any dividends paid to him as a shareholder. The set off is available in any year in which the seller retains beneficial ownership of the shares. For the sale to be 'wholly or mainly' in return for shares, at least 80% of the consideration should be in shares.

CGT roll-over into shares

Section 162 of the TCGA 1992 enables the seller to roll any chargeable gains on the sale of the business into the shares issued by the company in consideration, thus reducing the CGT acquisition cost of the shares by the amount of the gain. The effect of the relief is to postpone the CGT until the former proprietor of the business disposes of his shares in the company.

For the relief to operate, all the assets of the business (although cash can be ignored for this purpose) must be transferred to the company; it is not necessary, however, to transfer all the liabilities. Since the nature of the relief is to roll the gain into shares, to the extent that the seller receives cash or debentures in part satisfaction of the purchase price, an immediate potential liability to CGT will arise. This may suit a seller if, for example, he has capital losses brought forward from previous years which he can use to offset the gain.

7.3 IMPLICATIONS ON THE SALE OF A BUSINESS BY A COMPANY

7.3.1 Corporation tax

A company is charged to corporation tax on both its income profits and its capital gains. Thus, on a sale of a business by a company, the following will give rise to a corporation tax charge (note that taper relief does not apply to capital gains made by companies):

(1) capital gains (calculated in the same way as for CGT, save that companies continue to be entitled to indexation allowance after April 1998 and are not within the taper relief regime) arising on chargeable assets of the business;
(2) income profits on the sale of trading stock;
(3) balancing charges. A company is entitled to capital allowances on plant and machinery and industrial buildings in much the same way as an unincorporated business. The disposal of its business will entail an adjustment to the corporation tax relief given on those assets in the form of either a balancing allowance or a balancing charge.

A company which has been accustomed to paying corporation tax at the small companies rate may find that the sale of the business pushes its profits for the accounting period over the £300,000 threshold at which the higher rates of corporation tax (on income and capital profits) apply. The company does not have the benefit of an annual exemption to reduce its capital profits. However, if the selling company reinvests the proceeds of the sale of the business in a new business, roll-over relief from corporation tax on replacement of business assets is available in much the same way as already described in relation to CGT.

The right for the company to carry forward trading losses under s 393 of the ICTA 1988 is lost on the sale of its business. However, when a company ceases to trade, a trading loss sustained in its final 12 months may be set against profits of any description (income or capital) of the same accounting period or, if the loss is not fully relieved, it can be carried back for up to 3 years, provided the company was then carrying on the same trade.

7.3.2 Extracting the cash from the company

One of the attractions of selling a company by way of share transfer is that the sale price is received directly by the owners of the company, whether they are individual or corporate shareholders. Where, on the other hand, the business of the company is sold, it is the company itself, rather than the owners of the company, which receives the price. Consider, for example, a company (A Ltd) with a single business which has two individual shareholders (Bob and Charlie). D Ltd, which is aware that Bob and Charlie wish to sell A Ltd, agrees to buy its business as a going concern. On completion of the sale of its business to D Ltd, A Ltd will be a mere 'cash shell' in which the net proceeds of sale (ie after deduction of corporation tax) are deposited. Further steps involving an additional tax charge must be taken for this money to end up in the hands of Bob and Charlie (see below). If, instead, D Ltd acquired A Ltd's shares, Bob and Charlie would receive the consideration direct, subject only to paying CGT (see Chapter 11).

Liquidating the company

The shareholders may extract the proceeds of sale of the business by putting the company into voluntary liquidation. On a winding up, however, the shareholders are treated as disposing of their shares and individual shareholders will be liable to CGT (possibly at 40%) on any resultant gain. A corporate shareholder will be liable to corporation tax on any such gain if the disposal is not exempt from tax as a disposal of a substantial shareholding (ie broadly 10% or more of the ordinary share capital – see **11.3.4**). There is, accordingly, a potential double charge to tax where a business sale is followed by the liquidation of the company: a corporation tax charge on the company on the sale of the business and a CGT (or corporation tax) charge on the shareholder on the winding up.

Distribution by dividend

The shareholders may find it more tax efficient for the company to declare a dividend before it is put into liquidation. However, for individual shareholders, this will, once again, involve a second charge to tax (ie in addition to the corporation tax payable by the company on the sale of the business). It is also worth bearing in mind that a pre-liquidation dividend is unlikely to be attractive to individuals disposing of business assets owned for 2 years or more, as their chargeable gains will, in any event, be reduced by maximum taper relief.

If a pre-liquidation dividend is paid, individual shareholders are liable to Schedule F income tax on the gross dividend (being the net dividend plus the tax credit), albeit with the benefit of a tax credit.

Corporate shareholders will not pay corporation tax on the receipt of a dividend from a subsidiary. Where a shareholding will not qualify on disposal for exemption from tax as a substantial shareholding, a pre-liquidation dividend will be the most tax-efficient method of distributing the proceeds of sale, provided there are genuine distributable profits (see **11.3.5**).

Where the shareholders have extracted cash from the company in the form of a pre-liquidation dividend, the ensuing liquidation is less likely to give rise to a charge to CGT (or corporation tax) since the distribution by the company will have reduced the value of the shares.

7.4 IMPLICATIONS FOR THE BUYER OF A BUSINESS

The great advantage to the buyer of acquiring the business of a company rather than its shares is that he does not assume responsibility for all the hidden liabilities of the company. He can therefore save the cost and time involved in carrying out an in-depth investigation into the tax affairs of the company and in negotiating extensive warranties and indemnities.

The tax consequences of acquiring a business are similar whether the buyer is an individual or a company.

7.4.1 Capital allowances

Capital allowances are not restricted to the purchase of brand new assets. The buyer will be able to claim capital allowances on, for example, plant and machinery which he acquires from the seller. The allowances are calculated on the price which the buyer pays for them and not their tax written down value in the seller's hands. Assume, for example, that the seller originally acquired an item of plant and machinery for £8,000 and has received writing down allowances totalling £6,000 up to the date of the sale. On the sale of the business, £4,000 is attributed to this item (ignore the effect of pooling for this purpose). As the seller has sold the asset for more than its tax written down value (ie £2,000), a balancing charge will be levied on him. In the year of the sale, the buyer will receive an allowance based on the purchase price of £4,000.

7.4.2 Trading stock

The amount which the buyer pays for stock or work in progress will be a deductible expense in working out income profits liable to income tax or corporation tax as appropriate.

7.4.3 Base cost for CGT

The price paid by the buyer for chargeable assets of the business will form his base cost for CGT or corporation tax purposes. This contrasts with a share acquisition where the base cost of the chargeable assets of the target company for capital gains purposes will be their original cost to the target. This may be relevant if the buyer is proposing to dispose of certain unwanted assets after the acquisition.

7.4.4 Roll-over relief from CGT (or corporation tax) on replacement of qualifying assets

If the buyer has disposed of qualifying assets in the previous 3 years or is intending to do so in the next 12 months, he will be able to roll any chargeable gain arising on such a disposal into those assets of the acquired business which are themselves qualifying assets.

7.4.5 Apportioning the purchase price

The parties will usually agree initially upon a global consideration for the assets of the business. For tax and stamp duty purposes, however, they will need to negotiate the apportionment of this overall figure between the various assets transferred. Although s 52(4) of the TCGA 1992 requires that any method adopted for this apportionment must be 'just and reasonable', in practice the parties have some flexibility as to the figures upon which they settle.

It will be clear from what has been said above that the seller and buyer may be pulling in different directions on this issue. For example, the buyer may prefer the consideration to be balanced in favour of goodwill, which will not attract stamp duty, but also stock, which will form a deduction from his income profits, and plant and machinery, on which capital allowances will be available. By contrast, the seller may prefer the apportionment to be weighted more in favour of qualifying assets for roll-over relief if he is proposing to reinvest the sale proceeds. Much will depend, of course, on the individual circumstances of the parties. If, for example, the seller has unrelieved trading losses which he would not otherwise be able to use, he may be happy for a relatively high value to be attributed to stock and plant and machinery. The carried forward losses would then be available to absorb some or all of the resulting trading profit.

7.4.6 VAT

Is VAT chargeable?

A taxable person must charge VAT on taxable supplies of goods and services made in the UK in the course or furtherance of a business carried on by him (s 4(1) of the Value Added Tax Act 1994 (VATA 1994)). Prima facie, therefore, on the sale of a business, VAT is chargeable on the stock and capital assets (including goodwill) of the business.

There is, however, a special exemption contained in Art 5 of the Value Added Tax (Special Provisions) Order 1995. This treats the transfer of the whole or part of a business as a going concern as being outside the scope of VAT.

Transfer as a going concern

For the Art 5 exemption to apply, the following two important conditions must be satisfied:

(1)   the assets must be used by the buyer in the same kind of business as that carried on by the seller with no significant break; and

(2)   the buyer must be a taxable person, or become a taxable person as a result of the transfer.

In determining whether the sale is of a business as a going concern or merely assets in the business, regard must be had to all the circumstances including, for example, the following:

(1)   the wording of the acquisition agreement (however, the label which the parties put on the transaction is not conclusive);

(2)   whether goodwill (and the right to use the business name), contracts and customer lists are transferred;

(3)   whether the work-force is transferred;

(4)   whether the buyer can carry on the same type of activities without interruption;

(5)   where part of a business is transferred, whether it is a severable unit, capable of standing on its own.

It is very important to distinguish between the sale of a business as a going concern and a mere transfer of assets for VAT purposes (see **1.2.3**). It used to be common practice where there was any doubt (and, particularly, in the case of a sale of part of a business) for the parties to a transaction to seek a ruling from Customs & Excise as to whether the proposed sale would come within Art 5. Recently, however, Customs & Excise has stated that routine clearance applications will no longer be considered. In future, Customs & Excise will only give an opinion when the transaction has unusual features, to which attention should be drawn in the application. This strict approach requires solicitors to take even greater care than before.

Provision in the acquisition agreement

The seller's solicitor should ensure that in the acquisition agreement the consideration is stated to be exclusive of VAT. Otherwise, if Customs & Excise argues successfully that VAT is chargeable because the Art 5 conditions have not been satisfied, the purchase price will be deemed to be inclusive of VAT (VATA 1994, s 19(2)). The unfortunate result will be that the seller must account for the VAT to Customs & Excise but is unable to recover this from the buyer. In the absence of advance clearance from Customs & Excise, even if the seller believes that the sale comes within Art 5, the seller should seek an indemnity from the buyer against any VAT charge arising from the sale (plus any penalty or interest payable).

If the seller wrongly charges VAT on a sale in respect of which Art 5 applies, the buyer may be unable to recover the tax from Customs & Excise by claiming an offset against input tax (although he should have a right of recovery from the seller).

7.4.7 Stamp duty

Stamp duty is a document-based tax which is payable by the buyer either on the contract for the sale of assets or on the subsequent transfer. Certain assets, however, can be transferred without any liability arising. Although failure to stamp a document gives rise only to a civil penalty (in the shape of a fine), an unstamped document cannot be presented as evidence before a court or tribunal. It is therefore necessary for the sale contract to be duly stamped before it can be used, for example, as evidence in proceedings for breach of warranty.

Assets within s 59 of the Stamp Act 1891

Section 59 of the Stamp Act 1891 charges stamp duty on the contract or agreement for the sale of the following assets:

(1)   any equitable estate or interest in any property whatsoever;

(2)   any estate or interest in any property except, inter alia:

    (a)   land;

    (b)   property outside the UK;

    (c)   marketable securities (see Chapter 11 for stamp duty on shares);

    (d)   goods, wares or merchandise;

    (e)   stock.

On a business transfer, therefore, duty is payable on the dutiable assets of the business such as fixed plant and machinery, cash in a deposit account and, currently, book debts. Duty is also charged on liabilities, such as amounts owing to trade creditors, which are taken over by the buyer. As part of the modernisation of the stamp duty regime, however, transfers of debts should cease to attract duty with effect from late 2003. Transfers of, and agreements to transfer, goodwill and other intellectual property are already exempt from stamp duty.

Assets excepted from s 59

LAND

Although land is excepted from the s 59 charge, it is, nevertheless, subject to stamp duty, not on the contract, but on the subsequent conveyance or transfer (Stamp Act 1891, Sch 1).

GOODS, WARES OR MERCHANDISE AND STOCK

Goods, wares and merchandise (this includes loose plant and machinery of the business) and trading stock are also outside the scope of s 59. Stamp duty is avoided altogether on these assets if title to them is transferred pursuant to the contract by delivery. Consequently, these assets should not be included in a subsequent transfer.

Rate of duty

Stamp duty is payable by the buyer on the relevant consideration at the following rates:

(1)   nil where the relevant consideration does not exceed £60,000;

(2)   1% where the relevant consideration is more than £60,000 but does not exceed £250,000;

(3)   3% where the relevant consideration is more than £250,000 but does not exceed £500,000;

(4)   4% where the relevant consideration exceeds £500,000.

The relevant consideration is the aggregate consideration for all the dutiable items of the business, whether liability is imposed on the contract or the transfer. Where the relevant consideration does not exceed £60,000, £250,000, or £500,000, the relevant instrument (ie the contract and, in the case of land, the subsequent conveyance or transfer) must contain a certificate of value to this effect for the buyer to claim the nil, 1% or 3% rates respectively.

Minimising liability

Stamp duty is payable on the consideration paid for assets transferred by written instrument to the buyer. This consideration will include any liabilities that the buyer assumes. For example, if a business consisting of assets of £750,000 and liabilities of £250,000 is sold to the buyer for £500,000 in cash plus the assumption of liabilities, the consideration on which stamp duty is payable will be £750,000. A stamp duty saving will result, therefore, if the book debts and liabilities remain with the seller, who will be able to use the receipts from the book debts to pay off some or all of the creditors. However, this arrangement may not suit the commercial objectives of the parties (see **5.3.7**).

Since cash on deposit is dutiable, this should be switched to a current account immediately before completion in order to avoid a charge.

7.4.8 Financing the acquisition by borrowing: is tax relief available?

Individual buyer

If an individual borrows money to purchase a share in a partnership, he can obtain relief for interest payments he makes under the loan by treating the interest payments as an income tax deduction. This enables the interest payments to be set off against the total income of the individual. Alternatively, the interest payments can be treated as a deductible expense in arriving at the profits of the partnership (ICTA 1988, s 362).

Corporate buyer

Tax relief on interest payable by a company on a loan to acquire a business will normally be available as a deductible expense under the loan relationship legislation contained in the Finance Act 1996.

7.5 WARRANTIES

Since the buyer does not 'inherit' any of the tax liabilities of the seller of the business (whether the seller is an individual or a company) he does not need the protection of extensive warranties and indemnities in the acquisition agreement. Any warranties that are included are likely to be aimed at eliciting disclosures from the seller, particularly with regard to any concessions or dispensations agreed between the seller and either the Inland Revenue (eg in relation to benefits provided to employees) or Customs & Excise. The buyer will usually also seek assurances that PAYE, national insurance and VAT records are complete and up to date.

PART III

ACQUIRING A COMPANY BY SHARE PURCHASE

Chapter 8

THE ACQUISITION AGREEMENT

8.1 INTRODUCTION

This chapter deals with the structure and content of an agreement for the acquisition of the entire share capital of a company. No two transactions are ever identical but similar considerations are relevant in the drafting of most acquisition agreements. Many of the general principles discussed below apply whether individual owners of a company are selling their shares or a parent company is disposing of its shares in a wholly owned subsidiary. The acquisition may be by individuals or by a company; if the entire share capital is acquired by a company, the target company becomes a wholly owned subsidiary of the buyer.

8.2 STRUCTURE OF THE AGREEMENT

The agreement usually follows the same order as on the acquisition of a business, namely date, parties, operative provisions, schedules and execution by the parties.

8.2.1 Parties

The parties are the seller(s) of the shares (individual or corporate) and the buyer(s) of the shares (individual or corporate). Usually, all the sellers will give warranties to the buyer; however, some sellers, such as trustee shareholders or sellers in the context of a management buy-out, may be unwilling to give warranties (see **4.3.3**). In these circumstances, the parties will be described in the agreement as the seller(s), the warrantor(s) and the buyer(s).

The parties may also include guarantors of the obligations of the seller or the buyer. The seller may, for example, be required to provide a guarantor in relation to his potential liability under the warranties. Where, on the other hand, some part of the purchase price is left outstanding on completion, the seller may insist that the buyer's obligation to pay this amount is guaranteed.

The target company itself is not a party to the agreement; it is, of course, the focus of the transaction which remains intact after the change in its ownership.

8.2.2 Operative provisions and schedules

As with business transfers, the operative provisions will commence with a definitions and interpretations clause. The drafting of the interpretation clause demands attention to detail and the importance of this aspect of the agreement should not be underestimated (see **5.2.2**).

The schedules to the agreement are likely to be more numerous than on a business transfer. Some schedules will contain factual information about the target company

Chapter 8 contents
Introduction
Structure of the
  agreement
Sale of shares
Purchase price
Conditional contracts
Warranties
Completion
Restrictive covenants

(and any subsidiaries) which will not be available to the buyer when preparing the initial draft of the agreement.

8.3 SALE OF SHARES

8.3.1 Agreement to sell

In contrast to a business acquisition, where all the assets and liabilities to be transferred must be separately identified, the part of the agreement dealing with the transfer of the shares is short. Each of the sellers agrees to sell to the buyer his shares in the target (details of their relative shareholdings will normally be contained in a schedule) free from all charges, encumbrances, liens, etc. Alternatively, the sale can be expressed to be with full or limited title guarantee which will imply covenants for title under the Law of Property (Miscellaneous Provisions) Act 1994.

8.3.2 Simultaneous completion

The agreement will usually provide that the buyer will not be obliged to buy any of the shares unless the purchase of all the shares is completed simultaneously.

8.3.3 Pre-emption rights

The buyer's solicitor should check whether the articles of the target company contain any restrictions on the transfer of shares. It is common for the articles of a private company to oblige a member proposing to transfer his shares to offer them pro rata to the existing members. Although the articles invariably allow for the pre-emption provisions to be overridden by special resolution, it is usually easier for the sellers to waive their rights. The acquisition agreement will often contain a clause whereby the sellers agree to waive any pre-emption rights they may have, whether conferred by the articles or otherwise (the rights may be incorporated in a shareholders' agreement rather than in the articles).

8.4 PURCHASE PRICE

The acquisition agreement will stipulate the amount of the purchase price, the form that it will take and the timing of the payment. The form which the consideration takes may affect the asking price for the shares. The seller may, for example, be willing to accept a lower price if the deal is structured in such a way that he receives favourable tax treatment.

8.4.1 Form

The consideration may take the form of cash, shares or loan notes or a combination of these.

Cash

Cash is the most common form of consideration and one which will usually suit the seller. Payment in cash may involve the buyer in complex financial arrangements which the buyer's solicitor must ensure are properly in place before allowing his client to enter into any commitment to acquire the target company.

Shares

A company which is acquiring shares may wish to pay for them by issuing shares in itself to the seller (a 'share for share' exchange). The seller will only accept consideration in this form if the shares are readily marketable, ie they can in the future be realised for cash. This rules out shares in most private companies which will rarely have a ready market and will often, in practice, be subject to restrictions on transfer. Shares in companies listed on The Stock Exchange may, on the other hand, be virtually equivalent to cash for the seller.

A share for share exchange may suit both parties for different reasons. The buyer will often prefer to issue shares rather than, for example, increase its borrowing commitments or fund the acquisition by making disposals. The seller, on the other hand, may be attracted by the tax treatment of a share for share exchange: if certain conditions are fulfilled, the seller is able to roll over any capital gain made on the disposal of shares in the target, thus deferring the capital gains tax which he would otherwise pay at this time until he disposes of the shares in the acquiring company received in exchange (see **11.3.4**).

Where shares are issued as consideration, the agreement should specify how they rank with the other shares of the acquiring company and what rights the seller will have to any dividend declared in relation to a period in which completion falls.

If the buyer is worried that the market for its shares may be adversely affected by the seller disposing of all the consideration shares at once, it may insist on a clause in the agreement restricting the seller from, for example, disposing of more than a certain percentage of his allocation within a specified period after completion.

Where the acquiring company wishes to issue shares as consideration but the seller is only really interested in receiving cash for the target company, this can be achieved, albeit in a roundabout way, by what is called a 'vendor placing'. This is an arrangement whereby the acquiring company issues shares to the seller but arranges (through its financial advisers) for the shares to be sold on immediately to institutional investors. The acquiring company undertakes in the acquisition agreement that the sale of the consideration shares will yield a specified sum. For further reading, see LPC Resource Book *Corporate Finance: Public Companies and the City* (Jordans).

Loan notes

An acquiring company may issue loan notes to the seller for the purchase price or part of it, usually on terms that the seller can demand repayment of all or part at six-monthly intervals after a certain period from completion (eg 12 months). It may suit the seller to receive staggered payments in this way with interest on the balance outstanding, particularly as roll-over relief from CGT is available on a 'share for loan note' exchange (see **11.3.4**).

8.4.2 When is the purchase price paid?

Completion accounts

In many cases, the purchase price will be payable in full on completion. However, it is also common for the parties to provide for accounts to be produced after completion and for the purchase price stated in the agreement to be adjusted once they have agreed these accounts. The buyer may have based his valuation of the target company on the basis of its current earnings or net assets, using the most recent set of audited accounts or, possibly, unaudited management accounts for this information. The buyer may want confirmation (in the form of completion accounts) that the figures on which he based his valuation have not altered significantly since the date to which the original accounts were made up.

The agreement may provide for a maximum amount of consideration to be paid by the buyer on completion and for the buyer to be entitled to a repayment if the net assets or profitability, as revealed by the completion accounts, fall short of amounts on which the valuation was based. If, for example, the parties agreed their valuation of the target by applying a multiplier of 8 to the 'earnings' of the target, the agreement may provide for the purchase price to be adjusted by applying the same multiplier to any shortfall in earnings identified by the completion accounts. In other words, for every £1 shortfall in the earnings, the seller would agree to repay £8 to the buyer. The parties may agree that a certain proportion of the amount paid on completion is held in a joint account pending agreement of the completion accounts.

A typical clause will provide for the following:

(1) completion accounts to be drawn up within a specified period after completion (eg one month). The seller's accountant, who is likely to have been the target company's auditor until completion, is usually nominated to prepare the accounts and will be instructed to do so using a basis which is consistent with the latest set of audited accounts;

(2) the buyer (or the seller if the buyer's accountant has prepared the accounts) and his accountant to have the right to dispute the accounts within specified time-limits;

(3) in the absence of agreement, the matter to be referred to an independent firm of accountants acting as experts.

Earn outs

The term 'earn out' is used to describe an arrangement whereby at least part of the consideration is left outstanding on completion and is determined by reference to the results of the target for a specified period after completion (eg for the three accounting periods following completion). Earn outs are often considered appropriate where the sellers of the shares continue to manage the target company after completion. Earn outs can also be used in business acquisitions (see **5.4.3**).

Determining part of the purchase price on the basis of future profits not only avoids the buyer having to pay 'over the odds' for a target which fails to perform as expected, but also acts as a motivating factor for the sellers/managers of the target who are staying on, post acquisition, and on whom the business (particularly one that is 'employee orientated') may be heavily reliant.

The earn out clause will usually provide for accounts to be prepared by the buyer's accountant (ie the target company's auditor after completion) for relevant accounting periods after completion and for these to be submitted to the seller and his accountant. The clause should specify the basis on which the accounts are to be prepared and contain precise definitions of those items which will determine the amount of the deferred consideration (eg 'net profit' or 'earnings'). As with completion accounts, the parties will incorporate a mechanism for resolving disputes, such as a reference to an independent accountant.

The parties may agree that the deferred consideration is to be in the form of shares issued to the seller by the acquiring company. The buyer may also insist on the right to deduct any warranty claim which he is able to substantiate from the deferred consideration.

A difficulty with an earn out arrangement is that the sellers who continue to manage the target after completion and the buyer may be pulling in different directions. The former will be keen to maximise profitability in the earn out period, whereas the latter will often be more concerned that decisions are taken which will benefit the target in the long term, at the expense, perhaps, of short-term profits. The parties may try to meet this problem by defining the objectives of the company during the earn out period and agreeing to certain limitations on the conduct of the business post completion. The buyer may, for example, undertake not to dispose of the whole or part of the business nor to permit any non-arm's length trading between the target and the buyer (or other members of an acquiring company's group) during this period.

Instalments as a means of financing the acquisition

The seller may agree to receive payment by instalments to assist the buyer in financing the acquisition but will usually demand interest on the outstanding amount and some form of security, such as a guarantee from a third party. If a charge is to be taken over the assets of the target, this constitutes financial assistance by the company for the acquisition of its shares, which is only permitted if special procedural requirements are complied with (see **9.3**).

8.4.3 Division between sellers

The amount of the purchase price payable to each seller (whether immediately or on a deferred basis) will usually be stated in a schedule to the agreement.

8.5 CONDITIONAL CONTRACTS

As with business transfers, it is desirable for exchange and completion of a share transfer to be simultaneous. However, the agreement may have to be made conditional on one or more of the following matters, for example:

(1) the Inland Revenue issuing a clearance, for example, in relation to roll-over relief from CGT on a 'share for share' exchange (see **11.3.4**);
(2) the Office of Fair Trading notifying the buyer that it does not intend to refer the acquisition to the Competition Commission (see **2.2.5**);
(3) the shareholders of a corporate buyer passing a resolution, for example, authorising the directors to issue shares to the seller in consideration for the shares in the target;

(4)   a substantial customer confirming that it will not exercise a contractual right to terminate an agreement with the target company on the change in control of the target company.

It was noted in the context of business transfers that the agreement should state which party has the responsibility of trying to procure the satisfaction of each condition and a date by which each condition must be met (or waived by the party for whose benefit it was included), in default of which the agreement terminates (see **5.5**).

The buyer is likely to want to have some influence on the conduct of the target company's business during the period between exchange and completion, particularly if he considers the consent or clearance which is awaited to be a mere formality. The buyer may insist that the seller supplies him with any information concerning the business and that he (or, in the case of a corporate buyer, an authorised representative) is allowed to attend all board meetings of the target company. The buyer may also seek undertakings from the seller in relation to the carrying on of the business, for example, that the seller will procure that the company does not do any of the following (unless the buyer gives prior consent):

(1)   appoint any additional directors;
(2)   lend or borrow money except in relation to routine matters in the ordinary course of business or grant any mortgage, charge or debenture over its assets;
(3)   settle any claim or dispute;
(4)   acquire or agree to acquire any property, commit itself to any capital expenditure or enter into any hire-purchase or leasing arrangements;
(5)   enter into any agreement or dispose of all or part of its business or assets except in relation to routine matters in the ordinary course of its business;
(6)   alter the terms of employment of any employee or director.

If the buyer is given a substantial degree of control in the period between exchange and completion, the seller may be justified in objecting to any proposal by the buyer to include a right to withdraw from the agreement in the event of any warranty becoming incorrect prior to completion (at least where this arises as a result of the exercise of control by the buyer).

8.6 WARRANTIES

8.6.1 Some areas covered by warranties

Many of the warranties which were considered in the context of a business acquisition will be equally as appropriate on a share acquisition. The list of warranties is, however, likely to be longer in a share purchase agreement as a direct result of the greater degree of risk which the buyer of shares assumes. The nature of the seller's liability for breach of warranty and limitations on that liability which he may seek to include in the agreement were considered in Chapter 4.

Constitution of the company

Particulars of the authorised and issued share capital of the target company will usually be included in a schedule to the agreement. Each seller will be required to warrant that he is entitled to transfer the full legal and beneficial ownership in the shares to the buyer and that the shares are not subject to any option, lien, charge or other encumbrance (alternatively, this may be included in the operative clause by which the sellers agree to transfer the shares with full title guarantee). The buyer will also want confirmation of, inter alia, the following:

(1) that the statutory books of the company have been properly kept and are accurate and up to date;

(2) that the memorandum and articles (attached to the disclosure letter) are true and complete;

(3) that all documents and returns required to be filed with the Registrar of Companies have been duly filed and were correct;

(4) that the directors listed in the agreement (usually in a schedule) are the only directors of the company.

Accounts

The buyer may seek to include, inter alia, the following warranties in relation to the most recent set of audited accounts:

(1) that they have been prepared using the same bases and policies of accounting as were used in preparing the accounts for the previous three accounting periods;

(2) that they comply with the CA 1985, as amended, and with all relevant standards set by the accountancy profession and contained in Financial Reporting Standards and Statements of Standard Accounting Practice and are not affected by any exceptional or non-recurring item;

(3) that they give a true and fair view of the assets and liabilities (including contingent, unquantified or disputed liabilities) of the company at the date of the balance sheet and of its profits for the relevant accounting period.

The seller is advised to be wary of the scope of warranties relating to the accounts. For example, the seller will often resist the inclusion of a warranty that management accounts are accurate or give a true and fair view. It is arguable that the buyer is not justified in placing much reliance on management accounts, which will have been drawn up for a specific management purpose and will not have been audited.

Financial matters

The buyer may seek assurances from the seller that the company has not done any of the following, for example, since the last accounts date:

(1) incurred any liabilities except in the ordinary course of business;

(2) incurred or agreed to incur any capital expenditure or disposed of any capital assets;

(3) paid or declared any dividend or made any other distribution.

The buyer may also seek warranties in relation to the debtors and creditors revealed in the accounts, for example, that the company has paid its creditors in accordance with their credit terms and that the debtors have paid their debts in full. He may also ask for assurances that any amounts owing to the company on completion will be fully recoverable in the ordinary course of business (possibly with a long-stop date of, say, 3 months) and that no amounts owing by the company on completion have been due for more than a specified period (eg 2 months).

Trading

The buyer may seek warranties (or disclosures) in relation to, inter alia, the following matters:

(1) that the business of the company has been carried on in the ordinary course and that its turnover, financial position or trading position has not deteriorated since the date of the last accounts (the seller should resist the extension of this warranty to include 'trading prospects');

(2) that the company is not engaged in any litigation or arbitration proceedings as claimant or defendant and no such proceedings are pending, threatened or, to the seller's knowledge, likely to arise;

(3) that the sellers have no knowledge, information or belief that any supplier will cease to supply the company (or substantially reduce supplies) after completion;

(4) that the sellers have no knowledge, information or belief that any customer will cease to deal with the company (or substantially reduce the level of business) after completion;

(5) that compliance with the terms of the agreement will not result in a breach of any agreement to which the company is a party, relieve any person from any obligation to the company, or enable any person to determine any right or benefit enjoyed by the company or to exercise any right;

(6) that the company has obtained all licences and consents required to carry on its business properly and is not in breach of their terms;

(7) that the company is not a party to any contract or arrangement of an unusual or loss-making nature or which it cannot terminate on 60 days' notice or less;

(8) that the company has not supplied or manufactured products which, in any material respect, are defective or do not comply with any warranties or representations made by it (whether express or implied);

(9) that the company has conducted its business in accordance with all applicable laws and regulations.

Taxation

Most tax matters will be dealt with separately, either in a deed of tax indemnity or by means of tax covenants. Whichever method is employed, the seller will often be obliged to compensate the buyer for any breaches on an indemnity basis (see **4.3.2**).

Where, however, the buyer is keen to elicit disclosures from the seller, he will include some tax warranties; problems may then be revealed which he is able to use as a lever to renegotiate the purchase price (or which may even prompt him to withdraw from the acquisition). In particular, the buyer will want confirmation that the company is not in dispute with the Inland Revenue or Customs & Excise and has complied with obligations to, inter alia, file returns, make payments and operate the PAYE system. The buyer may also require a warranty that the latest accounts make full provision or reserve for all taxation which could be assessed on the company in respect of the period covered by the accounts.

Tax matters (including the contents of the tax indemnity or tax covenants) are considered further in Chapter 11.

Assets other than land

The buyer may require the following warranties, for example, in relation to the underlying assets of the company other than land:

(1) that the company still owns and has good title to all the assets included in the latest audited accounts (except for current assets subsequently sold in the ordinary course of business) and has good title to all assets which it has since acquired;

(2) that plant, machinery, vehicles, etc are in a good state of repair and have been properly and regularly maintained;

(3) that the stock-in-trade of the company is in good condition and capable of being sold in the ordinary course of business by the company at prices contained in its current price list;

(4) that the stock of raw materials and finished goods held by the company are adequate (and not excessive) in relation to the trading requirements of the business on completion.

Warranties are constantly being tailored to take into account particular concerns of the buyer. For example, in the run-up to the millennium, warranties were included to the effect that the computer systems of the target company were 'year 2K-compliant', the buyer being wary of the potential costs associated with the so-called 'millennium bug'.

Insurance

The buyer will usually require warranties that full particulars of the company's insurances are included in the disclosure letter, that they are in full force and effect, and that they contain adequate cover against such risks as prudent companies carrying on the same type of business would normally cover by insurance. The buyer will also seek a warranty that no insurance claims are outstanding or pending and that the seller is not aware of any circumstances likely to give rise to a claim.

Intellectual property

Details of patents, trade marks, service marks, design rights and copyrights owned or used by the company will often be contained in the disclosure letter (with copies of agreements relating to these intellectual property rights attached). Warranties will be included that there are no outstanding claims against the company for breach of the intellectual property rights of any other person and, that, to the seller's knowledge, the company is not in breach of any such rights in operating the business. The buyer may also require the seller to warrant that he is not aware of any infringement of the intellectual property rights of the company by any third party.

Land

Typical warranties which may be included in the acquisition agreement in relation to land and property owned and used by the company are considered in Chapter 3 (see **3.9.1**). The scope of the warranties will depend on the extent of the buyer's property investigation and on whether the seller's solicitor is prepared to give certificates of title.

Employees and pensions

The effect of a share acquisition on the target company's employees and on their pension rights, and the provisions which are commonly included in the acquisition agreement are considered in Chapter 10.

Information disclosed

Two controversial warranties relate to information disclosed by the seller to the buyer. First, the buyer may include in the initial draft of the agreement a warranty that all information about the target company provided to the buyer or his advisers prior to the parties entering into the contract is true and accurate in all material respects. This is clearly a wide-ranging warranty which would involve the difficulty of identifying the information which the seller and his advisers have passed to the buyer. A compromise might be for the warranty to be restricted to information contained in the disclosure letter.

Secondly, the buyer may seek to impose a warranty that the seller has disclosed everything which might materially affect the value of the shares or which might influence a buyer in deciding whether to proceed with the acquisition. This 'catch-all' warranty will often be resisted by the seller on the basis that it would cover matters which the buyer can be expected to find out for himself (eg information in the public domain) and information which the seller may not realise is significant.

8.6.2 Warranty protection on hive-downs

Where a company is in receivership, administration or liquidation, rather than sell the assets or business of the company direct to a buyer, the receiver, etc may transfer the viable parts of the business to a wholly owned subsidiary specially formed for the purpose and then sell the shares in the subsidiary to the buyer (see **1.3.8**). Although the transaction proceeds as a share acquisition, in terms of risks to the buyer it is more akin to a business transfer as the buyer does not inherit the past liabilities of the insolvent company. There is little risk of the hived-down company acquired by the buyer having any 'skeletons in the cupboard' since the only 'history' which it will have is the hive-down agreement with the parent company.

Receivers, etc, will be willing to give only very limited warranties. On the sale of a hive-down company, these are likely to be restricted to the following:

(1) the shares are the property of the selling company and are sold free from all charges, liens and encumbrances;
(2) the shares comprise the whole of the issued share capital of the company;
(3) copies of the memorandum and articles supplied to the buyer are complete and accurate and no alteration has been made to them since incorporation;
(4) the statutory books of the company (including the register of members) are up to date and accurate;
(5) the company has not at any time had any subsidiaries or been a subsidiary of any company other than the seller;
(6) the only activities carried on by the company relate to the business transferred to it by the seller.

8.6.3 Management buy-outs

A management buy-out may proceed as a business acquisition or as a share acquisition. The reluctance of sellers to give full warranties to the buyers on the grounds of the buyers' knowledge of the target has already been mentioned in the context of a business acquisition (see **5.9.4**). The dangers inherent in the buyers accepting this argument are, of course, even greater on a share acquisition.

Some management buy-outs involve the buyers acquiring shares in a hive-down company (ie the assets of the parent company of which they were the former managers have been transferred to it), in which case there is less need for the buyers to insist on extensive warranty protection.

8.7 COMPLETION

Completion may take place simultaneously with the exchange of the acquisition agreement or, if the contract is conditional, within a specified time of the fulfilment (or waiver) of the condition. The acquisition agreement will usually detail the documents which each party must deliver to the other and the steps which each party must take on completion. Agreed forms of minutes of board and general meetings of the target company required to be held on completion may also be attached to the agreement (for details of the procedure on completion, see Chapter 9).

8.8 RESTRICTIVE COVENANTS

The share acquisition agreement will often restrict sellers from competing with the target company, soliciting customers, suppliers and employees of the target company, and using or disclosing confidential information (see **4.8**).

Chapter 9

PROCEDURAL ASPECTS AND STATUTORY REQUIREMENTS

9.1 INTRODUCTION

Chapter 9 contents
Introduction
Compliance with the
   Financial Services and
   Markets Act 2000
Compliance with the
   Companies Act 1985
Completion

The roles of the buyer's solicitor and the seller's solicitor in an acquisition were discussed in Chapter 2. This chapter deals with provisions in the FSMA 2000 and the CA 1985 which may be relevant on the acquisition of a company by share transfer, and outlines procedures before, on and after completion.

9.2 COMPLIANCE WITH THE FINANCIAL SERVICES AND MARKETS ACT 2000

The Financial Services Act 1986 (FSA 1986) introduced a regime of consumer protection to regulate persons carrying on investment business through a system of self-regulation. Those conducting investment business, as defined (eg giving advice in relation to the purchase of listed public company shares), were required to obtain authorisation to do so from the appropriate organisation. In the case of solicitors, this meant applying annually for an investment business certificate from The Law Society.

In 1997, the Government decided that the system of regulation required an overhaul. In particular it was felt that there had been too much devolution of control. The solution was to create a single regulator (the Financial Services Authority) which would oversee all financial and banking services and provide framework legislation for the new system (namely the FSMA 2000).

Although the new legislation in certain circumstances makes life a bit easier for solicitors they must still be aware of the effect of the FSMA 2000. In particular, solicitors must be aware of when they need authorisation (see **9.2.2**) and when they should seek the help of others with the requisite authorisation in order to carry out acquisitions work (see **9.2.1**).

9.2.1 Investment advertisements and unsolicited calls

The proposal to acquire the shares of a private company may arise in a number of ways: the seller may, for example, have a particular buyer in contemplation or the initial approach may come from the buyer. It may be, however, that the seller is searching for potential buyers for the company and wishes to bring the possibility of a sale to their attention. In these circumstances, the seller and his advisers must be careful not to contravene the provisions of the FSMA 2000 relating to investment advertisements and unsolicited calls.

The basic restriction

Section 21 of the FSMA 2000 makes it a criminal offence for any person other than an authorised person to 'communicate an invitation or inducement to engage in investment activity' unless its contents have been approved by an authorised person. Any investment agreement entered into as a result of the breach is rendered unenforceable (although the court has discretion to permit enforcement in certain circumstances).

What sort of activities are covered by the restriction?

This would seem to include approaches by a seller to potential buyers in the hope of inducing them to enter into negotiations for the acquisition of shares in the target company. The consequences of breach are serious so the seller should seek the approval of an authorised person if there is any possibility of the section applying. An example of an authorised person used in these circumstances would be a merchant banker.

9.2.2 Regulated activities

If a firm finds that it is involving itself in 'mainstream regulated activities' it must obtain authorisation, direct from the Financial Services Authority, for each specific type of activity with which it is involved.

'Mainstream regulated activities' are activities involving defined financial matters as a stand-alone service.

The practical effect of the new legislation is that most solicitors firms will be exempt from the requirement to be authorised as they are unlikely to be providing regulated activities as a stand-alone service. However, if they are involving themselves in 'non-mainstream regulated activities' as an incidental part of their legal services, The Law Society will supervise the provision of such services and the Financial Services Authority will in turn monitor the effectiveness of such supervision.

The FSMA 2000 is considered in more detail in the LPC Resource Book *Corporate Finance: Public Companies and the City* (Jordans).

9.3 COMPLIANCE WITH THE COMPANIES ACT 1985

9.3.1 The financial assistance rules

Section 151 of the CA 1985 prohibits a company from giving financial assistance for the purchase of its own shares. The consequences of breaching this rule are serious (see below) and it is, therefore, vital that every acquisition of a company by share purchase is analysed carefully to ensure compliance. The rules are complex in their application and extend to financial assistance given before, at the same time as, and after the acquisition.

The prohibitions

FINANCIAL ASSISTANCE BEFORE OR AT THE SAME TIME AS THE ACQUISITION

Section 151(1) states that:

'... where a person is acquiring or is proposing to acquire shares in a company, it is not lawful for the company or any of its subsidiaries to give financial assistance directly or indirectly for the purpose of that acquisition before or at the same time as the acquisition takes place.'

FINANCIAL ASSISTANCE AFTER THE ACQUISITION

Section 151(2) states that:

'... where a person has acquired shares in a company and any liability has been incurred (by that or any other person), for the purpose of that acquisition, it is not lawful for the company or any of its subsidiaries to give financial assistance directly or indirectly for the purpose of reducing or discharging the liability so incurred.'

'FINANCIAL ASSISTANCE'

Financial assistance is defined in s 152(1)(a) as meaning:

'(i)   financial assistance given by way of gift,
(ii)   financial assistance given by way of guarantee, security or indemnity other than an idemnity in respect of the indemnifier's own neglect or default or by way of release or waiver,
(iii)   financial assistance given by way of loan or any other agreement under which any of the obligations of the person giving the assistance are to be fulfilled at a time when in accordance with the agreement any obligation of another party to the agreement remains unfulfilled, or by way of the novation of, or the assignment of rights arising under a loan or such other agreement, or
(iv)   any other financial assistance given by a company the net assets of which are thereby reduced to a material extent or which has no net assets.'

Some examples

The following arrangements fall within the general prohibition on financial assistance:

(1)   the target company makes a loan to the buyer to enable him to buy shares in the target. This is an obvious example of direct financial assistance in breach of s 151(1);

(2)   the target company makes a loan to the buyer to enable him to repay an earlier loan taken out to acquire shares in the target. This breaches s 151(2) as the target is giving financial assistance to the buyer to enable him to discharge a liability incurred for the purpose of acquiring shares in the target;

(3)   a subsidiary of the target makes a loan to the buyer to enable him to buy shares in the target. Section 151 prohibits the giving of financial assistance by a subsidiary of the company in which shares are being acquired;

(4)   the target company makes a loan to a subsidiary of the buyer which 'on-loans' this money to the buyer to enable it to buy shares in the target. This is an example of indirect financial assistance which is prohibited by the rules;

(5)   a charge is taken over the assets of the target company as security for a loan taken out by the buyer to enable him to buy shares in the target. This falls within the definition of financial assistance in s 152(1)(a)(ii);

(6) the seller takes a charge over the assets of the target company as security for part of the purchase price which has been left outstanding on completion. This again falls within s 152(1)(a)(ii);

(7) the target company acquires assets from the buyer for more than their market value to put the buyer in funds to acquire shares in the target. This falls within s 152(1)(a)(i) as there is an element of gift by the target in paying over the market value, and s 152(1)(a)(iv) if the target company's net assets are reduced to a material extent. If, on the other hand, the target pays market value, this does not come within the definition of financial assistance unless the target company has no net assets;

(8) the target company, prior to completion, sells an asset to the buyer at an undervalue. This again meets the definition of financial assistance in s 152(1)(a)(i), and s 152(1)(a)(iv) if either the target has no net assets or its net assets are reduced to a material extent.

Exceptions

Section 153 of the CA 1985 sets out a number of transactions which are not prohibited by s 151.

THE PRINCIPAL OR LARGER PURPOSE EXCEPTION

Section 153(1) provides that financial assistance is not in breach of s 151(1) if:

> '(a) the company's principal purpose in giving that assistance is not to give it for the purpose of the acquisition, or the giving of the assistance for that purpose is but an incidental part of some larger purpose of the company, and
>
> (b) the assistance is given in good faith in the interests of the company.'

Section 153(2) provides an equivalent exemption in relation to financial assistance given after the acquisition within s 151(2).

It is submitted that the ambit of these exceptions is so unclear that it is dangerous to rely on them. The House of Lords gave a very narrow interpretation of the 'incidental part of some larger purpose' part of the exception in *Brady v Brady* [1988] 2 All ER 617. Lord Oliver made it clear that a buyer's view that the target company would be much more profitable after the change in ownership would not be regarded as a 'larger purpose' when he said:

> '... the financial and commercial advantages flowing from the acquisition, whilst they may form the reason for forming the purpose of providing assistance are a by-product of it rather than an independent purpose of which the assistance can properly be considered to be an incident.'

DIVIDENDS

Section 153(3) provides a number of other exceptions to the general prohibition on financial assistance. Perhaps the most important of these is the exception for

> 'a distribution of a company's assets by way of dividend lawfully made or a distribution made in the course of the company's winding up' (s 153(3)(a)).

In order to facilitate a sale, a target company may pay a 'pre-sale dividend' to its shareholders prior to completion of the acquisition, thereby reducing the price of the target company payable by the buyer. The exception in s 153(3)(a) prevents this arrangement being unlawful financial assistance. Similarly, dividends declared after completion which enable the buyer to discharge loans taken out to acquire shares in the target will also come within the exception.

OTHER EXCEPTIONS

Other exceptions include:

(1) where a company issues bonus shares;
(2) where a company redeems or buys back its own shares in accordance with the CA 1985;
(3) where a company makes a loan in the ordinary course of a lending business;
(4) where a company makes a loan to its employees (other than directors) to enable them to buy fully paid shares in the company or its holding company;
(5) where a company provides money to bona fide employees or former employees (including directors) for the purchase of its shares as part of an employee share scheme.

Special relaxation for private companies: the 'whitewash procedure'

By following a special procedure (commonly known as the 'whitewash procedure') outlined in ss 155–158, a private company is able to give financial assistance to the buyer for the acquisition of its shares (or, if it is a subsidiary, for shares in its holding company provided the holding company is itself a private company and there is no intermediate public company).

This procedure can be used, however, only if:

- either the company has net assets which are not reduced by the financial assistance, or, to the extent that net assets are reduced, the assistance is provided out of distributable profits. It should be noted that the giving of guarantees by the company will not generally reduce its net assets for this purpose; and
- the correct procedure is followed.

The procedural requirements are as follows.

(1) The directors of the company giving the financial assistance must all make a statutory declaration. Generally, the declaration must contain a statement that the company will be able to pay its debts as they fall due during the year immediately following the date on which the assistance is proposed to be given.
(2) A report by the company's auditors must be annexed to the declaration, stating that the auditors are not aware of anything to indicate that the directors' opinion is unreasonable in all the circumstances.
(3) Within 7 days of the date of the statutory declaration, the members of the company must pass a special resolution approving the assistance. If the assistance is being given by a subsidiary for the acquisition of shares in its holding company, the holding company must also approve the assistance by special resolution (in this case, the directors of the holding company must also swear a statutory declaration). A special resolution by the company giving the assistance is not required, however, if that company is a wholly owned subsidiary (see Chapter 12 for this definition), but its directors must still swear a statutory declaration supported by an auditor's report.
(4) Where all those entitled to vote at the meeting vote in favour of the resolution, the company can give the financial assistance immediately. It can also do so where a special resolution is not required.
(5) In all other cases, the financial assistance must not be given before the expiry of 4 weeks from the date of the special resolution and not later than 8 weeks from the date of the directors' statutory declaration. Holders of not less than 10% in nominal value of the company's share capital or any class of it may apply to court for the cancellation of the special resolution within 28 days of the passing

of the resolution. In the event of such an application, the financial assistance must not be given until the court has determined the application.

(6) The company must file the statutory declaration and auditors' report at the Companies Registry at the same time as filing the special resolution. If a special resolution is not required (ie the assisting company is a wholly owned subsidiary – see above), that company must file these documents within 15 days after the directors make the declaration.

If it is contemplated that the whitewash procedure be used to authorise the giving of financial assistance by a target company on completion of a share acquisition, it is important that the appropriate steps are taken in the correct order. Any directors who are to resign on completion will not be willing to swear the statutory declaration. Similarly, the auditors will not normally be prepared to provide a report if they are to be replaced as part of the completion arrangements. In these circumstances, the statutory declaration will have to be made after new directors and auditors have been appointed.

Consequences of breach

Breach of s 151 is a criminal offence; the company is liable to a fine and every officer who is in default is liable to imprisonment for up to 2 years upon conviction on indictment, or a fine, or both.

The transaction itself is void and unenforceable (this includes any security or guarantee given in breach of the rules) and directors who were parties to the breach are liable to compensate the company for any loss. A third party recipient of the financial assistance may be required to account for any money or property received in breach of s 151 as a constructive trustee.

9.3.2 Issue of shares by buyer

Where a company which is acquiring a target proposes to issue shares to the seller as consideration, resolutions of its shareholders may be required to increase the share capital (CA 1985, s 121) and to authorise the directors to issue the shares (CA 1985, s 80).

The statutory pre-emption rights contained in s 89 of the CA 1985 do not apply to non-cash consideration. However, the articles of the acquiring company may oblige the directors to offer shares pro rata to existing members whether they are issued for cash or otherwise. A special resolution may, therefore, be necessary to override the pre-emption rights or to change the article conferring them.

9.3.3 Directors' interests

Section 320 of the CA 1985, which was discussed in **5.10.2** in the context of business acquisitions, may also be relevant in the context of a share acquisition. Consider, for example, the following transactions.

> *Example 1*
> A Ltd is acquiring the entire share capital of Target Limited. B is a shareholder in Target Limited and a director of A Ltd.

A Ltd is acquiring non-cash assets from one of its directors. If B's shares in Target Limited are of the 'requisite value', an ordinary resolution of the shareholders of A Ltd is required to authorise the transaction.

Example 2

A Ltd is acquiring the entire share capital of Target Limited. B is a director of A Ltd. C, who is B's son, is a shareholder in Target Limited.

Consent of the shareholders of A Ltd may again be required because A Ltd is acquiring non-cash assets from a person 'connected' with one of its directors if C is under the age of 18 (the definition of 'connected persons' for this purpose is contained in s 346(3)(a) of the CA 1985).

Example 3

D Ltd sells shares in Target Limited to E, who is a director of D Ltd.

D Ltd is disposing of non-cash assets to one of its directors. If D Ltd's shares in Target Limited are of the 'requisite value', consent of the shareholders of D Ltd is required by s 320.

A director who is directly or indirectly interested in a contract or proposed contract with the company should also remember to declare his interest to the board in accordance with s 317 and to comply with any relevant provisions of the company's articles (eg restricting him from voting or counting in the quorum of a board meeting discussing the contract).

9.3.4 Payments to directors in connection with the transfer of shares by way of compensation for loss of office

Payments made to a director in connection with a transfer of the company's shares by way of compensation for loss of office may be governed by s 314. This section applies if the transfer of shares results from one of the following:

(1) an offer made to the general body of shareholders;
(2) an offer made by or on behalf of some other body corporate with a view to the company becoming its subsidiary or a subsidiary of its holding company;
(3) an offer made by or on behalf of an individual with a view to his obtaining the right to exercise or control the exercise of not less than one-third of the voting power at any general meeting of the company;
(4) any offer which is conditional on acceptance to a given extent.

Section 314 provides that the director concerned must take reasonable steps to ensure that particulars of the proposed payment are sent to shareholders with the offer and that the director is only entitled to receive the payment if it is approved by ordinary resolution of a meeting of the holders of the shares to which the offer relates.

A director who receives a sum in breach of these requirements holds it on trust for the shareholders who have sold their shares as a result of the offer. Section 314 does not apply to bona fide payments by way of damages for breach of contract.

It is also provided (s 316(2)) that if the price which is offered to the director for his shares is in excess of the price obtainable by other holders of like shares, the excess is deemed to be compensation for loss of office or consideration for or in connection with his retirement from office. This provision is designed to prevent compensation to a director being 'dressed up' as part of the purchase price of his shares.

9.3.5 Service contracts for directors

After a target company has been acquired or as part of the completion arrangements, new directors may be appointed and granted service contracts or existing directors may be awarded fresh contracts. If these contracts are to last for more than 5 years, consent of the members by ordinary resolution is required under s 319 of the CA 1985 (see **5.10.2**).

9.3.6 Interests of employees

Section 309 of the CA 1985 obliges directors to have regard to the interests of the company's employees in general. The directors of a target company should, therefore, try to strike a balance between the interests of the members and those of the employees when taking decisions relating to the share acquisition (eg at the completion board meeting). The directors owe this duty to the company and not to the employees, who are unable, therefore, to take any direct action to enforce it.

9.4 COMPLETION

The parties will usually aim to complete the acquisition on the same day as they sign the agreement. However, the parties may enter into the agreement conditionally on certain events taking place, such as the Inland Revenue granting tax clearances or third parties giving consents (eg customers whose contracts with the target contain a 'change of control' clause). The acquisition agreement will, in any event, set out the matters which are to be dealt with and the documents which are to be handed over on completion. The parties' solicitors may also agree a detailed completion agenda (the first draft is usually prepared by the buyer's solicitor) with forms of minutes of completion board and general meetings of the target attached. The remainder of this chapter will deal with the final preparations of both parties, the completion meeting itself and post-completion formalities.

9.4.1 Preparations by the seller or his solicitor

Once the seller has obtained all necessary consents and tax clearances and has agreed with the buyer a date for completion, he and his solicitor will need to make a number of preparations for completion.

Statutory books and filing requirements

The seller should ensure that the statutory books of the target company, which will be handed over on completion, are complete and up to date. In particular, the registers of members, directors and directors' interests in shares and debentures should be accurate, the minutes properly written up, stock transfer forms duly stamped, and share certificates available for all the issued shares of the target. It is preferable that these matters are sorted out in advance rather than cause problems on completion or involve the seller in warranty claims after completion.

The seller should also check that filing requirements at the Companies Registry have been complied with. In particular, he should ensure that the accounts and annual return have been filed, notices of increases of capital, share allotments and changes of directors and secretary have been duly given, and the charges register does not reveal any debenture which has been repaid (in respect of which a memorandum of satisfaction should have been forwarded to the Registry).

Title deeds

The seller will need to collect the title deeds for all the properties of the target company which are not subject to a charge as these will be given to the buyer on completion. If any charges are to be released on completion, the seller should make arrangements with the chargee for the deeds to be handed over to the buyer.

Powers of attorney

On completion, the selling shareholders will sign the acquisition agreement and related documentation and a meeting of the board of directors of the target company will be held. Resolutions of the members in general meeting may also be required (see **9.4.3**). If a seller is unable to attend the completion meeting, he may execute a power of attorney (eg in favour of his solicitor or another seller). The attorney will usually be given power to sign the completion documents and to appoint a proxy to attend and vote at any general meeting held on completion (he may, of course, appoint himself as proxy). The articles of the company will normally stipulate that the proxy form must be deposited at the registered office at least 48 hours before the meeting.

The seller will also have to ensure that the completion board meeting is quorate and that there is a sufficient majority to pass the requisite resolutions. Any director of the target company who is unable to be present at this meeting may appoint an alternate director to attend and vote on his behalf if the articles of the company allow (see, eg, Table A, Arts 64–69).

In the case of a corporate seller, the board of the selling company will appoint a representative to attend any extraordinary general meeting of the target company held on completion. A certified copy of the minutes of the board meeting at which the appointment is made should be given to the buyer on completion as evidence of the representative's authority.

9.4.2 Preparations by the buyer or his solicitors

In addition to preparing the documents which will be required on completion and arranging for the acquisition funds to be available, the buyer or his solicitor will need to take a number of other pre-completion steps.

Searches

The searches which a prudent buyer should make were described in Chapter 3. The buyer will usually repeat some of the searches which he made in the early, information-gathering stages of the transaction immediately before completion. In particular, he should repeat searches at the Companies Registry against the target company itself (and any of its subsidiaries) and against a corporate seller, and bankruptcy searches against individual sellers. In appropriate cases, the buyer is well advised to repeat patent and trade mark searches.

The buyer may also wish to make an appointment with the seller to inspect the statutory books of the target company prior to completion.

Corporate buyer

Where the buyer of the share capital of the target is a company, a board meeting of the buyer should be held prior to completion. The purpose of the meeting is to approve the terms of the draft acquisition agreement and to authorise the signing of the agreement and the completion of the acquisition. The board may appoint a director or a committee to attend to completion arrangements on behalf of the company. A certified copy of the minutes of this meeting will be handed to the seller on completion as evidence of the authority of the buyer's representatives to act (and sign documents) on behalf of the buyer.

If the consideration for the target company includes shares (in the buyer), an extraordinary general meeting of the buyer may be necessary to increase the share capital and authorise the directors to issue the shares (see **9.3.2**).

9.4.3 Completion meeting

The following matters will be dealt with at the completion meeting where there is no delay between exchange and completion:

(1) the seller's solicitor delivers the disclosure letter;
(2) the parties sign and exchange the acquisition agreement (and any separate deed of tax indemnity). If any document has been signed by an attorney the power of attorney should be delivered;
(3) each seller signs a stock transfer form and delivers this and the relative share certificates;
(4) a completion board meeting of the target company is held (see below);
(5) a completion extraordinary general meeting of the target company may be held in certain circumstances (see below);
(6) directors' service agreements are signed and exchanged;
(7) outstanding loans by the seller(s) to the company or vice versa may be discharged;
(8) the seller's solicitor delivers the statutory books of the target company, the title deeds to its properties (including any certificates of title given by the seller's solicitor), documents of title relating to other assets, financial records, agreements to which the target is a party and insurance policies;
(9) the buyer's solicitor delivers a banker's draft for the cash consideration and share certificates for any consideration shares.

If there is a delay between exchange and completion, points (1) and (2) would occur at exchange and points (3)–(9) at completion.

Completion board meeting

A board meeting of the target company will be held on completion to deal with, for example, the following matters:

(1) approve the transfers of shares;
(2) appoint new directors and a company secretary;
(3) receive notification from directors of their interests in the shares of the company (as required by s 324 of the CA 1985);

(4) accept resignations of directors and the company secretary;

(5) approve and authorise the signing of directors' service contracts;

(6) accept the resignation of the auditors of the target company and appoint new auditors;

(7) change the registered office of the company;

(8) change the accounting reference date of the company;

(9) alter existing bank mandates;

(10) call an extraordinary general meeting (see below);

(11) allow directors to make CA 1985, s 317 declarations of interest, if applicable.

Completion extraordinary general meeting

The buyer of shares does not become a member of the target company until his name is entered on the register of members (CA 1985, s 22). As registration cannot take place until the stock transfer form has been properly stamped, the buyer will not be able to exercise voting rights on completion of the acquisition. Consequently, the parties will normally agree that the selling shareholders will pass any resolutions which are required by the buyer on completion (the buyer's solicitor usually forwards draft minutes of the proposed meeting in advance of completion). An extraordinary general meeting may be called (on short notice) for the following purposes:

(1) to give consent to a substantial property transaction involving a director under s 320 of the CA 1985;

(2) to authorise the giving of financial assistance by the target for the acquisition of its shares as part of the 'whitewash procedure';

(3) to consent to a term in a director's service contract whereby his employment may continue for more than 5 years under s 319 of the CA 1985;

(4) to alter the articles of the target company. A corporate buyer may, for example, want the articles to be changed so as to be suitable for a wholly owned subsidiary.

9.4.4 Post-completion formalities

Filing

The buyer's solicitor should file the following at the Companies Registry:

(1) Forms 287 (registered office), 288a and/or 288b (directors and secretary), and 225(1) (accounting reference period);

(2) a copy of the letter of resignation of the auditors (s 392 requires this to be filed within 14 days);

(3) a copy of any special resolution of the company;

(4) a print of new articles of association of the company.

Where a company has issued shares as consideration, the buyer's solicitor may also need to file the following:

(1) Form 123 (increase in share capital);

(2) a copy of the ordinary resolution authorising the directors to issue shares;

(3) a copy of the special resolution suspending any applicable pre-emption rights;

(4) a return of allotments (Form 88(2)) and a copy of the acquisition agreement.

Statutory books

The buyer's solicitor should complete the statutory books of the target company including the registers of members (after the stock transfer forms have been stamped), directors and secretary, directors' interests in shares and debentures, and minutes.

Matters outstanding on completion

There may be matters to be dealt with which were left outstanding on completion. For example, the sellers may not have been released on completion from guarantees in relation to obligations of the target company. The buyer will often undertake in the acquisition agreement to try to obtain the release of the seller from such guarantees and, in the meantime, to indemnify the seller against any liability arising under them.

'Bibles'

The parties' solicitors will often compile so-called 'bibles' after completion containing copies of the complete set of documents used in the acquisition, which can be used as a source of reference should any problems crop up in the future (eg in relation to warranties).

Chapter 10

EMPLOYEES AND PENSIONS ON A SHARE ACQUISITION

10.1 EFFECT OF A SHARE ACQUISITION ON EMPLOYEES

When control of a company is acquired by share transfer, this has no direct effect on the employees of the target company. There is no change of employer in these circumstances and the employees retain exactly the same rights against their employer company, even though ownership of its shares has changed hands. The mere fact that the share acquisition has taken place will not, therefore, give rise to any claims from employees of the target company for wrongful dismissal, redundancy or unfair dismissal. There is no dismissal either at common law or within the statutory definition and all contractual rights of the employees are preserved. The Transfer Regulations described in Chapter 6 do not apply and, unlike on a business transfer, there is no obligation to inform and consult trade unions in relation to a proposed share acquisition (unless redundancies are proposed).

As the buyer of the target company indirectly assumes liability for its work-force (including the management team), he will require full employment details before committing himself to enter into the acquisition. The buyer may be perfectly happy with the employment structure of the target company (in terms of both the number and quality of employees and their contracts of employment) but if he is contemplating making changes, he should consider the potential liability of the target company and ways of keeping this to a minimum. These aspects are considered further at **10.3**.

10.2 PRE-CONTRACT ENQUIRIES

The buyer's solicitor will ask for full details of the directors, the managers and the general work-force of the target company. Requested information should include the following:

(1) copies of written service contracts (directors and senior managers in particular may have full written contracts);

(2) copies of written statements of terms of employment required by s 1 of the ERA 1996 (alternatively, the seller may provide a copy of a standard written statement with a list of those employees who have received it);

(3) details of any arrangements or agreements which are not recorded in the service contracts or written statements of terms. These are required because a written contract may not contain all of the terms agreed between employer and employee or there may be discretionary or customary arrangements regarding bonus payments and promotions, etc;

(4) a list of all current employees with their ages and lengths of service;

(5) details and copies of any pension schemes applicable to the target's employees;

(6) details and copies of any trade union recognition agreements;

Chapter 10 contents
Effect of a share acquisition on employees
Pre-contract enquiries
Changes contemplated by the buyer
Provision in the acquisition agreement
Pensions

(7) details of any dismissals or changes in terms and conditions of employment (say, in the previous 6 months) and of any claims against the company by employees or trade unions which are either threatened or outstanding;

(8) a list of persons who work in the business but are not employed by the target company. It may be, for example, that, where the target is a subsidiary company, some of those working in the business may have contracts with the parent company and will not, therefore, be available to the target after the acquisition.

10.3 CHANGES CONTEMPLATED BY THE BUYER

Although the change in the target company's ownership will not of itself give rise to any claims by its employees, in reality the acquisition may result in a major shake-up of the work-force. The buyer may intend, for example, to make redundancies or to reorganise the business so as to fit in with his own preferred methods or as a step towards integration with his existing employees. The target company may be faced with claims from the employees affected as a consequence of these actions.

Claims arising out of the termination of employment were discussed in Chapter 6. There follows a brief analysis of factors which the buyer should take into account when contemplating changes which will affect the general work-force or the management team.

10.3.1 Employees generally

Actual dismissals

If the buyer concludes that some of the target's work-force must be dismissed, he should take into account the potential costs of taking this action when negotiating the purchase price for the company. It will make little difference if the dismissals take place shortly before or after the acquisition. In either case, any liability is incurred by the target company, thus reducing the value of the buyer's investment (although warranties or indemnities may have the effect of redistributing the risk).

WRONGFUL DISMISSAL

The target company can avoid claims for wrongful dismissal by giving dismissed employees the correct period of notice, ie the notice period stipulated in the contract or, in the absence of express or implied contractual provision, reasonable notice. In either case, the notice period must not be less than the statutory minimum required by s 86 of the ERA 1996 (see **6.2.1**).

STATUTORY CLAIMS

Employees who do not satisfy the eligibility criteria (eg who do not have the required period of continuous employment) cannot generally claim redundancy or unfair dismissal. Provided they are given correct notice they can, usually, be dismissed without the target company incurring liability.

It should be noted, however, that there is no prerequisite length of service for an employee to be able to claim that he or she has been unlawfully discriminated against on grounds of sex, race or disability. Care should be taken to avoid any suggestion of unlawful discrimination in selecting employees for dismissal, particularly as the compensation for such unlawful discrimination is not subject to any maximum.

Where redundancy dismissals of eligible employees are necessary, the target company may be able to avoid liability to pay redundancy by making a suitable offer to re-engage (it will be recalled that an employee loses his right to a payment if he unreasonably refuses such an offer). The offer to re-engage may come from an 'associated employer' (see **6.2.2**).

Where liability for redundancies cannot be avoided, the buyer should try to ensure that the management of the target carries out the dismissals in such a way as not to give rise to additional claims for unfair dismissal. Although redundancy is one of the 'fair' reasons for dismissal, the target company employer will, nevertheless, be liable for unfair dismissal unless the tribunal is satisfied that it acted reasonably in accordance with s 98(4) of the ERA 1996. This involves, inter alia, adopting a fair selection procedure which is applied correctly, consulting relevant employees and trade unions and considering whether there is any suitable alternative employment which can be offered to the employees.

The employer is under a duty to consult recognised trade unions or elected employee representatives where redundancies are proposed, in default of which the employment tribunal may make protective awards to affected employees (see **6.2.2**). Perhaps the more potentially damaging consequence of failing to consult is that it may lead to findings of unfair dismissal. Ideally, the target's management should consult initially with the union or elected representative and then with those employees who are selected as a result of that consultation.

Constructive dismissals

A constructive dismissal is more likely to involve the target in liability than an actual dismissal, simply because the employer does not plan for it in the same way as an actual dismissal and cannot, therefore, take steps in advance to minimise liability. A constructive dismissal occurs where the employer commits a repudiatory breach of contract which the employee accepts as discharging the contract and walks out. The employee can claim damages for wrongful dismissal and he will be treated as dismissed for the purposes of the statutory claims.

An employer will be treated as committing a repudiatory breach of contract if he commits a serious breach of an express or implied term of the contract. This would include, for example, making a unilateral change to an important term of an employee's contract. This is an important consideration for a buyer who proposes that the terms and conditions of employment of the target's employees should be changed or that some or all of them should be relocated.

CHANGING THE PLACE OF WORK

Requiring an employee to move to a different location may not amount to a breach of contract. The definition of the employee's place of work in the contract may, for example, be sufficiently wide to include the new location. Alternatively, the contract may contain a 'mobility clause' permitting the employer to move the employee to a different place of work. Even in the absence of an express mobility clause, the court or tribunal may imply a right to move employees, but will normally only do so where the new location is close to the old one. In all these situations, therefore, there will be no constructive dismissal if an employee chooses to leave rather than move, although a term will be implied into the contract that the employer must give reasonable notice of the relocation.

If, on the other hand, the proposed relocation is in breach of contract, the employee who leaves as a result may have claims for wrongful dismissal, redundancy and unfair dismissal. As regards the redundancy claim, the proposal to relocate the employee will be treated as an offer to re-engage him at the new place of work. If this is a suitable offer which is unreasonably refused by the employee, the target company will escape liability to make a redundancy payment.

CHANGING OTHER TERMS AND CONDITIONS OF EMPLOYMENT

There may be scope for changes to be made to the duties of employees which do not amount to a breach of contract. Some contracts give the employer considerable flexibility in this regard by, for example, defining the employee's duties as 'such duties as the employer may from time to time reasonably require' (a 'job mobility' clause).

However, if the buyer does intend to change important terms and conditions of the contract, such as hours of work or pay structure, he should seek the agreement of the employees concerned rather than impose the changes unilaterally. The buyer will usually find it more productive to use the 'carrot' approach than the 'stick' approach. In other words, he is more likely to obtain the agreement of the employees to changes in their terms and conditions if he is able to offer them incentives in return (eg a pay increase) rather than threatening them with dismissal if they refuse to accept the changes.

If the target company imposes changes as a result of a genuine business reorganisation which is in the interests of the company as a whole, it may be able to establish that the reason for dismissal was 'some other substantial reason of a kind to justify dismissal' in defence of a claim for unfair dismissal by employees who are able to establish a constructive dismissal (or, indeed, by employees who have been dismissed for refusing to accept the changes). The target would also have to show that it acted reasonably within s 98(4) of the ERA 1996. Significant factors in determining reasonableness in the context of a genuine business reorganisation include notifying the employees well in advance of the proposed changes, listening to any representations made by the employees or unions and paying heed to any legitimate concerns which they express.

Transfer between companies

Unless the employee consents, the transfer of his contract from one company to another amounts to a repudiatory breach of contract. If, however, the change results from, for example, a group reorganisation and the terms and conditions of his employment remain the same, the employee will usually have no objection. In these circumstances, provided the employee is moved between 'associated employers' (see **6.2.2**) his continuity of employment will be preserved.

10.3.2 Directors and senior managers

Directors of the target company who are also employees, and senior managers, are subject to the same regime as all other employees; however, their important position in the company requires that the buyer gives them careful consideration. He should analyse the strengths and weaknesses of the management team and identify those managers and directors he considers important to the future success of the company and those whom he does not wish to retain. Where the buyer is a company, part of its strategy for 'turning the company around' may be to introduce some of its own managers or managers from other parts of the group. Similarly, individual buyers may insist on becoming directors on completion. As early as possible in negotiating the acquisition deal, the buyer should consider how he is going to retain the key managers and what will be the costs and consequences of dispensing with others.

Removing 'surplus' directors and managers

The buyer should check whether the articles of the target company give weighted voting rights to directors on any resolution to remove them as directors or to change the article conferring those rights. Such provisions may, of course, have the effect of entrenching the directors by preventing their removal by ordinary resolution under s 303 of the CA 1985.

The buyer will often be concerned about the cost to the target (and, therefore, indirectly, to himself) of removing directors and managers and the possibility that those dismissed may damage the company by their activities after leaving.

COST TO THE TARGET

The target company may face substantial claims for wrongful dismissal from directors or managers who are removed prior to the end of a fixed term or without proper notice. The cost of removing a director who is, for example, in the early stages of a 5-year fixed-term contract which entitles him to a lucrative package of salary and benefits may be prohibitive. Similarly, it may prove expensive to remove a director or manager who has a so-called 'evergreen' or 'rolling' contract. This is a contract for a fixed term which, on each anniversary of the commencement date, is automatically renewed for a further fixed term; automatic renewal will only not take place if the employer gives notice before the anniversary of the commencement date that the contract will determine at the end of the current period.

In the case of directors who have been granted service contracts for over 5 years, the buyer should check that the term was authorised by ordinary resolution of the members in accordance with s 319 of the CA 1985. In the absence of such approval, the contract can be terminated at any time on reasonable notice (see **5.10.2**).

To the extent that damages exceed £30,000, they are taxable in the hands of the employee and, consequently, in order to compensate for his actual loss, the award will be 'grossed up' to take account of this liability. Damages may be reduced significantly, on the other hand, to take account of accelerated receipt and the duty on the employee to mitigate his loss by seeking suitable alternative employment (see **6.2.1**).

RESTRICTIVE COVENANTS

The buyer should check whether the service contracts of the directors and managers of the target contain effective restraints on their activities after termination of their contracts. Typical clauses include covenants by the employee not to work in a competing business and not to solicit or entice away customers of the target company. The employee may also be prohibited from using or disclosing confidential information about the business of the target. In the absence of express terms, few post-termination restraints are implied into an employment contract (there is an implied term, however, that the employee will not reveal highly confidential information).

Restraints of this nature are valid and enforceable at common law only if they protect a legitimate trade interest of the employer (eg they protect the goodwill of the business), are not against the public interest and are reasonable between the parties. A non-competition covenant, for example, is likely to be considered void as being in restraint of trade unless its scope is limited in terms of duration and the geographical area which it covers. Similarly, a non-solicitation clause should be limited to customers who have recently dealt with the target (eg within the previous 12 months). It is now well established that clauses preventing the disclosure of information after termination can only be effective in relation to highly confidential information or trade secrets (*Faccenda Chicken Ltd v Fowler* [1986] IRLR 69, CA).

If any of the directors who are leaving are also selling shares in the target, the buyer should ensure that they agree to restrictive covenants in the acquisition agreement (see **4.8**). The courts will more readily uphold restraints which have been freely negotiated between parties to an acquisition than those included in employment contracts.

Even if restrictive covenants are prima facie valid, they will not survive a repudiatory breach of contract by the employer. This is on the basis that, by committing such a breach, the employer is indicating that he no longer considers himself to be bound by the contract and cannot, therefore, hold the other party to obligations contained within it. There is a danger here for buyers proposing that the target dismisses some of the management team; if dismissals are carried out in breach of contract, this may discharge the former employees from compliance with restrictive covenants (*General Billposting Co Ltd v Atkinson* [1909] AC 118, HL). Even if the covenant purports to enable the employer to enforce the covenant whatever the reason for the termination of the contract, this will not be effective (*Briggs v Oates* [1991] 1 All ER 411). Some directors' service contracts, however, permit the company to pay them salary in lieu of notice. Since, in this event, the company is not in breach of contract in terminating the contract without notice, it should be able to rely on post-termination covenants.

Retaining directors and managers

The buyer should consult with those directors and managers that he is keen to retain as early as possible in the negotiations for the acquisition of the target (subject to considerations of confidentiality). He may be able to negotiate a term in the acquisition agreement that certain key personnel enter into new service contracts on completion. If a director or manager chooses to leave, however, the rights of the parties will, inter alia, depend on the terms of any existing contract.

'GOLDEN PARACHUTE' CLAUSES

A director's service contract may include a so-called 'golden parachute' clause, entitling him to treat himself as dismissed without notice on a change of control of his employer company and to receive a specified payment from the company in this event.

A disadvantage for the director of receiving a contractual payment is that it is taxable in full as income. The first £30,000 of a claim for damages for breach of contract or a settlement of such a claim would, in contrast, be tax free within ss 148 and 188 of the ICTA 1988.

'GARDEN LEAVE' CLAUSES

A 'garden leave' clause is intended to enable the employer to hold an employee to his contract if, for example, the employee attempts to resign in breach of contract. Although the employer must continue to pay the employee for the notice period, he will not usually intend to provide him with work. The advantage to the employer is that the employee is unable to work for anyone else during the notice period and must comply with all obligations of confidentiality, etc which apply during the contract, which can be more extensive than those imposed after termination of the contract. However, the enforceability of clauses of this nature is still open to question, particularly where the employer refuses to provide work for the employee.

10.4 PROVISION IN THE ACQUISITION AGREEMENT

Particulars of employees including dates of commencement of employment and remuneration (including bonuses etc) payable by the target will usually be included in a schedule to the disclosure letter. Particulars of the directors of the target company may be contained separately in a schedule to the main agreement. In both cases, the buyer will normally insist on a warranty that the particulars shown are true and complete.

The buyer may also seek warranties as to the following, inter alia:

(1) that all subsisting contracts of service can be determined at any time by the target on 3 months' notice or less (this warranty should prompt disclosures of any fixed term or 'evergreen' contracts or contracts with a substantial notice requirement);

(2) that the company has not given notice terminating the employment of any employee;

(3) that no employee of the company is entitled to give notice terminating his employment as a result of the agreement (this warranty should 'flush out' any 'golden parachute' clauses);

(4) that there are no outstanding claims against the company by any current or former employee;

(5) that no changes have been made to the terms and conditions of employment of any employee over a specified period (eg within 3 or 6 months of completion).

Finally, the acquisition agreement may provide for new directors to be appointed or for existing directors to enter into fresh service contracts on completion (the terms will usually be agreed prior to completion and annexed to the contract).

10.5 PENSIONS

The pension considerations discussed in Chapter 6 in the context of a business acquisition are equally applicable to a share acquisition. There follows a reminder of some of the main points.

(1) The employees of the target may be members of a final salary scheme or a money purchase scheme. In a final salary scheme, the members are guaranteed a particular level of benefit on retirement, whereas the benefit received by the

members in a money purchase scheme is entirely dependent on the return on the fund invested.

(2) The target company may have its own discrete pension scheme or may be part of a group scheme.

(3) The pension fund is a separate entity from the target company and is administered by trustees who are obliged to act in accordance with the trust deed and rules; the trustees will not be parties to the acquisition agreement.

(4) If a discrete final salary scheme is in surplus, the seller may seek an increase in the purchase price of the target company to reflect this. If, however, there is a deficit, the buyer may ask the seller to make a payment into the fund or, alternatively, seek to reduce the price.

(5) If the target company is a member of a group scheme, the parties must agree a basis for making a transfer payment from the group scheme to the buyer's scheme. The buyer should insist on a guarantee from the seller to make up any shortfall if the seller cannot procure that the trustees transfer the agreed amount.

(6) The target company's employees may remain in the group scheme for a short period after completion to allow time for the buyer to set up his own scheme.

(7) Details of a discrete pension scheme or provisions relating to a transfer payment out of a group scheme are normally included in schedules to the main acquisition agreement.

Chapter 11

TAXATION ON A SHARE ACQUISITION

11.1 INTRODUCTION

This chapter considers the tax implications for the seller and buyer on the sale of a company by share transfer. In some ways, the tax position is simpler than on the sale of a business; there is only one type of asset involved (the shares in the target company) and there is a single charge to tax levied on the individuals or company disposing of those shares. There is an added layer of complexity, however, which arises from the fact that the buyer is acquiring an entity with a tax history and with all its tax liabilities intact. This obliges the buyer to carry out a more detailed investigation into the tax affairs of the target than on a business acquisition (when tax liabilities remain with the seller) and to seek protection in the acquisition agreement by negotiating numerous warranties and indemnities. In some cases, the buyer may be attracted to a particular company because of its tax status; the target company may, for example, have unrelieved trading losses which the buyer intends to use to shelter future profits. In these circumstances, the buyer would wish to ensure that nothing has happened in the past which would mean that anticipated reliefs are prejudiced by the change in control of the company.

Chapter 11 contents
Introduction
Liability of the seller on the sale of shares
Reducing the charge
How is the seller taxed when the consideration is deferred?
Tax implications for the buyer
Warranties and indemnities

11.2 LIABILITY OF THE SELLER ON THE SALE OF SHARES

11.2.1 Individuals

Subject to available reliefs and exemptions, an individual shareholder pays CGT on the gain arising from the disposal of his shares at his marginal rate of income tax, ie as though the chargeable gain represented the top slice of his income. The date of the disposal for CGT purposes is the date that the parties enter into the acquisition agreement (or, if the agreement is conditional, the time when the condition is fulfilled) and not, if later, the date of completion.

On the disposal of shares by an individual, after 5 April 1998, taper relief will apply to reduce the gain (see **7.2.1** for a discussion of taper relief). The reduction for gains on business assets is greater than for non-business assets.

Shares

Not all shares qualify as 'business assets' for the purposes of taper relief. The following shareholdings qualify as business assets:

- all shareholdings in unquoted trading companies (including those listed on the Alternative Investment Market);
- all shareholdings held by employees or officers (full- or part-time) in trading companies quoted on the Stock Exchange;

- where the shareholder is not an officer or employee, shareholdings in trading companies quoted on the Stock Exchange which carry at least 5% of the voting rights.

To be a 'trading company' for the purposes of taper relief, the company must exist 'wholly for the purpose of carrying on one or more trades, professions or vocations'. If a company carries on non-trading activities, the shares will only qualify as business assets if held by an employee of the company who does not have a material interest in the company of more than 10%. There is some easing of the test for minor non-trading activities. An investment activity alongside a major trading activity may well disqualify the shares from the definition of 'business assets'. The Inland Revenue has issued guidance notes that may prove useful in determining individual cases.

11.2.2 Companies

A company which sells a shareholding, the disposal of which does not qualify for exemption from tax as a disposal of a substantial shareholding, pays corporation tax on any chargeable gain (calculated as for CGT, save that indexation allowance continues after April 1998 and taper relief does not apply) which arises on the disposal of the shares. The rate of tax depends on whether the total profits of the company's accounting period exceed the 'small company' threshold. The company pays the tax 9 months after the end of the accounting period, unless it is a large company.

For large companies, corporation tax will be paid in instalments, calculated according to their anticipated final tax bill for the accounting period. The first instalment is payable 6 months and 14 days into the accounting period. There are provisions for the Inland Revenue to repay tax to a company that believes that it has over-estimated the instalments that become due. Interest will be payable on late paid instalments and the Inland Revenue will pay interest on overpaid tax.

(A large company is a company whose taxable profits in any accounting period will equal at least £1,500,000.)

11.3 REDUCING THE CHARGE

There are a number of provisions in the TCGA 1992 enabling shareholders selling shares to exempt either the whole or part of the gain or, at least, to postpone the occasion of the charge. There may also be scope for corporate sellers to take steps prior to entering into the contract which have the effect of reducing liability on the disposal.

11.3.1 Deferral relief on reinvestment in EIS and VCT shares

This relief, which was considered in **7.2.1**, will avail an individual who, for example, disposes of shares of any kind and reinvests the chargeable gain by subscribing for shares which qualify under the EIS. The individual's chargeable gain on the disposal of the original shares (up to the subscription cost) is deferred until he disposes of the EIS-qualifying shares. The EIS shares must be acquired within one year before or 3 years after the original disposal.

A similar deferral relief is available where the individual invests in VCT shares. In this case the shares must be acquired one year before or one year after the original disposal.

The relief will not avail a corporate shareholder, though a corporate shareholder may obtain tax relief if selling shares in circumstances which qualify under the Corporate Venturing Scheme (see the LPC Resource Book *Pervasive and Core Topics* (Jordans)). The detail of the Corporate Venturing Scheme is beyond the scope of this book.

11.3.2 Emigration

Previous editions of this book have referred to the possibility of the individual seller of shares arranging his affairs so that the shares are sold when he is not resident and not ordinarily resident in the UK. In such a case, the seller would first become not resident, then sell the shares. He would therefore avoid any charge to CGT. The requirements for an individual to establish that he is neither resident nor ordinarily resident in the UK have always been stringent. The detailed rules on what constitutes residence are outside the scope of this book and readers are referred to the LPC Resource Book *Private Client: Wills, Trusts and Estate Planning* (Jordans) for a fuller discussion.

The basic rules on whether an individual is resident in the UK are set out in TCGA 1992, s 10A (as inserted by the Finance Act 1998). Individuals who fulfil the following criteria will be liable to CGT on any chargeable gains on assets disposed of after their departure from the UK. Individuals will be subject to CGT if they:

- have been resident in the UK for any part of at least 4 out of the 7 tax years immediately preceding the tax year in which they left the UK; and
- have been not resident and not ordinarily resident for a period of less than 5 full tax years between the year of departure and the year of return; and
- own the assets disposed of before they leave the UK.

A gain made in the tax year of departure will be assessed in that tax year. A gain made after the date of departure will be assessed in the tax year of return to the UK. The new provisions have greatly limited the scope for tax planning in this area.

11.3.3 Share for share exchanges (TCGA 1992, s 135)

Section 135 of the TCGA 1992 provides another form of roll-over type relief where the seller of shares (individual or corporate) receives shares issued by an acquiring company as consideration for the sale.

Nature of the relief

The effect of the relief is to roll any gain on the target company's shares into the shares in the acquiring company which are issued in consideration. The seller pays no CGT on the sale of the target company's shares as he is treated as not making a disposal at this stage; he is deemed, however, to have acquired the consideration shares at the same time and for the same price as the original shares. The effect is to postpone any CGT (or, in the case of a corporate seller, corporation tax) until the disposal of the new shares.

This relief cannot be used in conjunction with the annual exemption.

Conditions for the relief

THE BUYER MUST HOLD A MINIMUM STAKE IN THE TARGET

For the relief to operate, the buyer must hold over 25% of the ordinary shares of the target company, either before or in consequence of the share exchange. Alternatively, the exchange must result from a general offer made to the shareholders of the target conditional on the buyer obtaining control of the target.

THE EXCHANGE MUST BE EFFECTED FOR BONA FIDE COMMERCIAL REASONS

Section 137 of the TCGA 1992 provides that, for s 135 relief to be available, the exchange must be effected for 'bona fide commercial reasons' and must not form part of a scheme or arrangement of which the main purpose, or one of the main purposes, is to avoid CGT or corporation tax. This provision does not, however, affect the availability of the relief to a shareholder who holds 5% or less of the shares or debentures (or any class of shares or debentures) in the target company (s 137(2)).

A clearance procedure is contained in s 138 under which the Inland Revenue can be asked to confirm that it is satisfied that the exchange is effected for bona fide commercial reasons, and not for a tax avoidance motive. The Inland Revenue must notify its decision within 30 days of the application for clearance, unless it requires further information. Although it is clearly in the seller's interest to obtain a clearance, the section provides that the application for clearance must be made either by the target company or the acquiring company. Another curious feature of the procedure is that clearance from the Inland Revenue does not guarantee that relief will be granted; it confirms that s 137 will not prevent the relief, but not that the conditions for the relief are met.

Other paper-for-paper exchanges

Relief is generally available in the same way if the shares in the target company are exchanged for debentures or loan notes issued by the acquiring company. Two caveats, however: first, special rules apply to certain debentures which come within the definition of 'qualifying corporate bonds' (these rules, which are contained in s 116 of the TCGA 1992, are outside the scope of this book); secondly, the Inland Revenue is unlikely to give advance clearance where loan notes issued in exchange can be redeemed by the holder within 6 months of issue. Subject to this, it may suit a seller to receive staggered payments (loan notes will often be redeemable at 6-monthly intervals, see **8.4.1**), thereby effectively enabling him to pay the CGT by instalments.

11.3.4 Exemption for company gains on substantial shareholdings

New legislation has been introduced by the Finance Act 2002 to facilitate corporate restructuring. The effect of the legislation is to exempt from tax capital gains arising on the disposal by corporate shareholders of substantial shareholdings in trading companies. The provisions apply to disposals arising on or after 1 April 2002, and the main conditions are as follows.

(1)   The vendor company must have held at least 10% of the ordinary share capital of the company being disposed of for at least 12 consecutive months in the 2 years prior to the sale.

(2) The vendor company must be a trading company or a member of a trading group throughout the shareholding period (referred to in (1) above) and immediately after the disposal. A trading company or trading group is essentially a company or group the activities of which do not include non-trading activities 'to any substantial extent'. Although the Inland Revenue has given no clear guidance as yet, this provision is likely to be interpreted in the same way as for business asset taper relief.

(3) The company whose shares are being disposed of must be a trading company or qualifying holding company throughout the shareholding period and immediately after the disposal. (The provision does, however, extend to cover gains only (ie losses are not allowable) on shares in a company which is not a qualifying trading or holding company immediately after the disposal by reason only of it ceasing to trade/being put into liquidation at the date of disposal.)

A qualifying holding company is a company the activities of which, together with those of its 51% subsidiaries, do not to any substantial extent include non-trading activities.

It should be noted that, although the test for 'substantial shareholding' is measured by reference to ordinary shares only, if the test is satisfied, relief will be available in relation to disposals of any class of, or interest in, shares.

11.3.5 Target as a member of a group

There are a number of useful tax exemptions and reliefs which are relevant to transactions between members of a group of companies; these are considered in detail in Chapter 13. The main point to note in the context of the sale of a target company which is a member of a group is that there is considerable scope for some restructuring to take place prior to the disposal with a view to reducing the overall tax burden of the group.

Transferring assets to another member of the group

Assets can be transferred between UK members of a group without the transferor incurring a charge to corporation tax (TCGA 1992, s 171, see **13.4.1**). There is scope, therefore, for the parties to choose which of the target's assets are retained for the benefit of the buyer. Assets in which the buyer has no interest, or assets which the seller does not wish to sell to the buyer, can be transferred to another member of the group prior to the share transfer.

Surrendering losses

In certain circumstances, losses of a group company can be surrendered to other members of the group who can use them to reduce their own taxable profits (ICTA 1988, s 402, see **13.3**). There may be scope for losses to be transferred in or out of the target company prior to its sale, although surrendering of losses is not possible, for example, to the extent those losses arise once 'arrangements' are in place for control of a company to be transferred out of the group (see **13.3.4**).

11.4 HOW IS THE SELLER TAXED WHEN THE CONSIDERATION IS DEFERRED?

It is common for some part of the purchase price to be left outstanding on completion. The seller may have agreed to receive payment by instalments, or to the buyer retaining a specified amount as security for breaches of warranty. The price may even be determinable by reference to future profits (an 'earn out', see **8.4.2**). What, then, are the tax implications of such arrangements?

11.4.1 The general rule

The general rule stated in s 48 of the TCGA 1992 is that, even if some part of the consideration is deferred, CGT (or corporation tax) is payable on the total consideration by reference to the date of the sale. This applies even if the seller only has a contingent right to receive part of the price (although, if the amount is uncertain, special rules apply, see **11.4.3**). The section does, however, provide that if the seller does not in fact receive the full amount of the deferred consideration, an appropriate adjustment will be made to the tax payable, thus entitling the seller to a tax refund.

The contingent liability which the seller has to the buyer in respect of warranties and indemnities will not affect the calculation of the gain. However, any payment which the seller makes to the buyer after completion under a warranty or indemnity will have the effect of reducing the proceeds of sale and, consequently, the gain for CGT purposes (see **4.3.2**).

11.4.2 Payment of the consideration by instalments

Where the consideration is payable in instalments for a period exceeding 18 months, the tax may be paid by instalments at the option of the taxpayer, who must agree the instalment schedule with the Inland Revenue.

11.4.3 Where the amount of deferred consideration is uncertain

The tax position is complicated if the amount of the deferred consideration cannot be determined on completion; the most obvious example is on an 'earn out', where the total amount payable by the buyer depends on the profits earned by the target company in the 2 or 3 years following completion.

Following the case of *Marren (Inspector of Taxes) v Ingles* [1980] 3 All ER 95, the Inland Revenue charges tax on the basis of the consideration actually received at the time of the disposal plus the current value of the right to receive the future consideration. The Inland Revenue regards this contingent right to future consideration as a *chose in action* (ie a future right to something which may be recovered, if necessary, by court action) which is itself a chargeable asset. Thus, when the seller receives the deferred consideration, he is treated as disposing of the chose in action and may face a further charge to CGT (or corporation tax).

For an individual, any gain on the disposal of the chose in action will be subject to taper relief. The chose in action is a new, capital asset. It follows, therefore, that it must have its own taper relief period which starts from the date of acquisition of the chose in action, ie the date of sale of the shares.

Consider, for example, an individual seller who disposes of his shares after April 1998 and who has agreed to receive £250,000 on completion plus 20% of profits (as defined) of the target for the next 2 years; the base cost of his shares is £30,000 (taking into account indexation up to April 1998).

In calculating the capital gain on the disposal of shares, the Inland Revenue will deduct the base cost of the shares (£30,000) from the consideration received on completion (£250,000) plus its valuation of the seller's right to the deferred consideration.

The 20% of profits of the target for the next 2 years is treated as the seller's right to the deferred consideration. The Inland Revenue will estimate the value of this right as, say, £200,000. In this example, this would produce a gain of £420,000 which will be reduced by the application of taper relief.

When the individual seller receives the deferred consideration (at the end of the 2-year period), he is treated as making a chargeable disposal of a chose in action (ie his right to receive that deferred consideration). A further gain may arise resulting in a subsequent CGT payment being made.

Let us assume that the consideration received at the end of the 2-year period is, in fact, £350,000. The individual seller's gain is arrived at by deducting from this figure the base cost of the chose in action (ie £200,000) to produce a gain of £150,000. Again, this gain may be reduced by the application of taper relief from the date of completion.

Note, however, that the right to receive the deferred consideration (the chose in action) is treated as a non-business asset and therefore the taper relief available will not reduce the gain (ie taper at 100%) unless the asset has been held for 3 years.

A number of problems may arise out of this treatment. If the amount of deferred consideration received by the seller is less than the value placed on it by the Inland Revenue, a loss will accrue to the seller on the disposal of the chose in action. A capital loss, however, cannot be carried back and will only be relievable if the seller makes gains in the future against which the loss can be set.

The rule in *Marren (Inspector of Taxes) v Ingles* applies where the consideration is unascertainable at the time of completion. It would not apply if, for example, some part of the consideration is left outstanding pending the drawing up of completion accounts. In this case, although the consideration is not known on completion, the information is available for it to be ascertained.

11.4.4 Deferred consideration satisfied in shares

Where the deferred consideration is to be satisfied by the acquiring company issuing shares to the seller, the seller can elect to treat the chose in action as a security for CGT purposes, with the result that he should not be charged in respect of the deferred consideration until he disposes of the shares issued in satisfaction of this deferred element. Instead, roll-over relief on a share for share exchange is available provided the seller does not have the option to take cash instead.

11.5 TAX IMPLICATIONS FOR THE BUYER

The immediate tax consequences for the buyer of acquiring shares are uncomplicated; the buyer pays stamp duty (see **11.5.2**) on the price paid which also forms his base cost for CGT (or, in the case of a company, corporation tax) purposes. However, the tax position of the target company becomes the concern of the buyer following the acquisition of its shares and there are a number of matters which the buyer may need to consider.

11.5.1 Carry forward of trading losses

The target company may have unused trading losses which the buyer may intend to offset against future profits of the company. Although s 393(1) of ICTA 1988 normally allows trading losses of a company to be set against future profits of the same trade, s 768 restricts this right if there is a major change in the nature or conduct of the target company's trade within a 3-year period which includes a change of ownership.

Once again, the buyer should seek assurances from the seller that there has been no such major change in the nature and conduct of the trade before the acquisition and must keep an eye on the position after the acquisition. What, then, amounts to a 'major change in the nature and conduct of the trade'? Section 768(4) states that it would include a major change in the type of property dealt in, or services or facilities provided, in the trade, or a major change in customers, outlets or markets of the trade.

11.5.2 Stamp duty

The buyer pays stamp duty at the rate of £5 per £1,000 or part thereof of the consideration and should present the stock transfer forms for stamping within 30 days of completion. Where completion accounts are to be drawn up, the buyer should present the stock transfer form to the Stamp Office within 30 days, but undertake to pay the duty when the price has been determined. Stamp duty reserve tax (SDRT) is chargeable (at the rate of 0.5% of the consideration) on an agreement to sell shares. SDRT is payable on the seventh day of the month following that in which the agreement was made or became unconditional. Any SDRT charge will, however, be cancelled (and any SDRT paid refunded) if the transfer is executed and stamped within 6 years of the agreement.

11.5.3 Financing the acquisition by borrowing: is tax relief available?

Close companies

An individual who takes out a loan to buy ordinary shares in a close trading company will obtain tax relief on the interest as a charge on income if he either controls more than 5% of the ordinary share capital (shares acquired as a result of the borrowing are included) or works for the greater part of his time in the management of the company (ICTA 1988, s 360).

ENTERPRISE INVESTMENT SCHEME (FA 1994, s 137 and Sch 5)

The Finance Act 1994 introduced the Enterprise Investment Scheme to encourage individuals to invest in shares issued on or after 1 January 1994 by a qualifying unquoted trading company. If certain conditions are fulfilled (eg the shares must be held for 3 years), income tax relief (at 20%) is available on up to £150,000-worth of investment for any tax year. In addition, any gains on disposal of the shares are exempt from CGT and relief is given for any losses. Shares traded on the Alternative Investment Market are treated as 'unquoted' for this and other tax purposes.

Corporate buyer

A company will generally receive tax relief as a debit under the loan relationship rules contained in the Finance Act 1996 on the interest which it pays on a loan to acquire shares.

11.6 WARRANTIES AND INDEMNITIES

11.6.1 Buyer's objectives

The buyer's aims in seeking to obtain protection in the form of warranties and indemnities in the share acquisition agreement will include the following:

(1) to obtain as much information as possible about the tax history of the company. It will be clear from what has been said above that this will also be relevant to potential future liabilities of the target. For example, the buyer will want to know the base cost of chargeable assets owned by the target, particularly if he intends that the target will sell assets after completion;

(2) to ensure that the seller will be responsible for any tax liability in relation to the period prior to completion which exceeds the provision in the accounts;

(3) to obtain redress from the seller if expected reliefs, such as the target's ability to carry forward unrelieved losses, are forfeited on the change in ownership of the target as a result of events prior to completion.

11.6.2 Warranty or indemnity?

The difference between the protection afforded by warranties and indemnities was discussed in Chapter 4. There follows a reminder of some of the main points as they relate to taxation matters.

(1) A warranty is an undertaking by the seller that a particular state of affairs exists. On a breach of warranty, the buyer must prove loss, ie that the value of the target's shares has fallen as a consequence.

(2) An indemnity is a promise to reimburse the buyer in respect of a designated type of liability which has already arisen or may arise in the future; there is no need to assess any reduction in the value of shares.

(3) Warranties are appropriate to deal with compliance requirements of the target, such as the proper submission of returns and the correct implementation of the PAYE system and other areas where the buyer is mainly concerned to elicit information from the seller (eg as to the base cost of chargeable assets).

(4) Indemnities are appropriate to cover specific tax charges which may arise over and above those provided for in the accounts and which are referable to the seller's period of ownership.

(5) Tax indemnities may be incorporated in a separate deed or embodied in the main acquisition agreement. In either case, they should be expressed to be in favour of the buyer and not the target. This avoids the target being assessed to

tax on an indemnity payment under the *Zim* principle; instead, the price of the target will be adjusted for CGT purposes if the liability crystallises.

PART IV

GROUPS

Chapter 12

AN INTRODUCTION TO GROUPS

12.1 HOW DO GROUPS COME ABOUT?

Groups of companies involving a parent (or holding) company, one or more subsidiaries and, sometimes, sub-subsidiaries are popular structures for the carrying on of business enterprises both in the UK and abroad. It is not only well-known public companies listed on The Stock Exchange which avail themselves of this structure, groups are also common among smaller concerns and private companies. A group can come into existence in a number of ways.

12.1.1 Enterprise formed as a group

The promoters of a business venture may decide from the start to incorporate a parent company and several subsidiaries (which may be wholly owned by the parent) to carry on different aspects of the enterprise.

12.1.2 Splitting up a large concern

A company may decide to transfer certain sectors of its business (eg manufacturing, retail, distribution, etc) to subsidiaries specifically formed for this purpose. Similarly, where a number of different businesses are being run under the umbrella of a single company, these may be separated out and hived down to subsidiaries.

12.1.3 Mergers and acquisitions

Where a company acquires control of another company by share acquisition, the relationship of parent and subsidiary is created between the acquiring company and the target company; if the entire share capital of the target changes hands, it becomes a wholly owned subsidiary of the acquiring company. Where the target company itself has subsidiaries, the acquisition brings into existence a group with three levels (and so on). The buyer will often be content to maintain this structure rather than incur costs in transferring the businesses out of the subsidiaries. A group which expands in this way by making acquisitions rather than by achieving 'organic' growth of its core business may end up with an array of diverse activities under its wing (such a group is known as a conglomerate group).

12.2 WHY ARE GROUPS SO POPULAR?

The attraction of operating through a group of companies rather than divisions of a single company has much to do with the fact that each company within the group is a separate legal entity with limited liability. The parent company, for example, is not liable for the debts of its subsidiaries unless it has agreed to assume responsibility for them or there are other special circumstances (see **12.7**).

Chapter 12 contents
How do groups come about?
Why are groups so popular?
Disadvantages
Company law status of groups
Group accounts
Obligations of the parent company and its directors to subsidiaries
Group indebtedness

The group structure enables risky businesses or activities to be packaged into separate subsidiaries so that their failure would not impact too heavily on the remainder of the group. The valuable, asset-rich parts of the enterprise can be isolated from more speculative and uncertain ventures.

A group arrangement will often prove less cumbersome than having all activities under the umbrella of one company. It may be convenient for separate businesses or parts of a business to be run as identifiable units with their own management teams. Another factor is that a group structure provides greater flexibility where acquisitions and disposals are contemplated, since it is usually easier to transfer a subsidiary than part of the business of a company.

12.3 DISADVANTAGES

12.3.1 Administration

The overall administrative burdens and costs involved in each company within the group maintaining a separate set of statutory books and having its annual accounts audited are likely to be greater than those of a single company operating through divisions.

12.3.2 Taxation

It will be seen in Chapter 13 that the general aim of the tax legislation is to treat a group of companies as a single company, with the consequences that certain intra-group transactions do not give rise to a tax charge and the benefit of reliefs can be passed between members of the group. However, the following problems remain:

(1) for a group to have the benefit of these provisions, it must meet the various definitions contained in the tax legislation;

(2) there are pitfalls in obtaining reliefs, etc. Relief may be forfeited if, for example, claims and elections are not properly made within the specified time-limits;

(3) there are certain 'gaps' in the legislation. For example, the benefit of capital losses cannot be transferred between members of the group (see **13.3.6**).

12.4 COMPANY LAW STATUS OF GROUPS

Company law makes very little specific provision for groups of companies. Each company within the group is treated as a separate entity with its own assets and liabilities. Generally, a company (even the parent company of a wholly owned subsidiary) does not have any additional liabilities or obligations imposed on it, or benefits granted to it, through being a member of a group. Some provisions of the CA 1985 do, however, make specific reference to groups.

12.4.1 Membership of holding company prohibited

Section 23 of the CA 1985 prohibits a subsidiary or its nominee from being a member of its holding company and renders any transfer or issue of the holding company's shares to a subsidiary or its nominee void.

12.4.2 Financial assistance for the acquisition of shares

The general prohibition in s 151 of the CA 1985 on a company giving financial assistance for the acquisition of its shares (see **9.3.1**) extends to the giving of such assistance by any of its subsidiaries.

12.4.3 Substantial property transactions involving directors

Section 320 of the CA 1985 requires the passing of an ordinary resolution of the members of a company where a director of the company or its holding company acquires an asset from the company or disposes of an asset to the company which is of the requisite value. If the director is a director of its holding company, an ordinary resolution of the holding company is also necessary to approve the transaction. No approval is required under s 320, however, by any company which is a wholly owned subsidiary (see **5.10.2**).

12.4.4 Loans to directors

The general prohibition on a company making loans to directors under s 330 of the CA 1985 extends to making loans to directors of the company's holding company.

12.4.5 Definition of group

Section 736 of the CA 1985, which defines groups for the purposes of, inter alia, the above provisions, employs the terms 'holding company' and 'subsidiary'. For a company to be its subsidiary, the 'holding company' must:

(1) hold more than half of the total voting rights which can be exercised at a general meeting of the 'subsidiary'; or
(2) be a member of the 'subsidiary' and have the right to appoint or remove its directors who are able to exercise more than half the voting rights at board meetings; or
(3) be a member of the 'subsidiary' and control, pursuant to an agreement with other shareholders, more than half of the total voting rights which can be exercised at a general meeting of the 'subsidiary'; or
(4) be a holding company of another subsidiary which is itself the holding company of the 'subsidiary'. Thus if, for example, A Ltd is the holding company of B Ltd which is the holding company of C Ltd, A Ltd is deemed to be the holding company of C Ltd.

In determining the voting rights, etc of the 'holding company', the voting rights of its subsidiaries and certain nominees and trustees are taken into account.

12.5 GROUP ACCOUNTS

One area where the CA 1985 (as amended) does impose additional obligations on group companies is in the preparation of accounts.

12.5.1 Definition for accounting purposes (s 258(1))

A slightly different definition of a group is used for accounting purposes from that used for other purposes. Broadly, the differences are as follows:

(1) the terms 'parent undertaking' (or, in the case of a company, 'parent company') and 'subsidiary undertakings' are employed. The definition of 'undertaking' includes companies, partnerships and unincorporated associations;

(2) a parent/subsidiary relationship arises in a similar way to a holding company/ subsidiary relationship as described above. In addition, a company will be a parent company for accounting purposes if:

(a) it has the right to exercise a dominant influence over the 'subsidiary undertaking'; or

(b) it has a minimum stake in the 'subsidiary undertaking' (generally, at least 20%) and either actually exercises a dominant influence over the 'subsidiary undertaking' or is managed on a unified basis with the 'subsidiary undertaking'.

12.5.2 Obligation to prepare accounts

A parent company is obliged to prepare consolidated annual accounts for the group, ie a profit and loss account and balance sheet incorporating the results, assets and liabilities of the parent and all the subsidiary undertakings in the group; this is in addition to preparing its own annual accounts. Group accounts must be approved by the directors of the parent company and audited by its auditors; they must be laid before the members of the parent company and filed with the Registrar of Companies (at the same time as the parent company's own accounts). The purpose of these provisions is to enable the members of the parent company to obtain an overall impression of the prosperity (or otherwise) and prospects of the group as a whole.

There is no obligation to produce group accounts where the group comes within the definition of 'small' or 'medium sized'. Also, an intermediate parent company which is itself included in consolidated accounts does not generally have to produce group accounts; it must, however, file a copy of these consolidated accounts with the Registrar of Companies together with its own accounts.

Finally, certain information must be included in notes to the accounts. For example, parent companies must list their subsidiary undertakings and give details of their shareholdings, whilst subsidiaries are obliged to reveal the name of their ultimate parent company.

12.6 OBLIGATIONS OF THE PARENT COMPANY AND ITS DIRECTORS TO SUBSIDIARIES

Company law does not impose any general obligations on a parent company towards the members, employees or creditors of a subsidiary. As each company within the group is regarded as a separate entity, ordinary principles of company law apply. The directors of the parent company owe fiduciary duties to the parent alone and are not under a duty to act in the interests of the subsidiary. Similarly, the directors of a subsidiary (who may include the parent company itself) must consider the interests of the subsidiary and may find themselves in breach of fiduciary duty if these are sacrificed for the interests of the parent company, other subsidiaries or the group as a whole. In these circumstances, outside minority shareholders may have a valid claim for unfairly prejudicial conduct under s 459 of the CA 1985.

It can be seen that company law is not in harness with commercial reality in its treatment of groups; clearly, in practice, many commercial decisions are taken for the benefit of the group as a whole rather than individual companies within it.

12.7 GROUP INDEBTEDNESS

One of the consequences of treating each member of the group as a completely separate entity is that a parent company is not liable for the debts of an insolvent subsidiary; the parent may even take priority to other creditors if, for example, it has loaned money to the subsidiary and taken security over its assets.

12.7.1 Guarantees

A creditor who is not satisfied as to the financial stability of a subsidiary is wise to seek some form of guarantee or security from the parent company or other company in the group whose standing is not in question. Indeed, many lenders, for example, insist on making a loan direct to a parent company rather than to its subsidiary.

Although very much second best to a formal guarantee, a creditor may be prepared to accept a 'letter of comfort' from the parent company stating, for example, that it is the policy of the parent company to ensure that the subsidiary is in a position to meet its liability to the creditor. Letters of comfort, which are common in commercial dealings, are used where the parties wish to avoid entering into a legally binding commitment. As long as they are carefully worded and the intentions of the parties are clear, the courts seem prepared to accept letters of comfort as statements of intention rather than as creating contractual obligations.

12.7.2 Fraudulent and wrongful trading

A parent company may also be made to contribute to the assets of an insolvent subsidiary if it is found liable for fraudulent or wrongful trading under ss 213 and 214 of the Insolvency Act 1986 respectively (see LPC Resource Book *Business Law and Practice* (Jordans)). In this context, it is important to note that wrongful trading applies not only to directors who have been formally appointed as such but also to 'shadow directors' of the company.

'Shadow director' is defined as 'a person in accordance with whose directions and instructions the directors are accustomed to act' (CA 1985, s 741). This may well apply to a parent company, particularly of a wholly owned subsidiary.

Chapter 13

TAXATION OF GROUPS

13.1 INTRODUCTION

Chapter 13 contents
Introduction
Defining a group
Group relief
Capital gains
Small companies rate of corporation tax
VAT group registration

Although each company in a group is a separate legal entity, the group is treated as a single entity for certain tax purposes. This has the advantage of avoiding a plethora of tax charges on intra-group transactions and enables the group as a whole to take greater advantage of reliefs. Thus, for example, capital assets can be transferred from one group member to another without this triggering a charge, and trading losses can be moved around the group so as to obtain the maximum tax advantage. Indeed, if each member of the group were treated as independent for tax purposes, the group structure, which has proved so popular commercially, would compare very unfavourably with the divisionalised structure. Inevitably, the legislation is complex and the companies within a 'group' must meet the specific definitions in the tax legislation.

13.2 DEFINING A GROUP

Groups are defined for tax purposes by reference to the percentage of ordinary share capital which companies hold in their subsidiaries. Subsidiaries are described, inter alia, as '51% subsidiaries', '75% subsidiaries', and '100% (or wholly-owned) subsidiaries' (ICTA 1988, s 838). For a company to have a 51% subsidiary, it must own, directly or indirectly, over 50% of the ordinary share capital of the company; for a 75% subsidiary, the holding must be not less than 75%. Clearly, a 75% subsidiary also qualifies as a 51% subsidiary. Certain 'economic ownership tests' must also be satisfied (see **13.2.4**).

13.2.1 'Ordinary share capital'

The definition of ordinary share capital is wide; it includes all the issued share capital of a company (whatever it is called), other than capital the holders of which have a right to a dividend at a fixed rate but no other right to share in the profits of the company (s 832(1)). Thus, shares with no voting rights or carrying no rights to a dividend may still be classed as ordinary shares for this purpose.

13.2.2 Owned 'directly or indirectly'

Ownership may be direct or indirect. Indirect ownership means ownership through another company. Consider the examples below (which assume that the relevant 'economic ownership tests', as discussed at **13.2.4**, are satisfied).

Example 1

A Ltd
↓ 100%
B Ltd
↓ 51%
C Ltd

B Ltd is a wholly owned subsidiary of A Ltd (direct).

C Ltd is a 51% subsidiary of B Ltd (direct).

C Ltd is also a 51% subsidiary of A Ltd (indirect).

Example 2

D Ltd
↓ 80%
E Ltd
↓ 80%
F Ltd

D Ltd owns 80% of E Ltd. E Ltd is a 75% subsidiary of D Ltd.

E Ltd owns 80% of F Ltd. F Ltd is a 75% subsidiary of E Ltd.

D Ltd owns $80\% \times 80 = 64\%$ of F Ltd. F Ltd is a 51% subsidiary of D Ltd (but not a 75% subsidiary).

Example 3

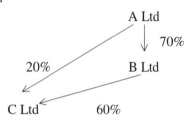

A Ltd owns 70% of B Ltd. B Ltd is a 51% subsidiary of A Ltd.

B Ltd owns 60% of C Ltd. C Ltd is a 51% subsidiary of B Ltd.

A Ltd owns 20% (directly) and $70\% \times 60 = 42\%$ (indirectly) of C Ltd. C Ltd is a 51% subsidiary of A Ltd.

13.2.3 Beneficial ownership

The company must be the beneficial owner of the appropriate percentage of the share capital in the other company. A company which enters into an unconditional contract (or a conditional contract if the condition can be waived by the buyer) for the sale of the entire share capital of a subsidiary ceases to have beneficial ownership of the shares. It is important, therefore, that any intra-group transactions take place before this happens.

13.2.4 'Economic ownership tests'

In order to prevent the creation of artificial groups, 'economic ownership tests' must also be satisfied for a company to come within the definition of a 51% or 75% subsidiary (ICTA 1988, Sch 18). In addition to beneficially owning the required percentage of the ordinary shares of the subsidiary, the parent company must fulfil the following two requirements:

(1) be beneficially entitled to more than 50% (or, in the case of a 75% subsidiary, not less than 75%) of the profits available for distribution to equity holders of the subsidiary; and

(2) be beneficially entitled to more than 50% (or, in the case of a 75% subsidiary, not less than 75%) of any assets of the subsidiary available for distribution to its equity holders on a winding up.

Beneficial entitlement to profits and assets may arise directly or through intervening companies. Special rules for determining this entitlement are at ICTA 1988, Sch 18.

13.3 GROUP RELIEF (ICTA 1988, s 402)

13.3.1 Nature of relief

Group relief enables a company (the surrendering company) which has incurred a trading loss in an accounting period, or which has charges on income or loan relationship debits, such as interest payments, to surrender these to another member of the group (the claimant company). This enables the claimant company to set the loss or charges on income or debits against its own taxable profits (ie income profits and chargeable gains) thus reducing its liability to corporation tax. The claimant company must first deduct its own charges on income and any current or brought forward losses. The surrendering company can surrender only trading losses, etc, of its current accounting period. The claimant company must set them against profits of the corresponding accounting period and cannot carry them forward or back. There are special rules which regulate the amount of losses which can be surrendered and claimed by companies with different accounting periods.

The whole of the trading loss, etc does not need to be surrendered and partial surrenders may be made to different members of the group. If the claimant company pays the surrendering company for the use of the trading losses, etc, the payment itself does not affect the tax position of either company, provided it does not exceed the amount of losses surrendered.

13.3.2 Applicable groups

Two companies are members of a group for the purposes of this relief if one is a 75% subsidiary of the other or if both are 75% subsidiaries of a third (ICTA 1988, s 413(3)). All relevant companies must be resident in the UK. Consider the example below.

Example

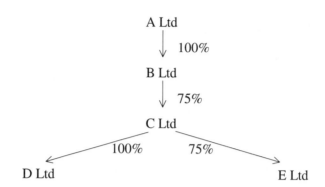

D Ltd is a 100% subsidiary of C Ltd and a 75% subsidiary of both B Ltd and A Ltd. A Ltd, B Ltd, C Ltd and D Ltd are members of a 75% group.

E Ltd does not form part of such a group since A Ltd and B Ltd only own 75% × 75 = 56.25% of E Ltd.

E Ltd is a 75% subsidiary of C Ltd. C Ltd, D Ltd and E Ltd form a 75% group.

13.3.3 Example of group relief

Example

A Ltd owns 100% of B Ltd. Both companies have the same accounting reference date of 30 September. In the accounting period ending 30 September 2001, B Ltd makes a trading loss of £50,000 (and no chargeable gains), whereas A Ltd makes total profits of £150,000.

B Ltd can carry the loss back against any profits of the preceding year, thus entitling B Ltd to reclaim tax (ICTA 1988, s 393A). Carry forward relief against trading profits is also available to B Ltd to reduce future corporation tax assessments (s 393). B Ltd may, however, choose to surrender all or part of the trading loss to A Ltd. If the whole of the loss is surrendered, A Ltd's profits liable to corporation tax for the year ended 30 September are reduced to £100,000.

13.3.4 Companies joining or leaving the group

Apportionment

Sections 403A–403C of ICTA 1988 provide for group relief to be apportioned when a company joins or leaves a group during an accounting period.

'Arrangements' for a company to leave the group

As an anti-avoidance measure, s 410 of ICTA 1988 was designed to prevent the artificial manipulation of group relief by the forming of groups on a temporary basis in order to obtain relief. In other words, a company with a loss arising, or due to arise, cannot join an unconnected group, surrender its losses and then depart from the group afterwards.

A company will not be regarded as a member of the group if 'arrangements' are in existence for the transfer of that company to another group: relief is not available during any period when such arrangements are in force (*Shepherd (Inspector of Taxes) v Law Land plc* [1990] STC 795).

In the context of an acquisition, therefore, losses will generally only be available for surrender between other members of the group, if they arose *before* 'arrangements' are in place for the sale of the target.

So, when do 'arrangements' come into existence for this purpose? It is clear that there does not have to be a binding contract for the acquisition of the shares; the signing of heads of agreement may, for example, be sufficient to prevent group relief. Although there is no statutory definition of 'arrangements', the Inland Revenue provides some guidance in a Statement of Practice (SP 3/93). The main points arising from the Statement are as follows.

(1) Arrangements will not normally come into existence in the case of a straightforward sale of a company before the date of the acceptance (subject to contract or on a similar conditional basis) of the offer.

(2) Where a disposal of shares requires approval of shareholders, no arrangement will come into existence until that approval has been given or the directors are aware that it will be given.

(3) 'Arrangements' might exist if there is an 'understanding between the parties in the character of an option' for a potential buyer to acquire shares.

13.3.5 Relief for members of consortia

Section 402 of the ICTA 1988 extends group relief in certain circumstances to companies which are owned by a number of other UK resident companies. At least 75% of the share capital of the consortium company must be owned by such companies which must themselves each own at least 5% of the consortium company. Companies owning less than 5% are not part of the consortium.

Example

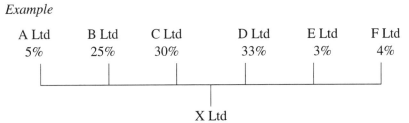

| A Ltd | B Ltd | C Ltd | D Ltd | E Ltd | F Ltd |
| 5% | 25% | 30% | 33% | 3% | 4% |

X Ltd

A Ltd, B Ltd, C Ltd and D Ltd are members of the consortium owning 93% of X Ltd, the consortium company. E Ltd and F Ltd are not part of the consortium as they do not own 5% of the shares in X Ltd.

Within a consortium, losses can be surrendered by the consortium company to the members of the consortium in proportion to their percentage shareholdings. In the above example, if X Ltd made losses of £100,000, X Ltd could surrender 25% of those losses (ie £25,000) to B Ltd.

Losses can also be surrendered by the members of the consortium to the consortium company in proportion to the members' share of the profits of the consortium company. In the above example, C Ltd is entitled to 30% of the profits of X Ltd. If X Ltd makes profits of £100,000, C Ltd's share of those profits would be £30,000. C Ltd would therefore be entitled to surrender up to £30,000 of any trading losses it makes to X Ltd.

13.3.6 Capital losses

The group relief provisions apply only to income losses. However, capital assets can be disposed of intra-group on a no gain/no loss basis (see **13.4.1**). It may, therefore, be possible to transfer losses across indirectly. Consider the following example.

> *Example*
> B Ltd and C Ltd are wholly owned subsidiaries of A Ltd. C Ltd has capital losses of £50,000. B Ltd proposes to sell premises to D which will realise a capital gain of £30,000.
>
> B Ltd will be liable to corporation tax on the chargeable gain on a direct sale to D. If, instead, B Ltd sells the premises to C Ltd which then sells to D, the position will be as follows:
>
> (1)   B Ltd pays no corporation tax on the disposal to C Ltd (even if full consideration is paid, the disposal is deemed to be on a no gain/no loss basis for tax purposes);
>
> (2)   C Ltd's disposal to D will realise a gain of £30,000, but this can be offset by its capital losses of £50,000 (leaving £20,000 unused loss for carry forward).

In addition, the Inland Revenue has introduced the possibility of a notional transfer of assets within groups in order to ease the administration of capital gains. Two members of a group of companies may jointly elect that a capital asset which has been disposed of outside the group by one company be treated as if it had been disposed of outside the group by the second company (ie as if the asset had been transferred to the second company immediately before the disposal). Thus, losses and gains on assets can be matched in a single company within the group without actually having to transfer the assets.

As an anti-avoidance measure, the Finance Act 1993 contains provisions preventing these schemes being effective where companies with unutilised capital losses are brought into a group specifically for the purpose of using the losses for the benefit of other members of the group (TCGA 1992, s 177A).

13.4 CAPITAL GAINS

13.4.1 Transferring capital assets

No gain/no loss

Section 171 of the TCGA 1992 allows capital assets to be transferred from one group member to another without any immediate charge to corporation tax. Such a disposal is treated as being for such a consideration (whatever the actual consideration passing) as not to give rise to either a capital gain or loss. Corporation tax is postponed until the asset is disposed of outside the group.

Exit charge on company leaving the group

A corporation tax charge on the postponed capital gain will be triggered, however, if the company leaves the group within 6 years of *receiving* the asset from another group member on a no gain/no loss basis. Section 179 of the TCGA 1992 provides that, on leaving a group, a company is treated as if it had sold and immediately re-acquired any asset which had been transferred to it from another member of the group within the previous 6 years. For the purpose of calculating the gain (or loss), this disposal and reacquisition is deemed to have taken place on the date the asset was last acquired intra-group. The gain or loss (often called a 'degrouping gain/loss') is, however, treated as arising immediately after the start of the accounting period of the company in which it ceases to be a member of the group. The buyer of a target must, therefore, investigate whether his acquisition will trigger any such charges and obtain suitable warranties or indemnities from the seller.

Example

A Ltd buys some land for £100,000 in 1993. A Ltd transfers the land in 1994 to its wholly owned subsidiary, B Ltd for £150,000 (its market value). B Ltd then transfers the land to C Ltd (B Ltd's wholly owned subsidiary) in 1996 for £250,000 (its market value).

In 1998, C Ltd leaves the group.

No corporation tax is paid on the transfer from A Ltd to B Ltd and on the transfer from B Ltd to C Ltd. These transfers are deemed to be on a no gain/no loss basis.

C Ltd's exit from the group in 1998 triggers an exit charge since it leaves the group within six years of acquiring the land. C Ltd is deemed to have sold the land for its market value in 1996 (£250,000) (and reacquired it at that value).

Ignoring indexation, the chargeable gain is £250,000 less the deemed acquisition cost of £100,000, ie £150,000. C Ltd is treated as making this gain in 1998.

Two new reliefs are available in respect of a degrouping gain or loss which accrues to a company which ceases to be a member of a group on or after 1 April 2002.

(1) The exiting company can make an election with another company in the vendor group to treat all or part of the exit charge as accruing to that other company (TCGA 1992, s 179A). Where the operation of s 179 gives rise to an allowable loss, such a loss can also be transferred to another company in the group.

(2) If the exiting company reinvests in qualifying business assets, the exit charge can be rolled over into those new assets (TCGA 1992, s 179B). The usual conditions for business asset rollover relief apply.

Claims for these reliefs must be made within 2 years of the end of the accounting period in which the exiting company leaves the group.

Transferring an asset out of the group

When a company transfers an asset out of the group, there is a charge to corporation tax on any gain that results. Here, the gain is the consideration received on transferring the asset out of the group *less* the price paid by the member who first brought the asset into the group.

So, using the figures from the previous example, if C Ltd were to sell the land in 1998 for £300,000 (instead of leaving the group), the gain would be £300,000 less £100,000 (the price paid by A Ltd), ie £200,000.

Definition of group

The definition of a group for the purposes of the provisions on capital gains is contained in s 170 of the TCGA 1992. The following rules apply:

(1) a company (the 'principal company') forms a group with all its 75% subsidiaries;

(2) the group also includes any 75% subsidiaries of those subsidiaries (and so on) if they are 'effective 51% subsidiaries' of the principal company;

(3) for a subsidiary to be an 'effective 51% subsidiary', the principal company must be beneficially entitled to more than 50% of any profits available for distribution to equity holders of the subsidiary and more than 50% of any assets available for distribution to equity holders on a winding up;

(4) a company which is a 75% subsidiary of another company cannot itself be a principal company unless it is prevented from being part of a group because it fails the 'effective 51% subsidiary' test.

All companies must be UK-resident.

Example

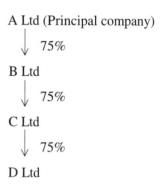

A Ltd, B Ltd and C Ltd form a group (C Ltd is a 75% × 75% = 56.25% subsidiary of A Ltd).

D Ltd is not part of the group as it is not a 51% subsidiary of A Ltd (A Ltd indirectly owns 75% × 75% × 75% = 42.18% of the shares in D Ltd).

As D Ltd cannot be part of the group it can be a principal company of its own group. Thus if D Ltd has a 75% subsidiary E Ltd, D Ltd and E Ltd form a group.

Note that B Ltd and C Ltd cannot be principals of their own groups because they are 75% subsidiaries of other companies and do not fail the 51% subsidiary test.

Stamp duty

Subject to certain anti-avoidance provisions, complete relief from stamp duty is available on a transfer of assets between companies where one company is a 75% subsidiary of the other or both are 75% subsidiaries of a third company (Finance Act 1930, s 42 as amended). In determining whether a company is a 75% subsidiary of another, direct or indirect shareholdings of ordinary shares are taken into account, and the economic ownership tests referred to at **13.2.4** must be satisfied.

13.4.2 Roll-over relief on the replacement of business assets

For the purposes of roll-over relief on the replacement of business assets (see **7.2.1**) all the trades carried on by members of a group of companies are treated as a single trade (TCGA 1992, s 175). Consequently, if one member of the group realises a gain on the disposal of an asset, the gain can be rolled into the acquisition cost of an asset purchased by another member of the group.

13.5 SMALL COMPANIES RATE OF CORPORATION TAX

Each member of a group does not have the full benefit of the starting, marginal and small companies rates of corporation tax, where profits do not exceed £10,000, £50,000 or £300,000 respectively, or the lower rates of tax where profits are between £300,000 and £1,500,000. Where companies are 'associated', the upper limit of each tax band is divided by the number of companies in the association. Two companies are associated if one has control (broadly, a majority of the issued share capital or voting power: ICTA 1988, s 416) of the other or if they are under common control (ICTA 1988, s 13).

> *Example*
> D Ltd has four wholly owned subsidiaries. The upper limit for the small companies rate for each company will be £60,000, and the threshold for the full corporation tax rate will be £300,000 (limits divided by 5, as there are five companies in the association – D Ltd plus four subsidiaries). In other words, if the profits of one of the subsidiaries are £59,000, then, for the tax year 2001/02, it will pay corporation tax at 20%. Similarly, if another subsidiary makes profits for the same tax year of £400,000, it will pay corporation tax at 30%, and so on.

13.6 VAT GROUP REGISTRATION

Two or more companies which are UK resident can apply to the Commissioners of Customs & Excise for a group VAT registration if, inter alia, one controls each of the others (VATA 1994, s 43). Broadly, control is defined as holding a majority of the voting rights or controlling the composition of the board of directors.

Group registration is in the name of a 'representative member'. Any supply made by a group member to a person outside the group is deemed made by the representative member. Equally, any supply made to a group member by a person outside the group is deemed made to the representative member. This does not mean that other group members escape liability; all members of the group registration are jointly and severally liable for VAT due from the representative member.

The other main consequence of registration is that supplies between members of a group registration are disregarded for VAT purposes.

Once a group registration is in place, other companies may be included or existing companies may be excluded from the group on application to the Commissioners of Customs & Excise. This will be a relevant factor if a subsidiary which is a member of a group registration is transferred outside the group. The buyer of a subsidiary should always check its VAT status and seek warranties that VAT has been properly accounted for (whether or not the subsidiary is part of a group registration).

In the Finance Act 1996, Customs & Excise were given wide discretionary powers to counter avoidance schemes. These include, for example, the power to direct that supplies between group companies are to be subject to VAT.

INDEX

References are to paragraph numbers.

Abatement notice 3.10.2
Accountant 2.1, 2.3
   accounts following completion 2.3.2
   investigation and report 2.3.2, 3.3
      contents of report 3.3.2
      deemed disclosure of matters in 4.4.2
      purpose of 3.3.1
      use of 3.3.3
   negligence 3.3.3, 4.6.2
   role of 2.3
   valuation of target 2.3.1
Accounting systems
   information on 3.3.2
Accounts 2.3.2, 3.4.3
   assets understated in 4.4.1
   completion hand-over of 5.6.2
   filed, usefulness 3.5.2
   group 12.5
      definitions for 12.5.1
      obligation on 12.5.2
   warranty as to 5.9.2, 8.6.1
Acquisition
   agreement, *see* Contract (acquisition)
   business, of, *see* Business acquisition
   meaning 1.1
   private company, of, by share transfer, *see* Share
      acquisition
   stages of 2.2, *see also* Procedure
      (acquisition)
Actuary 2.1
Advisory, Conciliation and Arbitration Service
   6.2.2
Air pollution
   control system 3.10.2
Alternative Investment Market 11.5.3
Annual return
   information from 3.5.2
Articles
   target company, of, alteration to 9.4.3
Asset(s)
   business acquisition contract, in 5.3, 5.9.2
      debtor, as 5.3.7
   condition of 5.9.2
   consideration for 5.4.1
   ownership 5.9.2
   replacement of, roll-over relief 1.3.6, 7.2.1
   retention of, for outstanding consideration
      5.4.3
   transfer of title to 5.6.1
   transfer within group, tax on 13.4.1
   warranties as to 5.9.2, 8.6.1
Asset-based valuation 2.3.1
Asset sale 1.2.3

assignment, need for consent to 1.3.6, 1.3.7
capital gains tax 1.3.6
choice of assets 1.3.7
contrasted with going concern sale 1.2
transfer of title of assets 1.3.6, 2.2.4
Assignment 1.3.6, 1.3.7, 2.2.4
   see also Lease
   business acquisition, on completion of 5.6.1
   consent to 1.3.6, 3.9.2
   warranty or indemnity, of 4.3.4
Attorney, power of 9.4.1
Auditor 2.3.2, 3.3.1
   see also Accountant
   duty of care of 4.6.2

Bank
   borrowing
      details on 3.4.3
      guarantee on 4.7
   joint deposit account, retained purchase price, for
      5.4.3, 8.4.2
Bankruptcy search 3.8
Board meeting
   completion, on 2.2.4, 9.4.1, 9.4.3
      business at 9.4.3
      corporate buyer 9.4.2
Bonus issue
   financial assistance rules exception for 9.3.1
Book debts
   see also Debtors; Liabilities
   stamp duty on 7.4.7
Books (statutory)
   see also Accounts; Records; Register (company)
   completion of, post-completion 9.4.4
   compliance with requirements 9.4.1
   delivery of, on completion 9.4.3
   inspection of, on completion 9.4.2
Borrowing
   commitments, details of 3.4.3
   guarantee on 4.7
   tax relief 7.4.8, 11.5.3
Business
   secrets, *see* Confidentiality
   types of 1.1.1
      company, owned by 1.1.1, 1.3, 1.3.1, *see also* Business acquisition
      unincorporated 1.1.1, 1.2, *see also* Partnership; Sole trader
Business acquisition 1.1, 1.1.1, 1.1.3, 1.3
   see also Asset sale; Going concern
   completion 5.5.1, 5.6

Business acquisition *cont*
  consideration   5.4
    apportionment of   1.3.7, 7.4.5
    form of   5.4.2
    receipt of   1.3.3, 1.3.6, 7.3.2
    retention of part   5.4.3
  contract   5.1 *et seq*
    assets and liabilities, details of   5.3
    conditional   5.3.1
    generally, *see* Contract (acquisition)
    implied terms   4.2.2
    interpretation clause   5.2.2
    order of clauses   5.2
    parties   5.2.1
    schedules, matters in   5.2.3, 5.3
  corporate seller   5.9.3, 5.10, 7.3, 7.4
    compliance with constitution   5.10.1
    director's interest in contract   5.10.2
    employee interests   5.10.2
    liabilities of company   7.4
    power to sell, check on   3.5.2, 5.10.1
    representative to attend EGM   9.4.1
    tax implications   7.3, 7.4
  due diligence   2.2.1, 3.4.1, 6.4
  employees, impact on   6.1 *et seq*
    employer's obligations to   6.2
    see also Employee(s)
  guarantor   5.2.1
  insurance   5.7
  land   5.3.1
  legal effect of   1.3.1, 1.3.6
  pensions   6.5, *see also* Pension schemes
  search at companies registry   3.5.1
  taxation matters   7.1 *et seq*, *see also* Taxation
  transfer in return for shares   1.2.1, 7.2.2
  transfer of title to assets   5.6.1
  warranties   5.9, 7.5, *see also* Warranty

Capital allowances   1.3.7, 7.2.1, 7.4.1
Capital gains, tax on
  base costs   1.3.7, 7.4.3
  buyer, for   1.3.7, 7.4.3
  deferral relief   1.3.6, 7.2.1, 11.3.1
  deferred consideration, and   11.4.1, 11.4.3
    instalments, paid by   11.4.2
    shares, satisfaction by   11.4.4
  reinvestment, on   1.3.6, 7.2.1
  residence, and   11.3.2
  retention from purchase price, and   4.3.5
  roll-over relief   1.3.6, 7.4.4
    group, for   13.4.2
  rolling gain, transfer in return for shares   1.2.1, 7.2.2
  seller, for   1.3.6, 7.2.1

    share for share exchange, relief on   8.4.1, 11.3.3
    share sale, liability on   11.2, 11.3
    taper relief   7.2.1, 7.3.1, 11.2.2, 11.4.4
    warranty payment, and   4.3.2
Charge(s)   3.5.2, 3.9.2
  asset transfer, removal or consent to transfer   5.5.1
  floating   5.5.1
  registration and validity   3.5.2
  release of   5.5.1, 5.6.2
  security for retained purchase price, as   5.4.3
Clean-up cost   3.10.2
  avoiding   3.10.2
  warranty as to   3.10.3
Close company   11.5.3
Companies registry
  search at   3.5, 3.8
    limitations of   3.5.1
Company
  associated   13.5
  business, acquisition from   5.9.3, 5.10, 7.3, 7.4, *see also* Business acquisition
  chargeable gains of   7.3.1
  constitution
    compliance with   5.10.1
    warranties as to   8.6.1
  corporation tax   7.3.1, *see also* Corporation tax
  director, *see* Director(s)
  dividend   7.3.2
  listed public   1.1, 2.1, 8.4.1
  methods for acquiring (private)
    comparison of   1.3.6, 1.3.7
    choice of   1.1.3, 1.3.4
    hive down   1.3.8
  share acquisition, *see* Share acquisition
  tax on sale of business by   7.3
Competition   4.8.1, 4.8.2, 4.8.3
  EC law   4.8.5
  Competition Commission   2.2.6
  reference to, procedure   2.2.6
Completion   2.2.3, 2.2.4, 9.4
  board meeting, *see* Board meeting
  business acquisition   5.5.1, 5.6
    documents for   5.6.2
    transfer of title   5.6.1
  power of attorney for   9.4.1
  share acquisition   8.7, 9.4
    matters at   9.4.3
Completion accounts   2.3.2
  clause for   8.4.2
  creditors and debtors, as to   5.3.7
  purchase price adjusted after   8.4.2
  stock valuation   5.3.5
Computer system and software
  details of   3.4.3

Conditional contract   2.2.3, 5.3.1, 5.5, 8.5
    business acquisition, and   5.5
        condition precedent   5.5.2
        period between exchange and completion,
            controls   5.5.3
        reason for   5.5.1
        undertakings by seller   5.5.3
        withdrawal   5.5.3
    share acquisition, and   8.5
        period between exchange and completion,
            controls   8.5
        undertakings by seller   8.5
        withdrawal   8.5
Confidentiality
    post-completion   4.8
        implied duty   4.8.1
        restrictive covenants   4.8.3
        undertaking as to   4.8.2
    prior to exchange   2.2.1, 3.2.2
Confidentiality agreement   2.2.1
Consideration   5.4, 8.4
    amount   5.4.1
    apportionment   1.3.7, 7.4.5
    cash   5.4.2, 9.4.3
        corporate sale, extracting on   7.3.2
    claims limited by reference to   4.4.1
    deferred   5.4.3, 8.4.2
        tax on seller   11.4
    discharge of liabilities by buyer as part of
        4.4.1
    payment   5.4.1, 8.4
    retention of, *see* Price
    shares or debentures, as   5.4.2, 8.4.1
        certificate for, on completion   9.4.3
        increase of share capital, authorisation
            9.3.2
        pre-emption rights, and   9.3.2
        ranking of shares   8.4.1
        vendor placing   8.4.1
    stock and work in progress, for   5.3.5
    VAT, and   7.4.6
    who receives   1.3.3, 1.3.6
        division between sellers   8.4.3
Contaminated land   3.10.2
    clean up costs   3.10.2
    definition   3.10.2
    new regime   3.10.2
    remediation notice   3.10.2
Contract (acquisition)   2.2.2, 5.1 *et seq*, 8.1 *et
    seq*
    breach
        limitation period   4.4.1
        recovery from third party, credit for   4.4.1
        remedies for, *see* Damages; Rescission
    business acquisition, for   5.1 *et seq, see also*
        Business acquisition
    conditional, *see* Conditional contract
    entire agreement clause   4.3.1

    exchange   2.2.7, 5.5.1
    express terms   4.3, 4.4.1
    implied terms   4.2
    indemnity in   4.3.2, *see also* Indemnity
    limitations on seller's liability in   4.4.1
    preparation of draft and amendments to
        2.2.2
    restraint of trade in, validity   4.8.3, *see also*
        Restrictive covenant
    retention from purchase price, provision for
        4.3.5, 5.3.7
    share acquisition, for   8.1 *et seq, see also*
        Share acquisition
    stages prior to   2.2.1, *see also* Procedure
        (acquisition)
    VAT, statement on   7.4.6
    warranties   4.3.1, 5.9.2, 8.6.1
        breach, and withdrawal from   4.3.1, 5.5.3,
        8.5
        subject to disclosure letter, provision
        4.4.2
    see also Warranty
Contract (general)
    commercial
        assignment or novation   5.3.6
        consents needed   5.3.6, 5.5.1
        existing, effect of acquisition on   3.4.3,
        5.3.6
        fundamental   3.4.3, 5.3.6, 5.5.1
        guarantee on   4.7
        liability under   5.3.6
        routine   5.3.6
        warranty as to   5.9.2
    employment, of   6.1 *et seq*, 10.1 *et seq*
        breach, claim for   6.2.1, 6.2.3
        enquiries on   6.4.1, 10.2
        restraint of trade in   4.8.3
        see also Director(s): service contract;
            Employee(s); Transfer of undertakings
    finance   5.3.4
Copyright   3.4.3, 5.3.3, 8.6.1
Corporation tax
    advanced
        dividends, and   11.5.1
    carry forward or back of trading losses   7.3.1,
        11.5.1
    charge to   7.3.1
    disposal of shares, on   11.2.2, 11.3
    exemption for company gains on substantial
        shareholdings   11.3.4
    roll-over relief on reinvestment   7.2.1
    small company rate   13.5
Credit agency
    report from   3.7
Creditors   5.3.7
    transfer or retention of, on business acquisition
        5.3.7
        stamp duty   5.3.7

Customer
    information on, pre-exchange   3.3.2
    solicitation of, post-completion, by seller
        4.8.1, 4.8.2
            restraint of trade covenant, and   4.8.3
    warranty as to continued custom   5.9.2, 8.6.1

Damages
    agreed in advance   4.3.1
    breach of warranty, for   4.3.1
    contractual, principles for   4.3.1
    misrepresentation, for   4.3.1
    tortious   4.3.1
Debenture
    consideration, as   5.4.2
Debtors   5.3.7
    group, of   12.7
    transfer or retention of, on business acquisition
        5.3.7
            stamp duty   5.3.7
    warranty as to   5.3.7
Deceit   4.3.1
Director(s)   3.5.2
    alternate   9.4.1
    asset (non-cash) of company, approval for
        dealing with   5.10.2
    board meeting for completion   2.2.4, 9.4.1,
        9.4.2
    compensation for loss of office   9.3.4,
        10.3.2
    environmental offences, liability for   3.10.2
    interest in transaction   5.10.2, 9.3.3
    loan to   12.4.4
    payment to, connected with transfer   5.10.2,
        9.3.4
    removal of   10.3.2
    resignation   9.4.3
    restrictive covenants   10.3.2
    service contract   5.10.2, 9.3.5
        approval   9.4.3, 10.3.2
        completion meeting, signing, etc at   9.4.3
        garden leave clause   10.3.2
        golden parachute payments   3.4.3, 10.4
        information about   3.3.2
        new, post-acquisition   10.3.2, 10.4
    shadow   12.7.2
    share acquisition, and   10.3.2
    substantial property transaction involving
        9.4.3, 12.4.3
    wrongful dismissal claim   10.3.2
Disclosure   4.4.2
    see also Information
    deemed   4.4.2
    letter of   2.2.2, 4.4.2
        employee, details on   10.4
        public information matters   4.4.2

        warranty overlap, and   4.4.2
Dividend
    declared prior to liquidation, tax and   7.3.2
    exception to financial assistance prohibition
        9.3.1
    pre-sale   9.3.1
    right to, on share for share exchange   8.4.1
    warranty as to   8.6.1
Documents   2.2.1, 2.2.2, 2.2.4
    completion
        business acquisition, for   5.6.2
        share acquisition, for   9.4.3
    contracts and loans, pre-existing, on   3.4.3
    post-completion   9.4.4
    signing of, board resolution for   5.6.2
Drafting
    solicitors, by   2.2.2, 4.4.1
Due diligence   2.2.1, 3.4.1, 6.4

EC law
    Acquired Rights Directive   6.3.2
    competition, on   4.8.5
    'concentration', definition   2.2.6
    mergers, on, compliance with   2.2.6
Earn out   5.4.3, 8.4.2
    clause   8.4.2
Earnings-based valuation   2.3.1
Employee(s)
    breach of contract by employer   6.2.1, 6.2.3,
        10.3.1
    business acquisition, on   6.1 *et seq*
    claims on dismissal   6.2.2, 6.2.3
        warranty as to   6.4.1
    constructive dismissal   6.2.1, 6.2.2, 10.3.1
    'continuous employment' for claims   6.2.2
    control change, rights on   3.4.3
    director, *see* Director(s)
    'dismissal'   6.2.2
    gross misconduct   6.2.1, 6.2.2
    information about, pre-exchange   3.3.2, 6.4,
        6.4.1, 10.1, 10.2
    interest of, regard to   5.10.2, 9.3.6
    liability of buyer and seller to   1.2.3, 1.3.6
    loan to buy shares   9.3.1
    notice, entitlement to   6.2.1
    pensions, *see* Pension schemes
    place of work
        change of   10.3.1
        determination of   6.2.2
    redundancy   6.2.2, 6.2.3, 10.3.1
        consultation provisions   6.2.2, 10.3.1
    removal of managers, cost of   10.3.2
    share acquisition, on   10.1 *et seq*
        common law position   6.3
        dismissals, and   10.1, 10.3.1
    terms and conditions, change to   6.7, 10.3.1

Employee(s) *cont*
    transfer between companies   10.3.1
    transfer of undertakings
        consultation prior to   6.7.5
        see also Transfer of undertakings protection
    undertaking not to entice from target   3.8.2
    unfair dismissal   6.2.1, 6.2.3, 6.6, 10.3.1
    written statements of terms   10.2
    wrongful dismissal claim   6.2.1, 6.2.3,
        10.3.1, 10.3.2
Employee share scheme
    financial assistance rule exception   9.3.1
Employer
    share acquisition, no change of   10.1
    unfair dismissal, and reasonableness   6.2.2
Enquiries before contract   3.4
    employees, as to   6.4.1, 10.2
    environmental matters, on   3.10.4
    replies to   3.4.2
    request for   3.4.1
    scope   3.4.3
        contracts, existing   3.4.3
        loans   3.4.3
Enterprise Investment Scheme   1.3.6, 7.2.1,
    11.5.3
Environment Agency   3.10.2, 3.10.4
    remediation notice   3.10.2
Environmental issues   3.10
    audit   3.10.4
    best available techniques (BATNEEC)
        3.10.2
    changes to legislation, and acquisition contract
        5.2.2
    criminal and civil liability   3.10.3
    contaminated land   3.10.2
    integrated pollution control   3.10.2
    licensing   3.10.2
    warranties   3.10.4
European Coal and Steel Community Treaty
    2.2.6
European law, *see* EC law
Exclusive bargaining right   2.2.1
Extraordinary general meeting   9.4.1, 9.4.2, 9.4.3
    completion, for   9.4.3

Fair trading
    merger regulation, and   2.2.6
    registration of agreement with Office of
        4.8.5,
    warranty as to   5.9.2
False or misleading statement
    criminal liability   4.5
Filing requirements
    compliance with   8.6.1, 9.4.1
    post-completion   9.4.4
Financial assistance   9.3.1

    after acquisition   9.3.1
    before or at time of acquisition   9.3.1
    company prohibition on   1.3.7, 9.3.1
        breach of, criminal offence   9.3.1
    definition   9.3.1
    examples   9.3.1
    exceptions   9.3.1
    groups, and   12.4.2
    instalments as   8.4.2
    private company procedure   9.3.1
        authorisation by EGM   9.4.3
    reductions in capital excepted   9.3.1
    'whitewash procedure'   9.3.1, 9.4.3
Fraud
    assessment to tax, and time-limit for   4.4.1
    misrepresentation, and   4.3.1
Fraudulent trading   12.7.2

Going concern
    sale of business as   1.2, 5.1
        employee protection   1.2.3
        indicators of   7.4.6
        outstanding contracts   5.9.1
        VAT exemption   7.4.6
        warranties, scope of   5.9.1, 5.9.2
Goods
    see also Assets; Plant and machinery; Stock
    warranty as to   5.9.2, 8.6.1
Goodwill
    assignment of   2.2.4, 5.6.1
    business acquisition contract, in   5.3.8
    capital gains on sale   7.2.1
    liabilities, adverse affect on   3.2.1
    preservation of by restrictive covenant   4.8.3,
        see also Competition
    value of   4.8.2, 5.3.8
    warranty as to   5.3.8
Group   12.1 *et seq*
    accounts, and   12.5
    administrative burdens   12.3.1
    asset transfer within   11.3.5, 13.3.6, 13.1,
        13.4.1
    capital gains   13.4
    capital losses   13.3.6
    company in, separate legal entity   12.2, 12.4
    conglomerate   12.1.3
    consolidated accounts, duty   12.5.2
    creation   12.1
        concern split up into   12.1.2
        enterprise formed as   12.1.1
        merger, on   12.1.3
    debts   12.7
    definition   12.4.5
        accounting purposes, for   12.5.1
        capital gains purposes, for   13.4.1
        taxation, for   13.2

Group *cont*
    economic ownership test   13.2, 13.2.2, 13.2.4
    financial assistance prohibition   12.4.2
    fraudulent or wrongful trading   12.7.2
    guarantees   12.7.1
    holding company   12.4.5
        membership prohibited   12.4.1
    leaving group   13.3.4, 13.4.1
    letter of comfort   12.7.1
    relief for trading losses   13.3
        anti-avoidance measure   13.3.4
        applicable groups   13.3.2
        apportionment   13.3.4
        consortia, extension to   13.3.5
        example   13.3.3
    roll-over relief   13.4.2
    stamp duty   13.4.1
    status in law   12.4
    structure
        attraction of   12.2
        disadvantages   12.3
    subsidiary, *see* Subsidiary
    substantial property transaction involving
        director   12.4.3
    target company member of   4.4.3, 11.3.5
        loss surrender   11.3.5, 13.3, 13.3.4
        tax exemptions and reliefs   11.3.5
    taxation of   12.3.2, 13.1 *et seq*
        beneficial ownership   13.2.3
        definitions   13.2
        ordinary shares   13.2.1
        ownership, direct or indirect   13.2.2
    value added tax, group registration   13.6
Guarantee   3.4.3, 4.3.5, 4.7
    balance of purchase price, for   5.4.3
    group, within   12.7.1
    lease, of obligations in   4.7, 5.3.1
    liability under   4.7
    party to agreement, as   5.2.1, 8.2.1
    release from   3.4.3, 3.9.2, 4.7
    subject matter of   4.7

Hire-purchase contract   5.3.4
Hive down   1.3.8, 5.9.4, 8.6.2, 8.6.3

Income tax
    balancing charge   1.3.7, 7.2.1, 7.3.1, 7.4.1
    capital allowances   1.3.7, 7.2.1, 7.4.1
    carry forward of trading losses   1.2.1, 1.3.7,
        7.2.1, 7.2.2
    closing year rules for sole trader or partnership
        7.2.1
    sale of unincorporated business, and   7.2.1
    stock, value of, and   7.2.1
Indemnity   4.3.2, 4.3.3

    assignment   4.3.4
    employee costs, for   6.4.1
    limiting scope of   4.4.1
    security for breach   4.3.5
    warranty distinguished   4.3.2, 11.6.2
Information
    see also Accountant; Confidentiality; Enquiries;
        Misrepresentation; Statement
    employees, as to   6.4.1
    environmental matters, on, public   3.10.4
    gathering of, prior to contract   2.2.1, 3.1 *et*
        seq, see also Investigation of target
    inaccuracy in, liability of target management
        4.3.1
    trade union, to   6.7.5
    warranties, as to disclosure and accuracy
        8.6.1
Inland Revenue
    see also Taxation
    tax indemnities and warranties, treatment of
        4.3.2
Insolvency
    seller of business, of   5.9.5
    target, and   3.5.2, 3.8
Inspection
    deemed disclosure, and   4.4.2
    property, of   3.9.2
Instalments
    payment by   8.4.2
        CGT on seller   11.4.2
Insurance
    business acquisition, on   5.7
    claim by buyer, and covered loss   4.4.1
    liability of seller, against   4.4.3
    share acquisition, and   8.6.1
    transfer or fresh cover, on business acquisition
        1.3.7
Intellectual property   3.4.3, 5.3.3, 8.6.1
    assignment of rights   2.2.4, 5.6.1
Interest
    see also Charge on income
    tax relief on   7.4.8, 11.5.3
Investigation of target   3.1 *et seq*
    see also Due diligence; Information; Searches
    accountant's report, *see* Accountant
    accounting system   3.3.2
    activities and market, etc   3.3.2
    charges   3.5.2, 3.9.2
    confidentiality, and   2.2.1, 3.2.2
    constraints on   3.2.2
    conveyancing enquiries and searches   3.9.2
    customers, suppliers, etc   3.3.2
    enquiries, *see* Enquiries before contract
    expense of   3.2.2
    liquidity   3.7
    management   3.3.2
    premises   3.3.2
    profitability   3.3.2

Investigation of target *cont*
  property, *see* Property
  reason for   3.1
  registers of company   3.6, *see also* Register
    (company)
  scope of   3.2
  share acquisition, problems associated with
    3.9.2
  staff, pensions, etc   3.3.2
  tax matters   3.3.2
Investment business   9.2
  advertisements   9.2.1
    restriction, basic   9.2.1
  authorisation requirements   1.3.6
  regulated activities   9.2.2
    mainstream   9.2.2
  unsolicited calls   9.2.1

Joint account   5.4.3, 8.4.2

Land
  see also Property
  business acquisition
    contract details   5.3.1
    conveyance of   5.6.1
  stamp duty   7.4.6
  warranty as to   3.9.1, 8.6.1
Lease
  see also Premises
  assignee of   3.9.2
  business acquisition, and, risk, insurance, etc
    5.3.1
  consent to assignment   1.3.6, 3.9.2, 5.3.1
    conditions, landlord stipulating (new lease)
      5.3.1
    cost of   5.3.1
    request for   5.3.1
    unreasonably withheld   5.3.1
  guarantee of obligations in   3.7, 5.3.1
  liability under   3.9.2
    release of original tenant of assignment
      3.9.2
  licence of   5.3.1
  original tenant, position of   3.9.2
Leasing contract   5.3.4
Liabilities
  see also Indemnity; Taxation; Warranty
  creditor as   5.3.7
  exclusion of, in contract   4.4.1
  guarantee, and   4.7, *see also* Guarantee
  indemnity for   4.3.2
  responsibility for, share and business acquisition
    contrasted   1.3.7, 3.2.1
  share acquisition, and   3.2.1
  seller, of, limiting   4.4.1, *see also* Insurance

Licence
  business acquisition, on
    intellectual property rights   3.4.3
    lease, of   5.3.1
  pollution control, and   3.10.2
  warranty as to   5.9.2, 8.6.1
Limitation period
  breach of contract claim, for   4.4.1
    restricted by parties   4.4.1
Liquidation
  see also Insolvency
  voluntary, on corporate sale, tax implications
    7.3.2
Liquidity
  target, of   3.7
Litigation
  warranty by seller   5.9.2, 8.6.1
Loan notes   8.4.1
Loans
  see also Borrowing; Financial assistance
  close company, for shares in   11.5.3
  director, to   12.4.4
  discharge of, on completion   9.4.3
  information about, of target   3.4.3
Local authority
  abatement notice   3.10.2
  air pollution control   3.10.2
  contaminated land remediation notices
    3.10.2, 3.10.4
Lock-out clause   2.2.1

Management
  target, of, information about   3.3.2
Management buy-out   5.9.4, 8.6.3
Memorandum and articles
  compliance with   5.10.1, 8.6.1
  study of   3.5.2
  warranty as to   8.6.1, 8.6.2
Merger
  compliance with provisions   2.2.6
  group formed on   12.1.3
  merger notice   2.2.6
Misrepresentation
  excluding liability for   4.3.1
  innocent   4.3.1
  meaning   4.3.1
  negligent   4.3.1
    distinguished from negligent misstatement
      4.6.1
  remedies for   4.3.1

Name
  business, of, use of   5.3.8
  change of, on acquisition   5.3.8, 5.6.2
  target, of, use of   4.8.2

Negligence
  accountant, of   3.3.3
  assessment to tax, and time-limit for   4.4.1
  misrepresentation, and   4.3.1
  negligent misstatement   4.6
    duty of care, and 'proximity'   4.6.2
    seller, by   4.6.1
    third party, by   4.6.2
  solicitor, of   3.9.1
Negotiation
  solicitors, by   2.2.2, 4.4.1

Offences
  environmental   3.10.3
  false impression as to market, etc   4.5
  false statement or dishonest concealment   4.5
  financial assistance prohibition, breach of
    9.3.1

PAYE
  compliance, information about   3.3.2
  warranty as to system, etc   4.3.2, 7.5, 8.6.1
Partnership
  see also Sole trader
  sale of business by   1.2, 5.1, 7.2
    tax matters, *see* Capital gains, tax on; Income
      tax
    valuation of goodwill   5.3.8
Patent   3.4.3, 5.3.3, 8.6.1
Patent agent   2.1, 3.4.3
Pension schemes   6.5, 10.5
  agreement as to transfer   6.5.3
  assets of   6.5.3
  business acquisition, on   6.5
    transfer of benefits   6.5.3
  final salary   6.5.1, 6.5.3
  group or discrete scheme   6.5.3, 10.5
  information about   4.3.2, 6.5.1, 6.5.2, 10.5
  money purchase   6.5.1
  share acquisition, on   10.2, 10.5
  trustees, position of   6.5.3
  warranties   6.5.3
Plant and machinery
  apportionment of consideration to   1.3.7
  business acquisition, assumption of risk, etc
    5.3.2
  capital allowances   1.3.7, 7.2.1, 7.4.1
  defects   5.3.2
  qualifying asset for CGT, as   1.3.6
  repair, state of, maintenance etc   5.3.2
  transfer of title   2.2.4, 5.6.1
  warranty   5.3.2, 8.6.1
Pollution   3.10
  air   3.10.2
  integrated pollution control   3.10.2

Premises
  see also Property
  target, of   3.3.2
Price
  see also Completion statement; Consideration
  accountant's report, and level of   3.3.3
  apportionment for tax   1.3.7, 7.4.5
    seller and buyer's interests in   7.4.5
  employees' contracts, rights, etc, and impact on
    6.1
  payment of
    instalments, by   8.4.2
    provision for   5.4.1, 8.4
  retention from   4.3.5, 5.4.3
    loan notes   8.4.1
    security for   5.4.3, 8.2.1
Procedure (for acquisition)   2.2
  acquisition agreement, *see* Contract (acquisition)
  exchange of   2.2.7, 5.5.1
  completion   2.2.4, 5.5.1, 9.4, *see also*
    Completion
  heads of agreement   2.2.1, 3.1
  investigation of target, *see* Investigation of target
  post-completion   2.2.5, 2.2.6, 9.4.4
  pre-completion   2.2.3, *see also*
    Information
  pre-contract negotiations   2.2.1
  'subject to contract'   2.2.1
  summary   2.2.7
Professional adviser
  see also Negligence
  duty of care   4.6.2
Property
  see also Lease
  certificate of title   3.9.1
  inspection   3.9.2
  investigation of   3.9
  warranties in contract   3.9.1

Receiver
  warranty by   8.6.2
Records
  completion hand-over   5.6.2
  warranty as to accuracy, etc   8.6.1
Redundancy   6.2.2
  claim   6.2.2
  consultation with workforce   6.2.2,
    10.3.1
    failure, protective award   6.2.2
  definition   6.2.2
  payment   6.2.2
  unfair dismissal, and   6.2.3
  wrongful dismissal, and   6.2.3
Register (company)   3.6
  compliance with requirements, check on
    9.4.1

Register (company) *cont*
  inspection of   3.6
  updating of, post-completion   2.2.5
  warranty as to   8.6.1
Registered office
  change of   9.4.3
Remediation notice   3.10.2
  register of   3.10.4
Representation
  post-completion, by seller   4.8.1
  pre-contract   4.3.1, 4.6.1
Rescission
  misrepresentation, for   4.3.1
Restraint of trade   4.8, 10.3.2
  injunction to enforce   4.8.4
  post-completion activities, covenant as to   4.8
    express   4.8.2
    implied   4.8.1
    validity of covenant   4.8.3, 4.8.4, 4.8.5,
      10.3.2
Restrictive covenant   4.8, 5.3.8, 8.8
  see also Restraint of trade
  employee, and   10.3.2
    dismissal, effect on   10.3.2
  enforcement   4.8.4
  goodwill, and   4.8.3
  registration of   4.8.5,
    effect of failure to register   4.8.5
Retention
  purchase price, from   4.3.5

Sale and purchase agreement, *see* Contract
    (acquisition)
Searches   2.2.3, 2.2.7, 9.4.2
  bankruptcy   3.8, 9.4.2
  companies registry, at   3.5, 9.4.2
  conveyancing   3.9.2
  environmental matters, on   3.10.4
Security
  warranty or indemnity, for   4.3.5
Service and repair obligations   5.3.7
Service contract, *see* Director(s)
Share(s)
  acquisition by transfer of, *see* Share acquisition
  business transfer in return for   1.2.1, 7.2.2
  chargeable assets, for CGT   1.3.6
    reinvestment relief   7.2.1
  consideration, as   11.4.4
    roll-over relief   11.4.4
    transfer of unincorporated business, for
      1.2.1, 7.2.2
    see also Consideration
  enterprise investment scheme   11.5.3
  issue, by buyer   9.3.2, 9.4.2
  pre-emption provisions   3.5.2, 8.3.3, 9.3.2
  restrictions on transfer, check for   3.5.2

share for share exchange   8.4.1
shareholder, *see* Shareholder
transfer of title   1.3.6, 2.2.4
vendor placing   8.4.1
Share acquisition   1.1, 1.1.2, 1.1.3, 1.3
  completion   8.7, 9.4
  consideration   8.4
    cash   8.4.1
    instalments   8.4.2
    loan notes   8.4.1
    payment   8.4.2
    receipt of   1.3.3, 8.4.3
    shares   8.4.1
  contract   8.1 *et seq*
    conditional   8.5
    employees' provision on   10.4
    exchange   8.5, 8.7
    implied terms in   4.2.1
    interpretation clause   8.2.2
    order of clauses   8.2
    parties   8.2.1
    pre-emption rights, waiving of   8.3.3
    price, amount, form, etc   8.4
    restrictive covenants   8.8
    schedules   8.2.2
    shares, clause for sale of   8.3.1, 8.3.2
    warranties   8.6, 11.6.1
  control clause   1.3.7, 3.4.3
  director, interest of, *see* Director(s)
  employees, implications for   10.1 *et seq*
  financial assistance, and   8.4.2, 9.3.1
  guarantor   8.2.1
  investigation of target   3.9.2, *see also*
    Investigation of target
  investment advertisement restrictions   1.3.6,
    9.2.1, *see also* Investment business
  legal effect of share acquisition   1.3.2, 1.3.6
  procedure   9.1 *et seq*
  taxation matters, *see* Taxation
  trade continuity   1.3.7
  transfer of title   1.3.6
  warranties   1.3.6, 8.6, 11.6
Share capital
  increase in, EGM for   9.3.2, 9.4.2
Shareholders   3.5.2
  breach of warranty, liability   4.3.1
  corporate   11.2.2
  individual   11.2.1
  non-resident   11.3.2
  party to transaction, as   8.2.1
  share sale
    consideration to   1.3.3, 1.3.6
    tax on   11.2, 11.3
  signing of acquisition agreement   9.4.1
  taxation of   11.2, 11.3, *see also* Capital gains,
    tax on; Income tax
  trustee   4.3.3, 8.2.1
  winding up, tax effect on   7.3.2

Sole trader
  sale of business by   1.2, 5.1, 7.2
    annual exemption (CGT)   7.2.1
    cash sale   7.2.1
    income tax   7.2.1
    see also Capital gains, tax on; Income tax
Solicitor
  buyer, for   2.2.7
    company registers, inspection of   3.6
    completion of share acquisition   9.4.2
    draft contract, preparation of   2.2.2
    enquiries before contract   3.4
    meeting with accountant   3.3.1
    see also Investigation of target
  role of   2.1 *et seq*
    commercial and legal aspects, interrelation 2.1
    coordination of advisers by   2.1, 2.2.2
    finalising documents   2.2.2
    information controller   2.2.1
    negotiation   2.2.2
    stage at which instructed, importance of 2.1
  seller, for   2.2.7
    certificate of title by   3.9.1
    completion of share acquisition   9.4.1
    corporate seller, check on   5.10.1
    disclosure letter, preparation of   2.2.2
    draft contract, amendments to   2.2.2
Staff, *see* Director(s); Employee(s)
Stamp duty
  assets not attracting charge   7.4.7
  business acquisition, on   1.3.7, 7.4.7
  certificate of value   7.4.7
  debtors and creditors, on transfer of   5.3.7
  group, transfer of assets within   13.4.1
  land   7.4.6
  reserve tax   11.5.2
  share acquisition, on   1.3.7, 2.2.6, 11.5, 11.5.2
  stock and goods, on   7.4.7
Statement
  see also Misrepresentation
  false or misleading   4.5
  negligent   4.6
  third party, by   4.6.2
Stock
  price of, as deductible expense   7.4.2
  stamp duty, and   7.4.7
  transfer of title   5.6.1
  valuation, etc   5.3.5
  warranties as to   5.3.5, 8.6.1
Stock transfer form   2.2.4, 9.4.3
  stamping   2.2.6, 11.5.2
Subject to contract
  use of phrase   2.2.1
Subsidiary
  see also Group

economic ownership test   13.2.4
  meaning   12.4.5
    tax, for   13.2
  parent company obligations to   12.6
  search, and   3.5.1
  small companies corporation tax rate   13.5
  transfer of assets involving, stamp duty
    exemption   13.4.1
  undertaking   12.4.5
  wholly owned, company becoming on purchase 8.1, 12.1.3
    change to articles   9.4.3
Survey
  deemed disclosure, and   4.4.2
  property, of   3.9.2
Surveyor   2.1

Target company
  group, member of   3.4.3, 11.3.5, *see also* Group
  information about, *see* Information; Investigation
  meaning   1.3
Taxation
  business acquisition, on   7.1 *et seq, see* Capital gains, tax on; Income tax
  buyer, and   1.3.7
  damages, employee's, and   10.3.2
  groups, and   13.1 *et seq, see also* Group
  indemnity for   4.3.2
    benefit of, old and new approach   4.3.2
  information about target compliance and liabilities   3.3.2
  reduction, credit for   4.4.1
  seller, and   1.3.6
  share for share exchange, of   8.4.1
  share acquisition, on   11.1 *et seq*
    buyer, position of   11.5
    seller, liability of   11.2–11.4
  warranty protection   4.3.2, 8.6.1, 11.6
    buyer's aims   11.6.1
    indemnity distinguished   11.6.2
Third party
  claim against target by   4.4.1
  recovery of sum from   4.4.1
  statement by   4.6.2
Timetable   2.2, 2.2.3, 3.2.2
  determination of   3.3.1
Title
  certificate of   3.9.1
  covenants for, implied   5.3.1, 8.3.1
  deeds   9.4.1
Tort
  damages in   4.3.1
Trade
  conduct of, warranties on   5.9.2
  continuity of   1.3.7

Trade *cont*
    information on, of target   3.3.2
        non-arm's length   3.4.3
Trade descriptions
    warranty as to non-contravention   5.9.2
Trade mark   3.4.3, 5.3.3, 8.6.1
Trade union
    collective and recognition agreements
        details of   10.2
        transfer of   6.7.5
    consultation with
        proposed redundancies, on   6.2.2
        prior to transfer   6.7.5
    enquiries as to   6.4.1
Trading stock, *see* Stock
Transfer of undertakings protection   6.3
    asset sale excluded   6.3.1
    automatic transfer of employment contract
        6.4.1
    buyer, position of   6.8
    consultation duty   6.7.5
    dismissal connected with transfer   6.6
        terms and conditions, variation to   6.7
    economic, technical or organisational reason for
        work-force changes   6.6.2
    'relevant transfer'   6.3.2
        effect of   6.4
        employees, which affected   6.4.2
        acknowledgment that is   6.8.1
    rights transferring   6.5.1
Trustee
    pension scheme, of   6.9.3
    warranty by   4.3.3, 8.2.1

Undertaking (entity)
    parent and subsidiary   12.5.1
Undertaking (promise)
    see also Warranty
    conditional contract, pending completion
        5.5.3, 8.5
    confidentiality, as to
        by buyer   2.2.1
        by seller   4.8.1
    implied, on seller   4.8.1
    merger reference, in place of   2.2.6
    name of business, as to use of   5.3.8
    non-competition, as to   4.8.2
Unfair contract terms
    control of   4.4.1
Unfair dismissal   6.2.2
    claim   6.2.2
    orders   6.2.2
    'relevant transfer', modified rules on   6.7
    wrongful dismissal, and   6.2.3
Utilities
    apportionment of outgoings   5.3.7

Valuation
    price, post-completion adjustment, and   8.4.2
    properties, of   3.9.2
    stock and work in progress, of   5.3.5
    target company, of   2.3.1, 2.3.2
        goodwill   4.8.2
        methods for   2.3.1
        understated assets, reduction of claim for
        4.4.1
Value added tax
    assets of business, on   1.2.2, 1.3.7
    charge on sale of business   7.4.6
    compliance, information about   3.3.2
    exemption for going concern   7.4.6
    group registration   13.6
    warranty protection   4.3.2
Vehicles
    warranty as to
Venture Capital Trust   1.3.6, 7.2.1

Warranty
    accounts, as to   5.9.2, 8.6.1
    assets, as to   5.9.2
    assignment   4.3.4
    breach
    damages for   4.3.1
        reduction in claim, matters affecting
        4.4.1
        security for   4.3.5
        withdrawal   4.3.1, 5.5.3, 8.5
    business acquisition, in   5.9, 7.5
    claim   4.3.1, 4.3.5, 4.4.1
    constitution of company, as to   8.6.1, 8.6.2
    contracts, as to   5.9.2
    contribution recovery   4.3.3
    disclosure by seller, and   4.4.2
    employee information, etc, as to   6.4.1, 10.4
    environmental   3.10.4
    goodwill   5.3.8
    hive down, on   8.6.2
    indemnity distinguished   4.3.2, 11.6.2
    information, as to   8.6.1
    insurance   8.6.1
    intellectual property   5.3.3, 8.6.1
    joint and several liability   4.3.3,
        4.4.1
    land, as to   3.9.1, 8.6.1
    liabilities and expenses, as to   8.6.1
    limiting scope of   4.4.1
    maximum limit   4.4.1
    minimum limit   4.4.1
    pension scheme, as to   6.9.3
    plant and machinery   5.3.2
    property   3.9.1
    receiver, by   8.6.2
    schedules, in   5.2.3

Warranty *cont*
    share acquisition agreement, in   1.3.6, 1.3.7,
      2.2.2, 4.3, 8.2.1, 8.6, 11.6
    shareholder, and   4.3.3
    third party claim against target   4.4.1
    time-limits   4.4.1
    trading, as to   5.9.2, 8.6.1

    trustees, and   4.3.3
Waste
    control and management   3.10.2
Work in progress   5.3.5
Wrongful dismissal   6.2.1, 6.2.3
    director, by   10.3.2
Wrongful trading   12.7.2